JOHN McLAUGHLIN:

The Emerald Beyond

Ken Trethewey

Jazz-Fusion Books

First published September 2008
Second edition published April 2013

Jazz-Fusion Books
Gravesend Cottage
Torpoint
Cornwall PL11 2LX
United Kingdom

©2008, 2013 Ken Trethewey

ISBN: 978-0-9570092-8-8

All rights reserved. No part of this publication may be reproduced, stored in a retrieval system, or transmitted in any form, or by any means, electronic, mechanical, photocopying, recording or otherwise, without the prior permission of Jazz-Fusion Books.

*For Chris, Joe and Helen, my musical family,
who love music as much as I do.*

John McLaughlin in Concert, Barbican Centre, London, 31 May 2008

Contents

Contents 7
Foreword 9
Introduction 11
Early Life 12
John McLaughlin: *Extrapolation* – 1969 (*****) 15
Tony Williams 19
The Tony Williams Lifetime: *Emergency!* – 1969 (*) 24
The Tony Williams Lifetime: *Turn It Over* – 1970 (*) 27
John McLaughlin: *Devotion* – 1970 (*) 29
More Miles 30
John McLaughlin, John Surman, Karl Berger, Stu Martin, Dave Holland: *Where Fortune Smiles* – 1971 (**) 31
Looking East 32
John McLaughlin: *My Goal's Beyond* – 1971 (**) 33
The Mahavishnu Orchestra 35
The Mahavishnu Orchestra: *The Inner Mounting Flame* – 1971 (*****) ... 38
The Mahavishnu Orchestra: *Birds of Fire* – 1973 (*****) 45
The Mahavishnu Orchestra: *Between Nothingness and Eternity* – 1973 (*****) ... 48
The Mahavishnu Orchestra: *The Lost Trident Sessions* – Rec. 1973, Rel. 1998 (****) 51
John McLaughlin and Carlos Santana: *Love, Devotion, Surrender* – 1972 (**) 53
The Mahavishnu Orchestra: *Apocalypse* – 1974 (***) 55
The Mahavishnu Orchestra: *Visions of the Emerald Beyond* – 1975 (***) . 60
The Mahavishnu Orchestra: *Inner Worlds* – 1976 (**) 62
Shakti with John McLaughlin – 1975 (**) 66
Shakti: *A Handful of Beauty* – 1976 (***) 69
Shakti: *Natural Elements* – 1977 (****) 71
John McLaughlin: Johnny McLaughlin, Electric Guitarist – 1978 (***) 73
One Truth Band: *Electric Dreams* – 1979 (***) 75
John McLaughlin, Jaco Pastorius, Tony Williams: *Trio of Doom* – rec. 1979, rel. 2007 (***) 78
Al diMeola, John McLaughlin, Paco de Lucia: *Friday Night in San Francisco* - 1980 (***) 79
John McLaughlin: *Belo Horizonte* – 1981 (***) 81
John McLaughlin: *Music Spoken Here* – 1982 (***) 84
John McLaughlin, Al diMeola, Paco de Lucia: *Passion Grace and Fire* - 1983 (**) 86

Mahavishnu Orchestra: *Mahavishnu* – 1984 (****) 87
John McLaughlin and Mahavishnu: *Adventures in Radioland* – 1986 (****) 93
John McLaughlin: The Mediterranean Concerto for Guitar and Orchestra – 1990 (****) 97
John McLaughlin Trio: *Live at the Royal Festival Hall* – 1990 (****) 98
John McLaughlin Trio: *Qué Allegría* – 1992 (***).. 101
John McLaughlin: *Time Remembered* – 1993 (**) 103
The Free Spirits: *Tokyo Live* – 1994 (***)... 104
John McLaughlin: *After the Rain* – 1994 (***)... 106
John McLaughlin: *The Promise* – 1996 (****).. 106
Paco de Lucia, Al Di Meola, John McLaughlin: *The Guitar Trio* – 1996 (**) 109
John McLaughlin: *Molom: A Legend of Mongolia* – 1996 (**) 110
John McLaughlin: *The Heart of Things* – 1997 (****) 111
The Heart of Things: *Live in Paris* – 1998 (*****).. 114
Remember *Shakti* – 1998 (***)... 118
Remember Shakti: *The Believer* – 2000 (**) 119
Remember Shakti: *Saturday Night in Bombay* – 2001 (**).................................. 119
John McLaughlin: *Thieves and Poets* – 2003 (**)... 120
John McLaughlin: *Industrial Zen* – 2006 (****) 120
John McLaughlin: *Floating Point* – 2008 (*****) [CD]; 122
Meeting of the Minds - The Making of Floating Point – 2008 (*****) [DVD] 122
John McLaughlin and the 4th Dimension: *Live @ Belgrade* – 2008 (****) [DVD] 126
Chick Corea and John McLaughlin: *Five Peace Band* - 2009 (*****)...................... 130
John McLaughlin and the 4th Dimension: *To The One* – 2010 (****) 135
John McLaughlin and the 4th Dimension: *Now Hear This* – 2012 (*****) 139
Concluding Remarks... 143
References 148
Discography 151
Recording Career of John McLaughlin 166
John McLaughlin's Recordings with Miles Davis... 169
Index 174

Foreword

John McLaughlin is a rare jewel in a vast landscape of guitarists. Some would argue that he is the greatest of them all. British jazz saxophonist Dick Heckstall-Smith is one: "First time I heard him onwards, I new John was the best guitar player in the world." [1] One of John's biographers, Paul Stump, an unusually critical fan and a man not given to ready hyperbole, admits to McLaughlin being his hero and states that he is "a musician of genuinely exceptional means." [2] Richard Cook is rather less enthusiastic, but at least concedes that John's music with the Mahavishnu Orchestra was "unrivalled and monumental". [3] Everyone's favourite writer, Stuart Nicholson, usually careful not to be too judgmental, nevertheless reports that, "His staggering virtuosity radically changed the sound and style of the jazz guitar." [4] In 1969, when Miles Davis saw John play at *Count Basie's* Jazz club in New York, soon after John's arrival in the USA, Miles described John as a "mf." That was, of course, the greatest compliment anyone could receive from Miles. [5]

As with much that is rare and spectacular, McLaughlin's music can produce extremes of emotional response. In my own case, it took thirty years to shift from a position of strong dislike to one of love and deep admiration. Part of the reason for that is the sheer complexity of what John is about. His speed of thinking and playing is so fast that many brains, operating at slower speed, give up trying to keep pace with the barrage of notes that flow from his guitar. Furthermore, his frequent use of complex rhythms makes it hard for listeners, conditioned to simple metres, to associate themselves with the music.

My original dislike of John's music was heightened by a simple lack of understanding and consequently I didn't listen to it properly. I feel the same can be true today, especially in an age when superficiality rules OK. John himself would see it all as very simple: a man with such an immense gift of skill and creativity inevitably sees what he does as straightforward. His audiences, however, have found it far from that, and over the years have polarised into two widely separated groups. Only when I made the sustained effort to study his music was I able to shift my position from one extreme to the other. As a huge fan of jazz-fusion, it was inevitable that one day I would be forced to take more than a passing interest in a musician I had tried to avoid through supposed dislike. It is a great satisfaction to me now that I did make the effort to understand John's work, and I am pleased to present the results of my work in this volume.

John's role in jazz-fusion is so extensive that I have also written about him in other volumes of this series. In particular, his contributions to the music of Miles Davis at a crucial time in music history have been spelled out in my book, *Miles*

Davis, Dark Prince (2010). It is not my intention to reproduce that material here. I therefore ask readers to forgive any perceived deficiencies in this volume, which is intended to be a study of John's own music as evidenced by his catalogue of available recordings. This book is not a biography. Even given those limitations, it's clear that there is a vast amount more that remains unsaid in a busy, productive life that publishes recordings only infrequently. This book can only scour the edges of such a great musician. Nevertheless, in the absence of other readily available material, and because John McLaughlin should be heard by more people, I hope you will find this book of some value.

Introduction

Around 70 AD (*Anno Davis*), the Great One had many disciples. Creating plenty where there was none, he miraculously fed the multitudes with loaves baked from wheat flour grown in the field of jazz, and fishes taken from the rock pools. His helpers helped themselves, planning their own gospels. With their eyes focussed sharply on their future careers, there seemed an almost indecent haste to get the Davis stamp on their indentures, and then to set off on the road to Damascus (that's the one in Illinois, of course) where they could start up for themselves in the evangelical business. Herbie Hancock and Chick Corea went their separate ways, whilst Wayne Shorter and Joe Zawinul chose to work closely together, a decision that brought them great success in Weather Report until the mid-1980s. John McLaughlin, Tony Williams and Billy Cobham were three musicians who would each be regarded as the best in their own fields of play. For reasons I shall discuss at length, John McLaughlin, a white, English guitarist, is one of the most important characters in a study of jazz-fusion.

In the mid-1960s, Western culture was in the midst of a musical revolution largely brought about by the invention of rock 'n' roll and the impact of new electronics on the process of making and recording music. One result was the blending of jazz with rock music to make a new musical genre known as jazz-rock, jazz-fusion, or just fusion. I have written about this in detail in my book, *Jazz-Fusion, Blue Notes and Purple Haze* (2009). Many musicians claim to have had a hand in the creation of the new genre. John McLaughlin did not invent jazz-rock, but he certainly played an important early role in its introduction to a wider audience. Furthermore, much of his career up to the present time has been spent working with music fusions.

Unfortunately, by the late 1970s, the word 'fusion' became synonymous with 'bad'. Gene Santoro expressed it well. "Fusion is a dirty word, almost an unword…Fusion has become a dirty word because of the 1970s jazz-rock hybrid it got pasted onto, and is practically unusable in any other context. Jazz purists then – like their descendants today – managed to forget that the music they so dearly love itself started and continues only as a hybridization of sounds, so for them the idea of welding rock beats and electronics to jazz's improvisational ways was the equivalent of scrawling a crayon moustache on the Mona Lisa." [6]

For an army of jazz fans, it had been painful to watch Miles Davis terminate his Second Great Quintet to take up a wishy-washy tuneless brand of fusion. They voted with their venom. However, the person perhaps most responsible for the severe reaction against fusion was John McLaughlin. This fiery electric guitarist, who could compete against any rock guitarist in the world (and win against most), led the Mahavishnu Orchestra and astonished everybody with a brand of guitar-based jazz-rock fusion that the jazz purists hated even more than Davis's fusion. Most didn't see McLaughlin's fusion as jazz at all, but as another weird outgrowth of the multi-headed hydra that rock music had become. Those who did at least recognise the jazz contained within the music saw it as a sell-out to rock music and feared the end of their beloved music. These feelings soured the atmosphere for years afterwards until around 1978 when, as many people argued, the fusion movement was declared dead (or perhaps just infected with The Plague). Even then, jazz-fusion music was denigrated at every opportunity, an odd, illogical manifestation of human behaviour that continues today. With the name 'fusion' cast into the bottom of the trash can, John, however, continues to make music that is as much a fusion of different genres than ever before. As I write this in 2013, John's latest band, the 4th Dimension, continues to play jazz-rock fusion that is as good, if not better, than any he has played in the past. And, at long last, nobody talks about it as fusion any more and simply recognises it for what it is – unbelievably great music!

Early Life

John McLaughlin was born on 4 January 1942 in Yorkshire, England where he lived with his sister and three older brothers. The family environment was a musical one and it was natural for him to start to learn piano at nine years old. With older brothers in the house, John, aged eleven, quickly discovered the blues and was initially inspired by guitarists Leadbelly, Big Bill Broonzy and Muddy Waters. Soon afterwards, John dropped the piano and took ownership of the 'family' guitar. His brother taught him a few chords. Aged 13/14 he began to enjoy Flamenco music and the concept of improvisation. Then he discovered the Miles Davis / Gil Evans 1950s fusion of jazz with Spanish music; it was a bridge into jazz sensibilities. He also listened to swing players and was very impressed by guitarist Tal Farlow. His growing skills in Spanish style guitar playing meant that his style was to pick the strings with all of his fingers, but he thought it wasn't working for him. Having heard Tal Farlow, the American became John's hero for a while and John was converted to using a single pick.

Thanks to his mother's playing of the violin, John became interested in the jazz violinists Django Reinhardt and Stephane Grapelli. The combination of the sounds of violin and guitar clicked with him, and was an important influence when he formed the first Mahavishnu Orchestra, and later Shakti.

At school he played in several bands, including a skiffle group, which was a popular thing to do in mid-50s England. He also played in jazz groups, both in the Dixieland and the mainstream styles. Perhaps from this moment in 1955/6, John McLaughlin became dedicated to the cause of the jazz guitar. No-one could have guessed just how great a guitarist he would become.

His first step was to leave school in 1957 at the age of 15 and move to Manchester where he played as a professional guitarist in a band called Big Pete Deuchar and his Professors of Ragtime. The band soon broke up and John travelled to London where there were more opportunities. McLaughlin: "In those days there were two clubs: The Marquee and the Flamingo. They were great. Everybody met everybody there, and the attitude was that everybody could play with everybody. So this is what I did. I remember jam sessions with everybody and anybody." [7]

Perhaps, like Miles Davis, John was lucky by being in the right place at the right time. John was always ahead of the game - literally. Soon after its formation, he played with Brian Auger's Trinity, but was gone when in 1968 the band (with singer Julie Driscoll) hit the big time with a UK smash hit *This Wheel's on Fire*. In 1962, John was playing with Georgie Fame and the Blue Flames - another of the popular R&B bands that started up in the early 60s, with Georgie, like Auger, playing Hammond organ. After John left, they became a big success from the mid 1960s, making regular appearances in the UK charts with songs such as *Yeah, Yeah*.

One of John's early colleagues was singer Duffy Power, and along with Terry Cox and Danny Thompson, Power formed a band called Duffy's Nucleus. Recordings were made, but none seem to be available today. Then John made a record with Duffy Power, alongside Bond, Baker and Bruce in the Graham Bond Quartet. Recorded on 20 February 1963, it was to be a 45-rpm single vinyl, and one of the very first covers of a Beatles number, *I Saw Her Standing There* (1963). However, the released version was actually of a tape recorded on 20 March that featured Jim Sullivan, instead of John, on guitar because the original version was rejected for unknown reasons. John did, however, appear on the record's 'B' side, *Farewell Baby*. [8] John went on to make a number of other records with Power, many of which appear on Duffy's album, *Innovations* (1971) or a later CD compilation entitled *Vampers and Champers* (2006).

In March 1963 the Graham Bond Trio, with Bond, Ginger Baker and Jack Bruce, became a Quartet with the addition of McLaughlin to the line-up. Once more, it was early in the life of the band. An organist who doubled on alto sax, Bond was just starting to have a big impact on the British music scene with his own brand of free jazz-influenced R&B. John can be heard on the tracks *The Grass Is Greener* and *Doxy*, recorded with this band on 26 June 1963, and available on Graham Bond's re-released album, *Solid Bond* (2008). The first of these is a fast blues-based piece of mainstream jazz, co-written with Bond, that shows just how immersed John, aged 21, was into the genre by this early phase in his life. The second piece, *Doxy*, is similar, but slower and meaner. It would be hard to identify him from his style at this point, as he had not yet developed his own individual sound, but he is confident and really swings through this Sonny Rollins standard. I feel it important to say that, despite what some may argue, neither of these tracks is characteristic of jazz-rock fusion at this point. I have argued in my book, *Jazz-Fusion: Blue Notes and Purple Haze*, that Bond was possibly an unwitting participant in the creation of jazz-fusion, something that happened after McLaughlin had, once again, moved on.

By now, John was becoming interested in spirituality. "I knew there was something magical about life, but I didn't know what it was." [9] He had listened to Coltrane's *A Love Supreme* (1964), but said he didn't understand it. "I joined the Theosophical Society in London and made an attempt to discover what religion really means." [9] Graham Bond was interested in the occult and they had many discussions together about spirituality. John found the Society meetings boring, but through people he met there, and his talks with Graham, he became aware of many books that helped him find India and philosophies derived from those cultures. He made friends with fellow guitarist, Big Jim Sullivan, whose interest in Indian music reminded John of the time he had first listened to it as a teenager. This time, his interest was deeper. Graham Bond had already fuelled his philosophical interest, but his love of Indian culture and music was to be one of several life-changing events he would be fortunate enough to experience. [10]

Around August 1963, John was fired from the GBQ by Ginger Baker, of all people. His replacement was a saxophonist, Dick Heckstall-Smith. At this point, he had developed into a formidable electric guitar technician and jazz musician, without making the crucial mark in jazz-fusion. His career so far had been all about playing with musicians who would later make it big without him!

As a jobbing musician, John took work wherever he could find it. His acquaintance with Mick Jagger and Co. got him a gig on three recordings used as demo tracks of the Rolling Stones. They were only released years later on the album *Metamorphosis* (1975). Around 1964-5, John played for a year with the Ray Ellington Quartet, which provided musical interludes for the famous British radio comedy *The Goon Show*. By the end of the gig he was able to read music so proficiently that he was a natural choice to become a session guitarist for many of the pop music hits during the time up to 1966, playing for such artists as Tom Jones, Dionne Warwick, Petula Clark and Englebert Humperdinck. These pop music singers were well known in every British household at the time, and went on to achieve international fame, but the musicians who helped to make their sound were almost never recognised. McLaughlin was one of them. It nearly drove him crazy and after a while he gave it all up to take a variety of ordinary jobs that had nothing to do with music, though he continued to play gigs in his spare time with the best of British jazz musicians such as John Dankworth and Tony Roberts, as well as South African saxophonist Dudu Pukwana. He appeared on two tracks of David Bowie's *The World of David Bowie* (1967). In 1967 John played with Gordon Beck whose drummer was Tony Oxley. John would hire Oxley for his first album. In 1968 he spent around six months playing free jazz in Germany with Gunter Hampel, times of which there appears to be nothing on record. McLaughlin lived in Antwerp for a time so that he could easily return to England to play in a trio with Dave Holland and Tony Oxley.

In an interview for *Down Beat* magazine, John told Chuck Berg of how, for a while, he became disenchanted with the role of guitar in jazz music. "I didn't feel anyone was approaching the height and inspiration of Miles and Coltrane. This was my own personal feeling. I don't know what it was but guitar players didn't have it." Playing in the style of Wes Montgomery, which was all most jazz guitarists could do at that time, was thoroughly unsatisfactory. "When I pursued it further, I couldn't get out of it what I wanted, what Coltrane and Miles gave me." [11] Though he didn't recognise it at the time, it was this yearning that led John (and others) into jazz-fusion.

John McLaughlin: *Extrapolation* – 1969 (*****)

John McLaughlin hung out in all the London haunts where good jazz was to be found. He knew everyone who was anyone: Mike Westbrook, Michael Gibbs, John Surman, Don Rendell, Ian Carr, Henry Lowther and Alan Skidmore. For a time he shared rooms with Dave Holland. One mark of a good jazzman is that his knowledge was of all kinds of instrumentalists, not just guitarists. Those in the know recognised John as one of the leading guitarists in Britain, still very much a jazz operative and well-known around the jazz circuit, but who had not made any recordings of his own.

At last, in January 1969, he was given the opportunity to make an album as leader. His quartet consisted of John Surman (baritone and soprano saxophone), Brian Odges (bass) and Tony Oxley (drums). Apparently, Holland was John's first choice for bass, but he had left for the USA when the recordings were made. Ron Carter left the Miles Davis band after the studio sessions for *Filles de Kilimanjaro* that took place on 19-21 June 1968; Holland was present at the next sessions in New York on September 24. As we shall see, Odges proved to be an excellent substitute. Together, McLaughlin, Surman, Odges and Oxley recorded *Extrapolation* (1969), a collection of innovative jazz pieces that at last allowed McLaughlin to show the world what he could do. The contrast between this and the work of all those pop singles could hardly have been greater. Here is a record of brilliant success and sweeping sophistication in many ways that I shall discuss below.

With some truly great albums, the magnitude of the achievement is not always immediately obvious. If you are unfamiliar with this album you can expect to spend a significant time delving into the many delights on offer and it will give you much pleasure in return, a pleasure that hopefully increases each time you play the disc.

McLaughlin's take on the title *Extrapolation* is of "past and present incidences focussed into the future." [12] In other words, real events with the timeline removed or blurred. This is a good indicator of the content of the whole album, which goes to considerable lengths to obscure the normal sense of time within the music. It is a formula that John would use a lot in the years to come. Indeed, I find myself making the same comments about *Señor CS*, for example, on *Industrial Zen* (2006).

The opening title track starts off innocuously in swing time, but the feeling of jazz mainstream is immediately dispelled as bass and drums, only loosely joined at the hip, play an introduction full of complexity. Then guitar and sax enter to play the quirky bebop-inspired theme that ends with a rather strangulated but inspiringly high baritone note. Baritone saxophone is an uncommon member of the gang of jazz instruments. Generally unpopular because of its surprisingly bass tones, it requires a huge amount of air from its master and often behaves more like a shire horse than a racehorse. Nevertheless, you should not underestimate the skill that Surman draws upon to make the sound of his beast as light and fleet as possible.

The angular theme is played twice, after which the piece suddenly fractures wide open and a sequence of quick-fire notes spews out from its core at double speed. After that, the band embarks on a round of solos, first from guitar, then from sax. The bass-playing is quite original, with no sign of the standard four-in-a-bar walking lines, just a sympathetic attempt to craft a harmonic accompaniment, whilst leaving the drums to keep the band together. Though there's an implied 4/4 rhythm, it always seems – as it does throughout most of this album - that the band is fooling us into believing that, whilst the rhythm might appear ordinary, the musicians are actually playing in a secret new rhythm known only to themselves.

The second track is *It's Funny* which begins with a slow 4/4 intro before Surman uses his soprano saxophone to introduce the title with its two-note motif based in 3/4. The subtitle indicates a relationship of the composition to some unpublished lyrics "reflecting its opposite result, Sadjoy". [12] There is thus a clear indication of a juxtaposition of opposites in the format of the music, presumably exemplified by the continual contra-flow between the two rhythms, 3/4 and 4/4. So well are they intertwined that it is frequently very difficult to count sensibly to this music, a property enhanced by Brian Odges' playing which never accedes to the normal bass player's role of keeping time, and drummer Tony Oxley's desire to cover his tracks throughout. It's a fascinating piece of jazz that, if you ignore all the technicalities of its construction, simply flows over you like a fresh spring breeze.

Arjen's Bag is dedicated to a mysterious Dutch musician. The subtitle implies that Arjen was a complex musician and this is appropriately borne out by the difficult 11/8 rhythm of this composition. (Try counting alternate sixes and fives.) Unlike the time signature, the melody played on Surman's baritone sax is both memorable and haunting, and the structure of the piece is a twelve-bar blues variation that, of course, sounds nothing like the blues until John's solo introduces some echoes of his old hero, Big Bill Broonzy. It's the first hint of jazz-fusion that is still an embryonic style in McLaughlin's subconscious musical mind.

Pete the Poet is named after one of the odd characters of the London music scene, a poet and lyricist called Pete Brown who wrote many lyrics for songs by Jack Bruce. Jazz and poetry were frequent bedfellows during this time of artistic experimentation and it was perfectly natural for poets to occupy stage time almost as much as jazz musicians. Another such character was Paul McCartney's brother Mike, who used his love of poetry to create a poetry-based pop group called the Scaffold, who had a number one hit with *Lily the Pink*, amongst other well-known numbers. This piece has a theme with a strong flavour of bebop, but the most mysterious time signature so far. Soloing is now something that all musicians do at once, and this piece is a forerunner of the group improvisation idea taken up by Weather Report several years later. The last part of the piece is a delicious drum solo by Oxley who magically returns the band to its flawless, synchronised theme.

This is for us to share is a love song, its intro played on Spanish guitar before the two Johns deliver the first strains of the theme and the rest of the quartet support the ever-divergent saxophone. As the tension builds, the band becomes increasingly animated. The music is *rubato* as timing is pretty much abandoned altogether. As Surman's saxophone reaches its highest notes, the piece ends in a beautiful symbiosis.

Spectrum is a brief burst of high-energy modal jazz. A short theme is followed at once by a freewheeling saxophone lead and then by a guitar solo before returning to the original fast bebop theme. *Binky's Beam* follows straight on and is a wholly extraordinary piece of music. It begins with a rock-blues oriented theme that is far better than anything he did for Miles Davis, if slightly reminiscent of his riff in *Right Off* on the Miles Davis album, *A Tribute to Jack Johnson* (1970). On closer examination, the main part of the music turns out to be played in a very complicated time signature that is a combination of alternate 6/4 and 7/8 and, taking this combination as a group, the piece cycles like a twelve bar blues. As the longest track by far on the album, the music is allowed full scope to consume its players, who turn the composition into an amazing piece of jazz. So far ahead of its time, this could be a blues for the twenty-second century.

Really to Know starts as a slow duet played as a loose waltz between bass and guitar. When sax and drums join in, Oxley's drums are ambiguous at first, but after some two and a half minutes support an evolution into swing time where McLaughlin resides until Surman pulls him back into the time warp.

Two for Two is labelled "an excursion into freedom" which indicates a bout of free jazz. The piece does begin with a short theme, after which McLaughlin improvises unaccompanied with a fierce blast of strummed chords. Then the rest of the band joins in for a brief spell of group improvisation that lasts until the theme returns and provides the ending.

Peace Piece is a straight non-improvised composition with strong Flamenco influences played on solo acoustic guitar and offers the audience the opportunity to appreciate the scope of John's guitar playing. Just in case listeners were beginning to think of him as a modern Jim Hall or Wes Montgomery, they discover that here is a musician who is comfortable with many different types of instrument and with the breadth of skills to take him far beyond the confines of electric guitar jazz.

It's very difficult for a British jazz artist to get the recognition he deserves for his work whilst working from a British base with a small market. So dominated is the jazz market by American musicians and so extensive is the American ignorance of anything from beyond their own shores that this album would normally have been consigned to obscurity. However, in John's case, his translation to an American base, and his consequent later fame, initiated a curiosity amongst his 70s and 80s fanbase that would constantly rediscover this album. As a result, it has continued to sell over the years, though even today there are substantial numbers of jazzers who have not heard the album, though they have heard *of* it. Here is an album filled with superlatives.

Too often the members of rhythm sections play Cinderella parts in group-work; that is absolutely not the case here. Odges must be the best, undiscovered bass player of the era, abandoning the conventional 'plunk, plunk, four-in-a-bar' rhythmic role for one of supreme creativity that hovers over, instead of on top of, the written bar lines. What might have happened if this album had been released just a few months earlier and Miles Davis, looking for the bass player for his new band, had heard Brian Odges instead of Dave Holland? Sadly for Odges, the arrow of fate pierced Holland's aura instead. This album is well worth listening to if only to study Odges' playing, especially since it is so well recorded. And with Odges so determined not play on the beat, Oxley deserves equal admiration for not feeling obliged to fill the void. His playing is equally as imaginative as any of the others, making the complex rhythms seem like a nursery rhyme to an opera singer, yet always guiding the musicians through the difficult arrangements.

Of course, all of the playing is superb, if not necessarily individually virtuosic. Surman won an award from *Downbeat* Magazine in 1969 for his playing, which is outstanding, whilst McLaughlin is constantly lyrical, and imaginative in whatever mode he operates. There's not much sign on this album of the sheets of aggressively plucked guitar notes he is now famous for, but that is irrelevant. His work on this album is majestic – and he was just 26 years old!

The music was far more cutting-edge than perhaps was realised at the time, and there is not the slightest hint of age in a single bar. The blend of instruments works beautifully and the musicianship in executing the charts of McLaughlin's compositions, most with extraordinarily complex themes and timings is of the highest order. Last, but not least, a great measure of coherence to the music is provided by running all the tracks together to make it a continuous piece with almost no breaks. Yet there are virtually no obvious edits and the smoothness of the result is a credit to the technicians that created it. It is beautifully recorded with clarity and warmth. Even the running order is pleasing and the album runs from beginning to end with the smoothness of Bentley engine. Whether at high or low revs, full power or gently ticking over, this motor is one of the sweetest power packs in recorded jazz.

Tony Williams

Like many others, John McLaughlin was listening to the best American jazz on record and meeting the musicians – even playing with some of them – when they came to Europe. He was already a big fan of King Davis and since his first acquisition of *Milestones* (1957) and *Kind of Blue* (1959) John had been a fan of all the King's Men too. As the seminal albums of the Second Great Quintet appeared through the 60s, he admired Tony Williams from afar as one of the world's great drummers. Tony had been taken on by the biggest name in jazz whilst still only a teenager, and, through an unrivalled sequence of albums by

Davis's quartet from 1964-69, had established a new level of virtuosity in jazz drumming thanks to his stunning polyrhythmic technique and a desire to break away from the old school of jazz drumming.

For jazz fans and musicians in the UK, the focus was Ronnie Scott's club in London – indeed, it still is! It was here on 28 October 1968 that John, with his friend Dave Holland, sat in to jam with the great American drummer, Jack de Johnette, in town with the Bill Evans trio. Jack recorded their bit of spontaneous fun on a cheap tape recorder and took it back to America with him. Then in September 1968, Miles Davis flew to London to hear Dave Holland play, and met McLaughlin at the same time. Davis later phoned Holland and made the invitation that was to change his life. Little did McLaughlin think then that the same stroke of luck would also fall upon his shoulders.

Many people regard Tony Williams as one of the greatest jazz drummers. Tony was born in Chicago on 12 December 1945. His father, a saxophonist, regularly took him to jazz clubs, and by the age of 15 he was taking drum lessons at Berklee with Alan Dawson and starting to sit in on jam sessions in the Boston area. During 1959-60, he was regularly playing with local saxophone player Sam Rivers. He accepted a job to tour with Jackie McLean's band, and it was Jackie who persuaded Williams, barely 17, to move to New York in December 1962 as a permanent member of the quintet. He made his recording debut in 1964 when aged 18 on the Blue Note album of free jazz *Out to Lunch* (1965) by Eric Dolphy. Tony's reputation was made, however, in Miles Davis's Second Great Quintet of 1963-68, as part of what many would regard as one of the most influential rhythm sections with Ron Carter (bass) and Herbie Hancock (piano). Williams was invited to join the Miles Davis band in 1963 during the recording of the material for *Seven Steps to Heaven* (1963). After the early material had been recorded in LA with Frank Butler in the drum seat, Tony joined Miles in New York with another new boy, Herbie Hancock. When Tony joined Miles he was so young that the other band members had to act as escort for him in the venues where they were playing.

I have written elsewhere about Williams' career with Miles Davis so I shall not duplicate that. I should remind you that his formative years were those in which the current direction of jazz was the abandonment of rules and the pursuit of abstraction. Young players like Williams, Hancock, Corea, and even the not-so-young Wayne Shorter, were strongly affected by this tide of change, just as they would be affected by the next tide of jazz-fusion.

Like the others in the band, Williams was fortunate to be able to make albums in parallel with his work with Davis. Indeed, he played in a Davis 'ghost' band, at gigs when Miles couldn't make it because he was ill (as frequently was the case). Freddie Hubbard replaced Miles. Then there were the other albums made in each of the names of Shorter, Hancock and Carter, most of them for Blue Note. Williams too was given a contract with Blue Note and made his own debut album *Lifetime* (1963) with Sam Rivers (saxophone), Bobby Hutcherson (vibraphone), Herbie Hancock (piano), Richard Davis (bass) and Gary Peacock (bass) when Williams was only seventeen.

By the end of the 1960s, as one of the most admired drummers in the world, he was in constant demand and the jazz world was his oyster. Then, like Davis, he became smitten with the staggering success of the loud rock bands and wanted his own piece of the action. In 1968, Williams was 22 and Davis was 42: there was a generation gap. Davis could see the changes that were going on in the world of rock music and was making his plans for the future. Williams, was certainly grateful to Davis for giving him his chance, but from a viewpoint twenty years distant Tony watched the rock bands create what was, to him, wondrous music. He saw them becoming wealthy beyond his dreams. Even Miles Davis, the biggest earner in jazz, couldn't get near the rock superstars for money. Jimi Hendrix, Jeff Beck, Eric Clapton, (and those who played in their bands, such as Jack Bruce and Ginger Baker did with Cream) ... Williams wanted to be a part of that action for sure, especially as (in 1968) Cream was about to disband. He could fill the gap they left behind. Furthermore, he could add something else to the mix - jazz! He believed he was more accomplished, more creative than any of the rock drummers and wanted to prove it to the world. It was the new Gold Rush, and like all such events, there was a great sense of urgency not to miss out on a golden opportunity.

In 1969, Tony Williams decided to leave Miles and form his own band. Inspired by a debut album, *Lifetime* (1964), he made for the premier jazz label of the time, Blue Note Records, he decided his new band would be called The Tony Williams Lifetime. Clearly he needed a heavyweight guitarist to be the centrepiece of a Cream-type group. He asked his friends for recommendations. Sonny Sharrock was first choice, but Sonny thought he was being asked to play rock 'n' roll and declined. Then Williams heard John McLaughlin on a tape that Jack de Johnette played him. Tony realised he had found his man. Late in 1968, he invited McLaughlin to New York. John left on 3 February 1969 and on his very first day in New York played a jam session at Basie's in Harlem during which he blew everyone away. Miles was in the audience, along with Larry Coryell, a guitarist from Texas born in 1943. Coryell had secured his first big break with Gary Burton on *Duster* (1967) and stayed in that band for three albums. When he saw McLaughlin play, Coryell said McLaughlin was the best player he had ever seen. John was clearly uppermost in Davis's mind too when he decided he needed a guitarist for his new recordings. McLaughlin's first sessions for Davis took place on 18 February when *In a Silent Way* was being recorded.

When McLaughlin accepted Williams' offer to join the band, he had no idea who else would be in it. He didn't care, " – it was Tony!" The offer of working with someone famous was too tempting to miss. He was stunned to discover that his other colleague in a trio would be Hammond organist Larry Young. Organ seems an odd choice of instrument today, but in those days before electronic keyboards had any real significance, the organ was considered really cool. We should remember that John had already spent a lot of time playing in bands led by organists. Furthermore, organ trios were popular because the bass player was dispensable when the organist could supply bass by means of his foot pedals. McLaughlin loved the sound of the organ. He could think of no better trio to start a new phase of his career with. In common with a number of other American jazz musicians at this time, Young was in the process of converting to Islam. He changed his name and became Khalid Yasin. (McLaughlin, of course, was soon to do something similar as a follower of Indian culture.)

McLaughlin's experience turned out to be different from that of his friend, Dave Holland. Dave had come over to play with Miles and found himself there at once. John had come to play with Tony, but Tony's plans to record were thrown off course. When Williams approached Columbia for a recording contract, according to Carr, they failed an audition, an indication that there were at least some people who were less than impressed with Williams' ideas. [13] He would have to look elsewhere for financial backing and it took a little while to get started.

Meanwhile, Davis invited McLaughlin to sit in on his own sessions that would result in the album *In a Silent Way* (1969). How could McLaughlin refuse? Williams and McLaughlin were both present at the first session of 1969, on 18 February, but on the 20 February, Joe Chambers replaced Williams, and by the time of the next recorded session on tour in Europe in July, the drummer was Jack de Johnette. John was a member of Davis's studio band, but not the touring band. He had come to the USA to play with Tony, and that was what he chose to do, despite being asked (more than once) to become a full member of Davis's band. It is truly astonishing that John was able to decline Davis's invitation, but as he later said, it was the musical freedom offered by Williams that he needed. The ever-pragmatic Davis wasn't bothered, and simply invited John to the recording sessions for the next couple of years. John was therefore incredibly lucky to have accidentally found this compromise position. He could play for Miles *and* Tony at the same time! Williams, on the other hand, did not play for a Davis recording again, except at a one-off session in September 1985.

The two Miles Davis albums that John played on in 1969 were *In a Silent Way* and *Bitches Brew*. The timing of this opportunity for John to make an impact could hardly have been more crucial. Miles was at another of his great career milestones and these two albums have been universally accepted as being amongst the most important in the history of jazz. Not only was jazz at the crossroads where it was intersecting with rock music, but there were other societal changes taking place that had a big impact on culture. The age of modern semiconductor electronics was starting to impact upon music and new equipment and technology was becoming available. Thus, possibly influenced by the imaginative use of tapes and new editing techniques, just as the Beatles were advantaged by George Martin's skills in the studio, so also was Miles greatly assisted by the creativity shown by his own producer, Teo Macero. New ways of working in the studio were adopted; tape recorders were left running for the whole time the studio was in use and this necessitated the use of significant editing. Miles's insistence that everything should be spontaneous was an invitation for Macero to be creative in his use of splicing and new kinds of compositions were artificially constructed in this way.

For John to have been present at these historical sessions was, of course, not just a stroke of luck, but reflected the way in which his reputation had carried across the Atlantic. However, Miles did not use John for his extreme gift of virtuosity. John had been selected because Miles considered him to have the kind of musical mentality he wanted. He instructed John to play in ways John had up to then not considered. For a virtuoso to be told to play like he didn't know how to was especially puzzling. In John's case, especially, less was more. Most importantly of all, musicians in Miles's bands should never play clichés. Thus, listening to John's contributions to these albums is more for historical reasons than to learn about new amazing guitar techniques. It is far more about the conveyance of feelings and moods than about formal musical compositions. Many years later, one of John's friends would remark that the effect of music on people was brought about by a combination of its sound and the lifestyle attached to it. [14]

For Miles, the sound was always crucial and there were many factors that he was looking for. As for lifestyle, other unexpected issues came to the fore. For example, John's very presence in the band was anathema to most jazz fans, who viewed the use of a solid-bodied electric guitar as a sell-out to those awful rock musicians. Miles had experimented with electric guitarists, like Joe Beck and George Benson, on a couple of tracks on earlier albums, but this was the first time he had given the guitar a central role in the band. It was an obvious, clear, conscious decision that many observers did not like. Then there was the matter of race. Miles was very keen to sell his new musical ideas to black people, but the white honky from England didn't go down well with many. Why couldn't Miles have found a black guitarist? Miles's response was simple: he couldn't find anyone better.

On *Bitches Brew* there is a track named after John. *John McLaughlin* was not intended to be a stand-alone musical composition, but was a result of Macero's new editing style as he constructed a montage of John's playing at the recording session and used it to showcase his style. Miles himself does not play on it. For much of the rest of the time, John's contributions are surprisingly low-key, in line with Miles's requirements.

John had certainly made his mark in more ways than had been expected. Other doors began to open for John too, thanks to John's new American friends. He recorded with Wayne Shorter on *Supernova* (1969) and on *Moto Grosso Feio* (1970), and with Miroslav Vitous on *Infinite Search* (1969) and *Purple* (1970). From the first day he got the call from Miles, his career could only go upwards. In the mean time, he had an appointment with Tony.

The Tony Williams Lifetime: *Emergency!* – 1969 (*)

The first Lifetime album, *Emergency!* (1969), was not recorded until May 1969. Al Kooper, founder member of Blood Sweat and Tears, had come to an early gig with the possibility of recruiting Lifetime to a record deal, but he was not impressed with what he heard. Williams finally succeeded in attracting the support of Polydor (now part of the Verve Group) and signed a contract for three albums. At the time, the company was inexperienced and the band suffered. The first album, *Emergency!* was recorded (badly) within weeks of the recordings for *In a Silent Way*. The contrast between the two leaders' ideas for the new genre could not have been greater: loud versus soft, hard tension versus cool vibe. But more important in terms of the result was Davis's management and his record company. Davis's management was the best, Williams' poor and ineffective; Davis's record company was the most powerful, Williams' a fledgling company with no real distribution capability. In contrast with *Bitches Brew*, which became a worldwide best-seller, the only input Lifetime could make to the creation of jazz-fusion was through its live gigs, which were cataclysmic events to all those fortunate enough to be present. But Lifetime remained invisible to the wider public because of its double whammy of both bad and invisible records. It was inevitable that the band would be consigned to an immediate impotence and a long-term place in the category of cult bands. Years later, when the band's important role in the early history of jazz-fusion had cemented a firmer place in the historical back catalogues for music enthusiasts, attempts were made to re-master the album for CD. The most recent was the 2011 version credited to Cherry Red Records on the Esoteric Recordings label. It was soon realised just how bad the original masters were and this remains evident on the CD today: there is only so much that can be done. However, even if the recording quality were perfect, my own analysis would remain the same.

Nicholson writes that it was Lifetime that was the most influential jazz-rock band and that *"Emergency*! remains one of the most important jazz-rock albums of all time". It was the first band to use "the dynamics of electricity to such coruscating effect." [15] I would not agree, in view of its extremely poor distribution in the 1970s. Perhaps Nicholson is viewing it with the benefit of hindsight. John McLaughlin himself lauded the band in 1978. "Working with Miles and Tony was the best of all worlds. In fact, Miles asked me to join his group permanently. But by this time Lifetime with Larry Young was underway. I thought that Larry was the greatest organ player in the world. So here was my favourite organist with my favourite drummer. I was in the perfect setup. We were making pennies, but I felt it to be a part of my destiny." [11]

The opening track *Emergency!* begins with a mush of guitar and drum noise playing a very unimaginative chromatic motif, presumably intending to announce the arrival of a new loud band on the scene. Sadly, that's all it is. Afterwards, the trio begins a section of fast jazz of the modal type that does not indicate any kind of attempt to create anything special. Williams is drumming pretty much as he did with Miles whist McLaughlin is improvising to nothing that is identifiable. After a slower section, the original theme returns and introduces Young's slow organ solo: hardly the auspicious start we might have expected. In essence, the first track is simply a compilation of long sections of free-form jazz improvisation bolted onto a crude loud rock theme. Is it experimental? Yes. Is it of value? No.

Williams' second attempt at a musical composition *Beyond Games* is made worse by his embarrassing attempts to add a vocal track. It seems he had decided to 'enhance' the appeal of the band towards the rock audiences by adding vocals to the music. This was to be one of the characteristics of Lifetime's three albums. The plan failed spectacularly. Crass lyrics and wailed non-existent melodies recorded over a quiet medium-tempo improvisation may have seemed ultra-modern at the time, but became a serious misjudgement, even from today's perspective. As if that was not bad enough, Williams proved to have an over-inflated idea of his own skills of composition. The trio's work during the rest of this long, tedious piece is mostly McLaughlin improvising over a rock-type theme with a distorted guitar sound as Young contributes a mostly chordal backing.

The third track is the ungrammatical *Where*. Written by McLaughlin, it might have indicated a little more forethought or creativity. Sadly, that is not the case. To hear Williams repeatedly wailing "Where am I going?" out of tune is not my idea of entertainment. Only when Lifetime performed music composed by others, did the poor quality of the content stand a chance of redemption. Thus,

Vashkar is a piece by Carla Bley that appeared on the album *Jaco* (1974) by Pastorius Metheny Ditmas Bley, a band led by Carla's husband Paul. The theme is presented fairly sensibly and developed by Young through a wholly ineffective improvisation that again is a mush of sound with loud drums for accompaniment. McLaughlin's role as guitarist was minimal.

Via the Spectrum Road sounds like it is intended to provide an introduction to the track that follows it, although there is no obvious musical relationship. After a brief early hopeful start nested in the blues, the tedious, amateur vocals start again. Afterwards, McLaughlin's *Spectrum*, which appeared on *Extrapolation* and which remains a fast piece of mainstream modal jazz here, is an honest attempt to recreate a clearly composed piece of jazz in the context of the new trio. There is no attempt to give it any kind of false stylistic context. Young makes a good attempt to provide a fast improvisation, but the result is another musical mush.

By this point in the album, this whole project seems like a crude attempt to join the ranks of the prog-rock bands and make money, not a serious attempt to create novel jazz, which had been the clear aim in recording *Extrapolation*. The penultimate track is *Sangria for Three*, a thirteen minute recording of dense brown noise that is impenetrable to analysis for any kind of harmony, melody or accepted musical construction. It is possible to discern drumming patterns and the pace varies from slow to fast and energetic. The final section is a freeform jam. Exactly what is being attempted here – other than what we might today call head-banging energy - is a mystery to me. Last is *Something Special*, which definitively it is not. Indeed, it could be argued that I enjoy the sound of my car engine or domestic washing machine more than this – at least those mechanical devices are doing something useful for me. Anyone who says this is a good album hasn't listened to it for thirty years.

The disaster that this eagerly anticipated album turned out to be merely emphasises the low likelihood of successful musical compositions from the pens of drummers who, with only a few exceptions, have a much narrower concept of musical scope at the high level of performance we are discussing here.

In the liner notes, Ralph Gleason makes a splash that "it is absolutely unlike any other instrumental sound I have ever heard." Well, that may be true but it neither guarantees quality or value or longevity, properties that score zero on all counts in my analysis of this. Those like Gleason who find this music worthwhile are clearly expecting something quite different from their musical experience. This music fails the test of critical, reasoned analysis. It's also horrible to listen to. The ideas are abstract, even allowing for some crystallisation around the lyrics that add nothing at all, and even detract from the overall result by their appalling naivety and poor execution.

The contemporary critical reception to *Emergency!* had been bad and the band's life-force had been possible only through the enthusiasm it inspired in rock fans that turned up to the gigs. Here lies a big clue to the difference between assessments of Lifetime. Much of the hyperbole written about the band emanated from people who had attended the gigs. They, at least, were enthusiastic about the energy (i.e. volume!) they obtained from the live music, as well as the obvious virtuosity that is often demonstrated live. Pete "the poet" Brown, McLaughlin's friend, also wrote lyrics for Jack Bruce's songs. He said the band was "never beaten live" and that "the records never did the band justice". [16]

Much of the strength of the new jazz-fusion genre lay in its volume, something that is hard to convey with an album, even when it is turned up to maximum. But, as we shall see with the Mahavishnu Orchestra, it should also have been about content and quality too. The music critics made their judgements based on the poor content and quality of this album, something Williams did not have the skills to improve. The critics were not backward in coming forward with printed damnation.

For me, with only albums to work from, the obvious difference lies in the comparison with Cream. Given the fact that Cream had disbanded some six months before this was recorded, it is impossible to conclude that this album was anything other than a regression. McLaughlin had been wooed by the hype of Williams' fame, and by the simple power of his playing, not by any evidence of his musical vision. Looking back to Miles's albums, where was the evidence that Williams was a good composer? Why should John ever have thought that Williams could give him more than he had with his British colleagues, except money, perhaps? For someone who had just released an astonishingly inventive and novel record *Extrapolation*, McLaughlin should have been disappointed with the result of this two-day recording session. The contrast between the two albums could hardly have been greater. Clearly, in this twentieth century Klondike, the dash for cash had blinded Williams to the need for a substantial product. It looked like he had staked his claim in barren territory. Fortunately, it was the band's live performances that saved his reputation.

The Tony Williams Lifetime: *Turn It Over* – 1970 (*)

The second album *Turn It Over* is billed as a protest album in which Williams is supposedly railing against the jazz establishment for not showering him with kisses for his creativity and foresight – a typical reaction from someone who does not understand his own lack of ability (at composition and production, not drumming!) Williams, desperate to replicate Cream's mega-success, must have begged Jack Bruce to join. In the event, Jack played on one track, or was it two? Stump says Bruce was keen to join, but that there were problems caused by conflicts between the musicians' managers. These problems were never satisfactorily resolved and ultimately resulted in Bruce's departure after the album *Ego* (1971), by which time McLaughlin had left for similar reasons.

Chick Corea provides two pieces at the start of the album: *To Whom it May Concern – Them* and *To Whom it May Concern - Us*. They run together and continue the very loud rock music approach, genuinely embodying jazz-rock characteristics. Then comes *This Night, This Song*, a hideously sung Williams composition in which I can find no merit whatever except for the puzzle created by the presence of an electric bass sound when, according to the sleeve notes, there is no bass player present. Was Bruce playing on this one? It sounds like it.

With *Big Nick* we finally get to hear a swinging jazz piece with a hard rock edge. It's hardly surprising since Williams has chosen a Coltrane number that is led by Young's good organ playing and with Williams doing what he does best. On the other hand, Williams' own *Right On* is just an excerpt of noise edited using the 'Macero Method for Miles' from some other unexplained source – presumably some studio jamming, for example.

The beautiful Bossa Nova number by Jobim *Once I Loved* is transformed into a piece of excruciating noise, as if a lovely melody was being pulled through a wormhole. Enough said. It is painfully followed by *Veulta Abajo* another Williams fiasco with a pretentious title, appropriately loud and frantic for a budding prog-rock prima donna, but entirely vacuous. Then, just when you think it can't get any worse, we reach *A Famous Blues*, a piece about which I am lost for suitable words of description. Perhaps that was the aim of the exercise. It is not even saved from damnation by having McLaughlin as its originator.

Allah Be Praised is by Young and offers a brief respite from the trashcan of recordings on this album. Offered a sensible idea with which to work, the band succeeds in creating an interesting piece of fast, novel jazz-fusion that has several distinct sections for all three musicians to show their mettle, including some novel 'thrash jazz' at the end.

To reach the final track on this album is something of an achievement. The carrot on the painfully large stick was the anticipation of hearing Jack Bruce sing a McLaughlin composition, with Williams just playing drums. However, Jack's unfortunate role as a victim of the Spanish Inquisition, stretched on the rack to the point at which every fibre of his vocal chords are at breaking point, is not a pretty sound. The end-product is a piece of prog-rock that some fans of that genre may enjoy, but not this listener. Like death to the tortured, it's a great relief when the agony is finally over.

Williams' exhortation to listeners to "Play it very loud" is not one that I wish to endorse in this case. Even in his Davis days, Williams was driven to play loud just because he could, not through the exigencies of the music and to this day it remains the biggest single criticism of the drummer in this purple patch of his life. However, the theme of 'loud at all costs' was carried forward by McLaughlin into the Mahavishnu Orchestra, which I shall describe later. Of course, playing very loud had become the norm, made possible by the developments in electronics. Most contemporary bands measured success, not just in sales, but also in terms of the number of watts they consumed to create the music. As a member of that young generation myself, I well remember how much enthusiasm accompanied the description of a band's use of tall stacks of Marshall amps. At the time, it was obvious to us that The Who was a better band than Cream when it had invested in more grunt.

In 1978, John said of Lifetime, "That group was one of the greatest in the world. I mean, I wouldn't have hung in for so long if I didn't believe it." We must take that statement seriously. What is more, John believed the band was going to get better still with Jack Bruce on board. Lifetime was about to make a record as a quartet with Bruce at the time John quit. Part of the reason for his departure was that the band's management was so bad. "Jack was singing and the material [for the new record] was very new. It was revolutionary and just incredible but there was such a bad scene going down between the management and the band that the recording never got made." [17]

But his assessment of the band's achieved greatness is based upon being a part of the band for two years, with hundreds of live gigs and many more hours of jamming together. The judgement I make here is based upon my listening to a few bad recordings, and, dear reader, I am describing what you and I both hear. We must recognise that Lifetime was a very important band for those who attended the gigs. I fear that these few Lifetime records constitute the band's only legacy for the distant future and reflect badly upon what this band was really about.

John McLaughlin: *Devotion* – 1970 (*)

On 25 March 1969 Tony's band was still just a twinkle in its creator's eye. He may well have been frustrated at the delay in his plans, but there was much going on in the music world that would later become rock folklore. For instance, McLaughlin met Mitch Mitchell that day. Mitch was an old friend from his days with Georgie Fame who, from 1966 to 1968, had been drummer with the Jimi

Hendrix Experience. He invited John to a late night jam session with Hendrix in the Record Plant studios. John went with Larry Young and Dave Holland. Little was known about the meeting for a long time in the public arena, and in later years, for many people, it was incredible that two such guitar legends should have been in the same room together, let alone have a tape machine running. Great speculation and rumour abounded for years afterwards, thanks to a bootleg CD entitled *Hell's Session* (1988) with wildly inaccurate sleeve notes. The facts, however, are fairly clear today. McLaughlin says they jammed during the early hours of the morning from 2 am until about eight. McLaughlin was playing his usual amplified acoustic Gibson Hummingbird guitar. It did not go well with Hendrix's kilowatts: there was a lot of feedback on John's guitar and the resulting twenty minutes or so of recorded material is of very poor quality. [18] John: "Basically, we played, but it was difficult because at the time I was using a hollow-bodied acoustic.....like a country guitar. The volume on it was so low and Buddy Miles was playing drums so loud. Dave Holland was there and Jimi played electric. It wasn't really a playing session....it was just hanging out....having a good time. I've only heard a little bit of tape, about two or three minutes, that's all they sent me. It sounded terrible to me." [19]

The following year, in September 1970, McLaughlin recorded *Devotion* at the Record Plant with Larry Young, Buddy Miles (drums) and Billy Rich (bass), a title that may have been inspired by the memories of Jimi Hendrix who had just died. This album has appeared in several editions. Recently it was repackaged once again and re-released under the title of *Marbles* (2007). McLaughlin had parted company with Tony Williams and the record was sponsored by the same Alan Douglas that had been involved at that meeting with Hendrix and was released on his own Douglas label. McLaughlin may want to forget the album if only because of the image of him that appears on the original edition. The photo shows him sporting a beard and what looks suspiciously like a Beatle-style haircut, in complete contradiction to the pure, clean shaven image that was to become his trademark soon afterwards with the Mahavishnu Orchestra. As for the album, McLaughlin wrote all of the music but does not succeed in creating any impression other than one of serious mediocrity. The music is almost wholly rock with no hint of jazz other than the use of the normal kinds of guitar improvisations that all rockers use. Any sign of the virtuosity on his instrument for which he had become renowned back in the UK had been expunged in his own personal rush to pan for gold.

More Miles

In April 1970, John played in further sessions with Miles as he recorded for the album *A Tribute to Jack Johnson* (1970). Possibly the most famous is the one in which the tracks for *Right Off* were recorded. Most commentators cite this track as the funkiest, rockiest thing that Miles did, and it bears his name as composer, to boot. Yet it was actually John McLaughlin and Billy Cobham together who kicked the piece off, quite spontaneously during a bout of what would otherwise have been warm-up sparring. John simply started to play a bluesy riff and Billy joined in, but the tapes were rolling. Miles, who was in the booth, realised that he liked what he was hearing and ran out, trumpet in hand, to join in. But this chance event did not alter the course of Davis's plans for he continued with his strategy of playing long, unstructured vamps behind extended free improvisations, a format that, in the long run, proved unpopular with wider audiences.

On several more occasions throughout 1970 and 1971, John was a regular at Miles' recordings and he made appearances on albums such as *On the Corner* (1972) *Big Fun* (1974), and *Get Up With It* (1975). With tapes rolling constantly, there was much that was recorded but not used until much later. There were other retrospective releases of Miles Davis material that included John, such as *Circle in the Round* (1979) and *Directions* (1981). (A list of John's sessions with Miles in included at the back of this book. Much more detail is available in my book, *Miles Davis: Dark Prince* (2010).) Later, the emphasis on electric guitar was enhanced by the presence of Reggie Lucas and Pete Cosey, although in the absence of McLaughlin, who had by then written a starring role of his own in the jazz-rock fusion movie.

John McLaughlin, John Surman, Karl Berger, Stu Martin, Dave Holland: *Where Fortune Smiles* – 1971 (**)

In late May 1970, McLaughlin took part in a small musical project with a group of friends, some old, some new. Most jazz musicians were inclined to give free jazz a run-out at some point in their careers and this was McLaughlin's. Dave Holland, of course, had been a friend since John's days in London, when both men shared a flat and attended sessions of the Spontaneous Music Ensemble in the Little Theatre Club that was the lesser-known alternative jazz venue to Ronnie Scott's club. Surman also knew John from London, but had to some degree exiled himself from the London scene in favour of the European circuit, where he has remained for most of his career since. Occasional reminiscences of his origins in the West of England are exemplified by albums such as *The Road to St Ives* (1992). Surman brought his fellow European friends Berger and Martin to this special party of spontaneity, which took place – no doubt, on a single day - in the Apostolic Studios in New York City.

You would have more success deciphering the Rosetta Stone than making sense of the accompanying notes to the Japanese CD edition of this disc. Cryptography is still in order even when you have managed to read the zero-size font overlaid with patterns on brown card. Some editions tried to promote sales by exaggerating McLaughlin's name, since it was always the most famous. However, this disc is by a band with no leader. McLaughlin and Surman seem to be the driving forces, although strictly speaking, equal credits should be applied. The music has no relevance to electric instruments, rock, fusion or funk. It is entirely about jazz that is not quite as free as Derek Bailey's, but is seriously demanding (or not if you choose to switch it off.) There are some minimal structures, heads and improvisations, in each of the five tracks. *Glancing Backwards (for Junior)* is structurally straightforward with a roundelay of harmonically undisciplined, free solos in between the very short phrase that cues the players in and out. It's a simple idea, executed with what was probably some exciting improvisations in 1971. The next two tracks are duets. Track two is John's *Earth Bound Hearts*, a slow, wistful duet between McLaughlin's guitar and Surman's untypically uneasy saxophone. This pleasant piece is adventurously harmonic and conventionally improvised, but the saxophone glitches indicate that the music was composed not long before it was recorded. So, sadly, this is no repeat of the fantastic success of *Extrapolations* (1969) as perhaps it was intended to be. Indeed, I suspect that none of this music existed before the day that it was recorded. Track three is the title track, a Surman piece that he, strangely, gives over to guitar and vibes. Similarly harmonic and structured to track two for at least three of the four minutes, it deteriorates into indecision for the third minute and the entirely miserable ending provides the truth of the song's provenance on the back of a fag packet.

From this point on, it's a tough ride. Track four is *New Place, Old Place* - over ten minutes of group therapy whereby the trashing of their musical educations on the scales of their instruments is presumably spiritually rewarding to the players, at least. As the name *Hope* suggests, the final track has the merest hint of a silver lining with an element of sincerity and soulfulness about it, even though it sounds like another freely improvised piece. Written by John, it contains the kinds of elements he enjoyed – a deeply spiritual feel that increases in tension and intensity until it reaches a majestic denouement. No doubt there are free jazz listeners who will love this album, which is far out enough to please them, whilst just clinging to the edge of acceptability for more traditional (and forgiving) ears. I think fortune must smile on those brave enough to take this music on.

Looking East

Crossover from one music genre to another was one thing, but the idea of crossover from one culture to another was very strange to most people in the early 1960s. George Harrison had led the Beatles towards the Indian culture in 1964 and, after taking up the sitar, introduced its sound into the band's music with *Norweigian Wood* on *Rubber Soul* (1964) and *Love You To* on the album *Revolver* (1965). Many fans found that quite a shock. They were absorbing the shock waves from the explosion of pop music within Western culture, and were quite unprepared to listen to music tinged with the sounds of the sitar, tamboura and tabla. Most learned to accept the new sounds as, at the least, interesting. Some who were already rejecting the Western ideologies that had resulted in so much war during the 20th century had grown tired of living under the threat of another global war that might this time result in the end of life on Earth. They saw Hinduism and Buddhism as fundamentally peaceful. Like John Lennon and Yoko Ono, they demanded *Give Peace a Chance* and voted with their feet by dipping them – sometimes above the knees - into those cultures. Being the most famous musicians on the planet during these years, the Beatles therefore did more to publicise Indian music and culture than anyone else up to this time and the level of interest in all things Indian was raised by an order of magnitude. The late 1960s turned into a period summed up by the phrase 'Make love, not war'. The 1967 'Summer of Love' and huge pop festival gatherings at places such as Woodstock were crystallised by the anti-Viet Nam War protests and led from the front by arch protest-song writer Bob Dylan.

Many Indian philosophers and musicians found themselves in demand. The philosophers were eagerly invited to lead the curious Westerners into the history, culture and religion of the East, whilst the musicians made that transition palatable by promoting and performing their music at concerts throughout Europe and the USA. Ravi Shankar was already famous as a sitar player. John Coltrane had studied his music briefly in the early 60s and was so impressed he named his second son after him.

Sri Chinmoy was a philosopher and musician invited to the USA in the mid 1960s. In 1970, just after recording *Devotion* John McLaughlin went to the Sri Chinmoy centre in Connecticut with Larry Coryell and was introduced to the spiritual leader. Already experienced in the arts of yoga and meditation, as well as being fond of Indian music, it was entirely natural for John to become more deeply involved with Eastern culture and practices. Coryell was less interested in the kind of commitment Sri Chinmoy was looking for, but John, who had previously been as deeply into drugs and alcohol as many other musicians, began to adopt a new 'clean' image and dressed himself in loose white clothing. Sri Chinmoy gave John the name Mahavishnu, which has a complicated translation but is roughly equivalent to a teenager from the east end of London taking the lid off a spray can, facing a wall and spraying "Clapton is God."

John McLaughlin: *My Goal's Beyond* – 1971 (**)

I'm always suspicious of albums with apostrophes in the title because so many people are incapable of handling them correctly. The rewriting of the title as *My Goal is Beyond* to distinguish it from *My Goals Beyond* indicates the new single-minded spiritual emphasis that was impacting upon John's music for the first time through the guidance of his new guru, Sri Chinmoy. For the first time, John appears with the name of Mahavishnu. It was not a complete and permanent change of name and the use of it (or not) seems to have remained fluid over the years since then. Even when John stopped using it, there was always a good commercial reason for keeping it in the public eye.

This album was the second of two he contracted to make for Alan Douglas and it was conceived as two sides of a vinyl disc that were as different as tai-chi from sushi. The first two tracks constituted side one. *Peace One* and *Peace Two* are examples of the fusion of Indian music with jazz. A large group of musicians is assembled to play on these twenty minutes of material, including Billy Cobham, with whom John had recently become good friends through his sessions with Miles.

Jerry Goodman had not yet been invited to join the new band John was planning and was taking part in an audition without knowing it. The Indian timbre and tonality is provided by John's wife Eve (aka Mahalakshmi) on tamboura and the tabla player Badal Roy, who would later appear on several Miles Davis recordings. Dave Liebman, Airto Moreira and Don Alias are present also, along with a surprising guest appearance by Charlie Haden on bass.

The last eight tracks were on side two. All are guitar duets – McLaughlin overdubbed with himself – with a trace of percussion – as John leaves behind the Indian sound to concentrate on pure jazz acoustic guitar. Only track six is a solo guitar piece. Without doubt, the highlight on the album is the wonderful presentation of track 8, *Follow Your Heart*, a retitled version of *Arjen's Bag* that McLaughlin included on *Extrapolation* (1969). Other tracks include the successful *Goodbye Pork Pie Hat*, the enigmatic *Blue in Green* from Miles Davis's repertoire, the disappointing Chick Corea tune *Waltz for Bill Evans*, as well as pieces by unknown composers *Something Spiritual* and *Hearts and Flowers,* and three pieces of his own, *Phillip Lane* (was this the western name John bestowed on Sri Chinmoy perhaps?) *Follow Your Heart* and *Song for my Mother,* which must have tempted her to dance around her piano. In complete contrast to the outpouring of loud psychedelic-style rock music that took place on *Devotion*, here is an album filled with peace and love, doing exactly what it says on the can.

The Mahavishnu Orchestra

Whenever you talk to contemporary fans of the Mahavishnu Orchestra, the phrase that always comes up is "I had never heard anything like it". It's impossible for us to imagine the stunning effect the band had on those fans; we can only list and describe those aspects of the band's style that helped create it. Kolosky was one such fan who had a life-changing experience the first time that he heard (and saw pictures of) the Mahavishnu Orchestra. [20] The guitarist was playing a large double-necked guitar that impresses testosterone-charged males, yet he was dressed in white with a short haircut and clean-cut image - quite the opposite of the fashion pertaining at that time. The bassist played an instrument that was transparent, the drummer was like an invincible ninja warrior wreaking controlled havoc and the sound of the electric violin was entirely new to most listeners who had never experienced it in a rock band before. Both then and now, many people are unable to accept the sound of an instrument that they inevitably associate with classical and folk or country music (which they hate) implanted into jazz or rock music (which they love). Others simply accepted it as part of an entirely new sound in music.

Drummer Billy Cobham was John's first choice for his new band. Billy was born in Panama in 1944. His family moved to Brooklyn when he was three years old and then to Queens when he was thirteen. Drumming was a big part of his early life as he listened to conga players in Robert Fulton Park at weekends. These immigrants from the Latin communities of countries like Puerto Rico, Columbia, and Cuba sought to keep their traditions alive by regularly practising their fierce Latin rhythms. As a consequence, Billy's early life was infused with rhythm. Cobham's father was a pianist so Billy's early listening was to Count Basie, Erroll Garner, George Shearing, and Dave Brubeck. The popular music of his time was by singers like Frank Sinatra, Billy Holiday, Dinah Washington, Ella Fitzgerald and Nat King Cole, but Billy loved drumming best of all. He listened to as many drummers as he could and was impressed at how Count Basie's drummer, Sonny Payne, could raise the performance of the band with such a small drum kit.

His first gig was playing drums for his dad when he was 8. Later he attended the School of Performing Arts and the High School of Music and Art in New York City. He joined a marching band and this naturally led him to join the US Army in 1965 where he became a percussionist with the Band. He left the Army in 1968, turned professional and began playing with Shirley Scott and Stanley Turrentine. He recorded with George Benson (guitar), but his first high point was reached when he joined Horace Silver's band with Randy Brecker, Bennie Maupin and others. In March 1968, he recorded some tracks for Silver at Rudy van Gelder's studio and in January 1969 recorded the Blue Note album *You Gotta Take a Little Love* (1969). However, Silver's poor pay caused him to leave before the year was out.

Jerry Goodman was born and brought up in Chicago by parents who were both serious violinists. His childhood environment was so imbued with classical music it was almost inevitable that he would become one too. For a time, he went along with it, but wrestled with the peer group pressure that propelled him towards rock music. He wanted to play guitar and began to learn, but his desire to please his father kept drawing him back to the violin. There was, of course, no place for violin in rock music at this time. Fortunately, his strong middle-class background allowed him more control over his future than many of his contemporaries. He took his time to decide. He drifted in and out of College and eventually found himself in the company of rock musicians with a band called the Flock. Initially he helped out as a kind of roadie, but it wasn't long before he was playing his electrified violin in the band - one of the first to do so. The band's unusual sound with a strong emphasis on improvisation got them noticed and lots of gigs followed. One day, John McLaughlin heard the band and knew at once that Jerry was the kind of musician he wanted for the Mahavishnu Orchestra. John invited Jerry to play on his album *My Goal's Beyond*. Only then did he tell Jerry about his plans. Jerry loved the way McLaughlin played and at once accepted his invitation to join.

McLaughlin invited Czech keyboardist Jan Hammer to join the band without even hearing him play. Fellow Czech and childhood friend Miroslav Vitous had recommended Hammer to John. Hammer had been born into a strong musical family in Prague where both his parents were jazz musicians, his mother a jazz singer and his father a musician and composer. In fact, so prominent was the family in music circles that all visiting jazz musicians would come to his home. Jan began to play piano aged 4-5 and his formal music education began at 6. He was writing music at 8 and accompanying his mother when he was 13. He became friends with the Vitous family and formed a band called the Junior Trio with Miroslav on bass and his brother Alan on drums. They played the cool jazz of Miles Davis and Bill Evans and even made some recordings. In 1967-8 Hammer was in a trio with George Mraz (bass) and Michael Dennert (drums) and made an album with Cees Sees replacing Dennert.

Jan was playing a residency in Munich in 1968 when the Russian tanks rolled into Prague. The future looked bleak for Czechoslovakia and the Hammer family took the first opportunity to emigrate to the USA. Jan, who had studied for two years at the Academy of Muse Arts in Prague, won a scholarship to Berklee. He studied piano with Ray Santisi and found the formal training easy. For him, it was much more important to get involved with the club scene in

Boston and he was soon gigging regularly. He briefly shared an apartment with John Abercrombie and then got a job in Sarah Vaughan's trio, which necessitated a move to New York. It was formal mainstream jazz and he enjoyed it, but he constantly experimented with new music at jams. On one occasion he even played drums for Paul Bley with Jaco Pastorius and Pat Metheny. As Jan played with Sarah Vaughan he met a bass player called Rick Laird when the Trio played alongside Buddy Rich's band at Disneyland. Once in New York and part of the scene, it was not long before he received an invitation to go to Miles Davis's house just after the Jack Johnson recording was released. There he met John McLaughlin and also Steve Grossman, with whom he later played quite a lot. Jan was hoping to be hired by Miles, but Keith Jarrett got the gig. Jan's gig with McLaughlin was probably more useful to him as it turned out.

McLaughlin first asked Tony Levin to play bass for the MO, but Tony was just forming a band of his own and declined. Then John thought of Rick Laird whom he had played alongside in Brian Auger's Trinity. Laird accepted immediately. Born in Ireland with a musical mother and a strong inclination towards music, he spent part of his youth in New Zealand where he taught himself the guitar and played with his friends in a number of ad hoc bands. As the one interested in bass, he spent a lot of time playing bass on the lowest four strings of his guitar. Eventually, he got a string bass and toured New Zealand in 1958 when he was 18. Two years later he moved to Sydney, seriously into jazz and the music of Miles Davis, Bill Evans and the bass playing of Scott Le Faro. He thought about going to the USA, but went to London instead in 1962. He joined Brian Auger's Trinity and when the band needed a guitarist it was John McLaughlin who was hired. Soon after that Rick had the good fortune to get a job in Ronnie Scott's house band from 1964-66, which was probably the best jazz job for bass in England. In this role he played for a wide range of visiting American stars, including Freddie Hubbard, Wes Montgomery, Art Farmer, Ben Webster, Stan Getz, Roland Kirk and Sonny Rollins.

In 1966, Laird sent a tape of himself playing with Stan Getz to the Berklee School of Music in Boston and he was awarded a scholarship. Once in Boston he was soon working the clubs and played in the house band at the Jazz Workshop where he heard Miles Davis on many occasions. He played with guitarist John Abercrombie and in the Mick Goodrick Trio with Alan Broadbent (piano). He met McLaughlin again in Boston where McLaughlin, Williams and Young all showed up at his apartment. Then Laird got a job as bassist for Buddy Rich with the help of a friend who was trumpet player in the band. He joined Rich on tour in San Francisco. There was no time to learn anything: he just had to get on with it. He didn't enjoy his time much. "I don't think Buddy spoke to me for a month." [21] Rich was an arrogant man with the habit of firing players at the drop of a hat. Laird was fired on many occasions, but got his own back by getting re-hired on more money each time. It was whilst playing for Rich that he took an electric bass on tour because it was easier to carry.

Kolosky says that it was Nat Weiss who persuaded John to make his new band an electric jazz-rock band. Nat Weiss was a New York lawyer and entrepreneur who specialised in handling the affairs of music stars such as the Beatles, Carly Simon, James Taylor and Miles Davis. It was Miles who told John that he should form a band and recommended he visit Weiss for help. Thus Weiss became the band's manager and going electric was his idea. [22] Weiss took McLaughlin to Columbia boss Clive Davis and with little fuss the new band was contracted to the biggest label in jazz. Actually, it was John who was under contract, and that would prove useful later when the band split up. The band's name was Chinmoy's idea. John thought it was a bit strange, but "in those days strange was cool." [23]

John made the decision to be even louder than Lifetime had been. It didn't go down well with Laird who, much experienced in the acoustic environment of jazz groups, found it very hard coping with the number of decibels. [24] Laird struggled to find an electric bass that could cope with the immense volume used by the rest of the band and, certainly in the early days, was frequently unhappy with the sound of his instrument. [25] Jerry Goodman seemed to be the odd man out and felt it. The others were all serious jazzers. He was the only one with no significant jazz experience and worked hard to find his place in the band. [26] His high level of classical ability however, enabled him to play lightning-fast lines in unison with McLaughlin – something that many listeners found astonishing and set the bar for this band so much higher than others. (John would use this technique throughout his career with different suitably talented musicians.) Goodman brought genuine rock experience and sounds to the party and, with John driving the band into ever increasing volume, the first true jazz-rock band came into being on 21 July 1971 in a New York jazz club. Some of the music they played live on that day was captured on the band's first album, *The Inner Mounting Flame* (1971), recorded at the same time in just two days, but nothing could capture the awesome experience of the audiences at the first gigs that July. They left in utter bewilderment at what they had just heard but knew they had experienced something entirely new in music. [27]

The Mahavishnu Orchestra: *The Inner Mounting Flame* – 1971 (*****)

McLaughlin composed all of the music for *The Inner Mounting Flame*. It was filled with complex time signatures and interwoven themes, but those jazz constructions were now set in the rock context that formally declared the start of jazz-fusion. Indeed, *Meeting of the Spirits* begins with a fanfare that could be announcing the birth of a new supergroup. You could almost say it heralded the start of a new genre, although when the album was released on 3 November, Weather Report had already pipped the band to the post by releasing its first album some six months earlier in May 1971. In fairness, there is little comparison to be made with *Weather Report* (1971) a record created according to a quite different set of rules. It is inevitable that a true jazz-rock album should have an electric guitar as its focus. Weather Report almost never used one. Hence this album can justly be claimed to be the real beginning of the jazz-rock fusion era of music, even though there had been numerous earlier attempts. It therefore requires more than the usual amount of space for analysis.

The album rightly begins with a bold statement of nine extended chords that become farther and farther out as the sequence proceeds. It could easily be interpreted as defining the spectrum from rock (at the start) to jazz (at the end), although I suspect it was not planned that way. The two chords at 0.30 and 0.35 are superb jazz chords that would have made Dizzy Gillespie proud. The timing of this music is simple compared to a lot that follows later in the album: it's a straightforward six-count (except for the slow sections). However, the mix of phrases and themes that occurs next is a remarkable piece of management in itself, with every player having a carefully defined role at a particular time, yet still being allowed to improvise. At 0.40 there begins a repeated two-note motif on guitar/keyboard over a pair of oscillating chords that I shall call A. This is a kind of foundation over which the other themes are played, though the musicians playing it vary. At 1.05 we hear a repeated rising and falling phrase (1), in a style that McLaughlin likes to use quite often. This is played on violin and bass. Then at 1.26 another phrase (2) starts on guitar; violin joins in unison, whilst the other instruments continue with phrase 1. This develops into a major solo from John that continues until 2.42 when he returns briefly to phrase 2. This leads into a slow section (B) that sounds disappointingly like the chimes incorporated in millions of striking clocks and modelled on London's well-known 'Big Ben'. Clocks, however, have got nothing on John's guitar as he finishes the section with serious distortion. From this point, it's back to A and this time the violin and bass accompany the solo on electric piano, which is quite restrained. The backing develops as violin and guitar play complicated lines in close unison and the music is about as complicated as it can get at this point. Amazingly, the band somehow gets back to the slow theme B, whereupon it leads for a third and final time to A. The violin solos briefly to a faded ending.

Dawn has a fairly simple structure consisting of a fast section sandwiched between two slow sections. The song begins with a lovely slow ballad played in 7/4 with just electric piano, bass and drums, which creates a beautiful feeling of peace and tranquillity. At 0.41 violin and guitar enter with a unison theme that takes on the now familiar rise and fall through unrelated keys. As I said above,

McLaughlin already likes this device, using it, for example, in *Don't Let the Dragon Eat your Mother* on *Devotion* (1970). As the sun comes up, the music gains strength and McLaughlin plays a distorted rock guitar solo over some sublime jazz changes from 1.25. Suddenly from 2.33 the music becomes animated with violin taking a solo. It gets a little untidy as he struggles to cope with the rigours of improvising over a very complex time such as 14/8, but it's admirable under the circumstances. Oddly, it doesn't seem as simple as just a doubling of the speed because it's played as two fours and a six, compared to the seven of the first and last parts. Finally, at 4.08, the ballad returns, joined by an organ line for a rerun to the faded end, naturally interpreted as a sunset.

Noonward Race begins with a fiery distorted guitar/ drums duet that's pure rock in style and tone but played as if the two men are telepathic to the entirely unpredictable rhythmic pattern. This on its own is a remarkable effect. Then, Cobham and Laird set up a hard-driving beat at 0.58, and Goodman sets off on a blistering drive through the streets. His electric violin sound has been tweaked to give it more street-cred. Hammer relieves him, playing a seriously distorted electric piano and sounding as macho as he can get. The guitar is hanging back at this point to maximise impact and Hammer improvises over a single chord. It arrives on the scene again around 3.15 with a fiendishly difficult, no, crazy theme that becomes even crazier as it changes slightly with each iteration. This introduces a manic, light-speed guitar solo with bass, drums and keys at full tilt. At 4.48 the crazy theme reverberates again and again, undergoing a metamorphosis each time yet all the musicians are playing the complex rhythm perfectly in time. The piece comes to a screaming end at 5.30 with a reprise of the opening drum/guitar duet and, at 6.19, exactly the kind of coda that Chick Corea would spend years perfecting. This is simultaneously both breathless and breathtaking.

A Lotus on Irish Streams is a calming, spiritual song played acoustically and entirely *rubato* on guitar, violin and piano with a melody that never stays in one place, but restlessly rises and falls through the keys according to the McLaughlin brand. The violin has lovely Irish resonances without taking on the folksy flavour of a fiddle. McLaughlin plays acoustic guitar in constantly restless streams of flow. From 3.40 Hammer takes the lead (with the help of some double-tracking) and at 4.38 the original theme returns even more poignantly than before, if that is possible. The ending is truly haunting.

Vital Transformation begins with Cobham delivering a fast and hard rock rhythm, though in a genuine 9/8 – by which I mean that it is not three bars of three! At 0.14 a unison quartet of fuzz guitar, violin, keyboards and bass simply repeat a nine-beat theme (A) over and over. Eventually, at 0.44 the guitar begins to break away and at 0.58 the beat collapses into a slow ten beat metre. A descending theme (B) is followed by a pause, and then the same in reverse. At 1.33 McLaughlin begins a rousing solo in the original nine-beat rhythm over violin and organ accompaniment, constantly driven from the roots by Billy and Rick. This gradually develops at around four minutes into a unison exposition of the nine-beat theme A from the lead instruments. When the slow theme B reoccurs at 4.34 it is in the same form again, this time rising to a climax at 5.03. At 5.11, Billy kicks in with his fast licks and the rest of the band play the piece out to a faded ending at 6.16 with a simple repeated phrase.

The Dance of the Maya is an ultra-clever construction of truly epic proportions. It is based on a series of 3 and 4 beat bars that starts out as two threes and a four, which makes 10/8. At 0.54 there begins an interplay between drums, guitar and bass. Guitar and bass continue playing their original 10/8 whilst at 0.54 Billy superimposes (almost impossibly, it seems) a 20/8 that's composed of six threes and a two. Rick Laird called it a 6½ /4 (i.e. 13/8) but it isn't that. The effect really fries your brain, which presumably is what John was trying to achieve. The tension builds and the music becomes bloodcurdling at the thought that you might shortly have your heart cut out. Then, almost as a pressure relief valve releasing its pent-up gases, at 2.34, just as the dagger is raised, the high priest rips off his hideous mask and reveals a jolly smile. "Let's all sing the blues!" he yells. From here on it's rather like a prehistoric Chuck Berry sound, assuming he could cope with 20/8 metre. Jerry plays a solo on fuzz-violin with matching guitar accompaniment. Just after four minutes, John takes over with a rather more serious rock-style solo that continues to 5.34 when Mayan Chuck returns. The piece starts to take on its ominous hues again as the chief's followers restart their ten-beat dance and threaten bodily violence once again. This time it all ends in a traditional crash-rock ending, which is much better than having your heart ripped out.

You Know, You Know begins enigmatically like a cat burglar skulking through the dark alleys that lead to his target. He creeps quickly along, taking care that his footfall is not heard behind the curtains of the lighted windows above. Once again, it's another complex superimposition of times, with a repeated nine-note theme spliced onto a simple four-beat metre, but the technical stuff is starting to wear a bit thin. Hammer's Fender Rhodes piano solo is gradually overtaken by his shadows. At each corner he jumps at every noise lest he is seen. The feeling of the piece greatly exceeds its mathematics and Billy's drumming is a highlight of this otherwise quiet, contemplative piece.

Awakening is a thermonuclear climax, which is quite appropriate for an album of this magnitude. McLaughlin's brain works at a greater speed than mere mortals like us. The speed of his ten-notes per second lines, played in unison by most of the band, is almost impossible to keep pace with and only the best musicians with a supreme level of skill could cope! Hammer's keyboard is undergoing meltdown and at two minutes John's solo almost goes into nucleonic disintegration. After a brief drum interlude criticality is finally reached and the album ends in a mushroom cloud.

Fission or fusion? Who cares! This album is quite stunning. There is no doubt whatever that the men on this album are extravagantly good players and the musicianship displayed in coping with such complex constructions and arrangements, recorded in a very short time under difficult conditions, is remarkable. McLaughlin carefully selected each of them and their CVs were impeccable. They didn't let him down, delivering his music with aplomb.

Once again, as he did with *Extrapolation* (1969), McLaughlin seems to have one of the finest creative imaginations in music. My technical descriptions of the music may not be easy to read, but they're necessary if we are to understand just how good this music is. I have some misgivings about his style, however. McLaughlin tends to attract attention with his rip-roaring fingerwork, but the improvisations always feel more like rock than jazz. Since this is a book about jazz-rock that is not necessarily a bad thing, except that McLaughlin's playing very rarely sounds like jazz. Mark Gilbert agrees: "Apart from Jan Hammer's solo in *Noonward Race*, there is little evidence in *The Inner Mounting Flame* of the chromaticism found in modern jazz. Furthermore, for someone who is often classed as a jazz-rock player, McLaughlin the soloist makes little use of the blues." [28] Furthermore, McLaughlin the composer doesn't write jazz tunes here, but seems locked into the creation of short motifs that rise and fall like shares on a volatile stock-market.

For someone who claimed to feel discomfort – even inferior - in such exalted company, Goodman mightily impresses with the way he copes with music of far greater complexity than he could ever have imagined he would be asked to play. He found the 'complex meter' hard to deal with, yet never sounds lost. In contrast, on the record at least, Hammer sounds as if he is running behind the violin and guitar, taking all the music in his stride and delivering competent, beautiful solos when required, but never quite reaching the heights of creativity of John, Billy and Jerry. His instruments changed rapidly during the months after the band's formation. At first he used Fender Rhodes electric piano, modified to create new, often distorted, sounds. Later, he adopted most of the new instruments I have described elsewhere – the B3 organ, the Moog and its smaller, more portable version, the Mini-Moog as they became available.

Rick Laird's electric bass playing is good but not outstanding compared to the huge talent that existed, even in these days before Clarke and Pastorius hit the headlines. Extremely well qualified in all respects for a jazz group, he was perhaps the least suitable candidate for a position in an experimental electric outfit. Brought up in swing-time, he must have often wondered how he had gotten himself into this. The music does not suffer because of it, but in such outstanding company he is bound to look slightly inferior.

The player who impresses most is Cobham, whose drumming is utterly breathtaking. His pace alone is startling, but his ability to maintain velocity with such apparent ease, whilst also delivering creative variation inside some of the most difficult complex rhythm patterns yet devised, is what led many people to proclaim Cobham as the world's greatest drummer at this point. No fewer than sixteen microphones were used to mike up the drums at an early 1971 gig. Any listener with an interest in drumming should purchase this album.

This album is awarded five stars. It is difficult music that requires deep concentration and may not appeal to some listeners – especially those who lean towards jazz rather than rock. Nevertheless, its contribution to the history of jazz music is incalculable. Amazingly, this is a band whose immense contemporary impact was created more by their astonishing live performances than by the legacy of their recordings. The Tony Williams Lifetime seem to have had a similar effect when live, but the evidence on record puts them several leagues below the MO for all the reasons I presented earlier. Ultimately, when we listen to this album today we can have no accurate comprehension of the impact that this band had on the music world in 1971 and 1972. There can be no comparison with what went on at the gigs where stunned audiences left with shredded eardrums and their understanding of what they could expect from current bands wiped clean. There are many first-hand accounts in Kolosky's book that record the experience as life-changing and these form a significant part of the analysis of the success of the Orchestra. The least we can do is describe, dissect and analyse the music on the CD in the search for explanations.

The Mahavishnu Orchestra had a profound effect on rock music because it showed just how simplistic much of it was and just how much better it could become. Once they heard about the Orchestra, all rock musicians knew they had to sharpen up their own acts. Members of bands like Yes, ELP, King Crimson, Frank Zappa and the Mothers of Invention, Grateful Dead, were all wowed – even intimidated - by the band's music. Joe Perry of Aerosmith said: "We had to play much better to try to win the audience." [29] Joey Kramer, also of Aerosmith said: "I got depressed. Billy…was so good I could not really believe I was playing the same instrument." [30] Billy: "We had a knack of making the most difficult music seem extremely easy to play" [31]

But where is the jazz in this music? The trouble is that, to many jazzers, some of the Mahavishnu Orchestra music sounds like rock. Rockers, however, did hear the jazz and, although they loved the rock sounds, many thought they were listening to an extreme form of jazz. There is no disputing the jazz elements within it. The most important and obvious difference from a listener's point of view is that there is no singing. For many people this is the most important element that distinguishes jazz from rock in this context. Yes, there is now and always has been plenty of jazz with singing, as well as plenty of rock without singing, but it remains the most obvious distinguishing mark for a great many jazz and rock fans. Rock fans expect vocals: jazz fans do not. The Tony Williams Lifetime fell between the stools in trying to cope with this; the Mahavishnu Orchestra reached the top of the ladder by ignoring it. The band's music is dense and often extremely fast with complex rhythms and structures. By contrast, rock music in the early 70s, was mostly lightweight, although the age of progressive rock had added new dimensions to the frothy stuff of the mid 1960s. Rock music was mostly medium tempo, based on simple 4-beat rhythms and AABA-type structures. Tunes were easily identifiable, and when you heard a tune at the start of a song you knew it would come back later. MO's music was long and deeply developed. Tunes were hard to find and pin down amongst the long improvisations. Only one track on this album is three and a half minutes in length; the rest are all five, six and seven minutes long – which was long in the days of vinyl. Rock was still only just beginning to realise that there was life after four minutes and radio stations wouldn't play anything much longer than three minutes, especially if it didn't have vocals. All this was consistent with this music being jazz and therefore receiving virtually no airplay.

Finally, there was the 'spiritual' element that many listeners recognised in the music. Bill Bruford, drummer with Yes and King Crimson, described the music as "electric modal jazz." [32] McLaughlin was using his jazz upbringing and his experience with Miles Davis, along with his deep interest in eastern music and philosophy to create music that was only loosely based on the standard scales and harmonic constructions. The result was music that sounded to most 1970s listeners as other-worldly or spiritual. It penetrated the souls of many thousands of young listeners like nothing else before it and converted them instantly.

The great success of the Orchestra resulted from a stupendous series of gigs around the eastern USA, mostly on College campuses, from July 1971 onwards. Word spread fast that there was an astonishing must-see band that would blow you away. Kolosky records many stories of how the Mahavishnu Orchestra opened gigs for other bands, only to watch the audiences leave when the Mahavishnu Orchestra finished their set. Emerson, Lake and Palmer (ELP) was one such cutting-edge 'prog-rock' band that suffered at the hands of the Orchestra. After hearing them, listeners didn't care about hearing anyone else! They left in a mixed sense of bewilderment and profound satisfaction. Today, all we have left are the albums and, although one album - *Between Nothingness and*

Eternity (1974) - was recorded live, no album can generate the musical spirit of being there or the experience of raw power that Pat Metheny described as "face-melting." [33]

The Mahavishnu Orchestra: *Birds of Fire* – 1973 (*****)

Towards the end of August 1972, the band arrived at the Trident Recording Studios in England to commence recording its second album, *Birds of Fire* (1973). In contrast to the two days they were allowed for the first album, they had the luxury of much more money and hence more time to spend on this project. John had written most of the music for the first two albums before the band got started so just over a year later the musicians were already familiar with it. The album was released on the third day of 1973.

There are some differences from the first album. Hammer had new gear in the form of a Mini-Moog synthesiser, which gave him entirely new sounds. John was now playing that amazing double-necked guitar that he had bought earlier in the year. Billy was playing a new kit. He had finally earned enough money to enable him to purchase new drums and dispense with the old ones he'd been using. What's more, he had invested in twin bass drums, which added a new dimension to the sound. He also had a gong that he used to introduce the first track *Birds of Fire*. Once again, an odd time signature of 9/8 was used for the alternating chords that ruminated beneath the music. Jerry and John played the theme in unison and then John played a solo. Everything sounded unrelated to everything else and gave the piece a most weird sound. The theme was repeated and ended in a superb flourish before the band all came together at 2.49 for a short bridging section before going back to the base chords over which Jan now used his synthesiser to create a solo in a similar vein to John's. The chordal base took the piece out with a fade.

Miles Beyond is misleading because it looks like it is actually a Davis composition, which it is not. It is, however, strongly influenced by Davis's piece *Mademoiselle Mabry* from *Filles de Kilimanjaro* and I have already commented on how similar this is to Hendrix's piece *And the Wind Cries Mary*. The focus or hook of the song, as in the other two, is a chromatic three-chord phrase that makes a very cool intro on Hammer's electric piano and he makes it incredibly funky just before bass and drums enter. Then the repetition is in real contrast to what the band is thought to be about. This phrase becomes the centrepiece of the whole track. However, after a brief heavy-rock phrase at 1.05, the melody starts at 1.23 and is like a severe bebop line transplanted into the wrong key and played by John and Jerry together in total opposition to Jan and Rick's harmonic focus. From 1.50 Jerry plays a great jazz pizzicato solo with just an electric piano accompaniment. Then from 2.40 a fuzz guitar/bass line plays over a solo by Billy that's tailored beautifully over the chordal theme. Listen out for some great band 'squeaks'. The final act is a joint solo over the melody to finish. This piece is quite sublime and the jazziest piece of jazz-rock in the Mahavishnu Orchestra repertoire.

Celestial Terrestrial Commuters is a reworking of John's tune, *Binky's Beam* from *Extrapolation* (1969). It makes use of Jan's new synthetic sounds in sympathy with the title of the piece as an intro. Then there's a passage of alternating violin and guitar improvisation. They all come together for a middle section alternated with synth and the piece is over almost before it feels it has started. *Sapphire Bullets of Pure Love* is a short triviality that Kolosky says was recorded during a sound check. [34] Throughout his career, McLaughlin has often indulged in the use of both very short as well as very long pieces on his albums.

Thousand Island Park is a beautiful acoustic composition without percussion - just piano, guitar and acoustic bass. Played *rubato* with some fiendishly difficult and fast runs, the written lines represent an almost impossible challenge to play tightly so there is clear water between the players at times, but the song is so beautiful that they pull it off. Between the written sections there are brief spells of improvised play in which some wonderful resonances and harmonies bubble around like the streams that presumably run through the park. And let's not forget Rick's lovely bass sound, for he is at last able to make his mark with the kind of bass playing he was expert in. The result is a timeless delightful interlude, beautifully recorded some twenty years before it might have appeared on a Pat Metheny album.

Hope is a short two-minute piece that is mostly written: it had to be. At first it seems almost completely unstructured and random except that there's a regular beat and, like DNA, you feel there's structure in there somewhere if you can only discover it. It's part of everyone's playing and matches a predefined format that, it turns out, is fundamentally 7/4. However, the way it is played makes it into a complex series of motifs with 2, 3, 4 and 7 beats, with sevens split into three and four and rests thrown in for good measure. It's a remarkable musical conception.

You really do need only one word to describe *One Word* and that's stupendous! It begins with a wonderful solo drum intro that is fast, quiet and perfectly controlled – the kind of thing Billy would have practised endlessly in the barrack room in his military days. Then, after the band play a section of heavy ensemble lines he breaks into a gentle high-speed pulse from 0.55. A theme develops between violin, guitar and keys that creates a sensational gurgling effect with a gradual crescendo until 1.30 when a short phrase ends the section and introduces an extended bass/drums solo from 1.38. It's a great opportunity for Laird who shows that, despite his earlier difficulties coping with the sound levels, he's still better than most of his pop contemporaries. The solo continues long after we all expect it to end and just builds and builds with the band growing steadily behind him. He's still leading when the guitar comes in at 4.13 and the three lead instruments start alternating with guitar, synth and violin taking turns. Notable in this section is Hammer's note-bending ability, a new technique for instrumentalists at this time. The solos gradually shorten and begin to overlap until 6.05 when they are all going at once. There follows an absolutely stunning drum solo, beautifully recorded in stereo with toms, snare and bass drums coming at you from all over the mix. It climaxes at 8.13 in a landslide of percussion, yet controlled to perfection. Finally, the solo instruments come in to create another startlingly fast passage with, from 8.40, all instruments playing perfectly together a section of two bars of 4/4 followed by one of 6/4. This simply amazing piece concludes with a composed, clean ending.

The title *Sanctuary* gives a pretty good indication of the song's identity, but the feelings created by its slow, pensive melancholic melody are far stronger and deeper than any title can convey. The notes are held for extraordinarily long times, like the echoes inside the ancient cavernous interior of the place where we escape from our fears of the world. And, just as we would not require a sanctuary if there was not something from which we needed to escape, so this piece is more about the fears of what we leave behind than the beauty of the place we have found.

Open Country Joy, aided and abetted by Jerry's country fiddle and John's twangy Nashville sound, seems at first to be anticipating a recording twenty-five years hence by the brilliant Alison Krauss and her Union Station friends. After a delightful quiet section of melody and lush harmony the track is placed firmly back on the jazz-rock footing at 1.10 as a machine-gun blast sprays bullets from all directions. It's a bit like the metallers giving their country cousins the finger, but at 2.30 the sweetness and light returns and the piece ends in pure, perfect harmony.

For the final track, *Resolution*, there's a single chord at the base as a rising swell of angst builds inexorably in pitch and volume until the world seems fit to burst. It's easy to see how this must have driven members of a live audience to ecstasy. And, by the way, it's a great ending to a very remarkable album.

This album clearly benefits for the more expert way in which it was recorded, with excellent clarity and delineation of the instruments. It also benefits from the time the band have spent developing this music and from the more cogent way in which the material is packaged. The blend of different types of music is even more interesting and better balanced than on *Inner Mounting Flame* and this album is constantly intriguing, remaining fresh with every time through – an essential factor for a disc that must withstand the test of time.

By the time the album ended its run in the US album charts where it peaked at 15, it did achieve gold record status – over 500,000 sales – which made it one of the biggest selling jazz albums. Only McLaughlin received any money from the sales because he was the only member of the band that had composed the music. It is ironic and not a little sad that, in comparison, Blood Sweat and Tears sold over 35 million copies of the nine albums they released. Who said the world is fair?

The Mahavishnu Orchestra: *Between Nothingness and Eternity* – 1973 (*****)

In June 1973 the band recorded the master tapes of what was intended to be the third studio album, but in August, the fighting took over. On a flight to Japan for a short tour, McLaughlin picked up a music magazine in which he found an article in which his band mates openly criticised him. He was shocked and hurt that they had not expressed their views to his face. When he tackled them about it, all the grievances that had been pent up for so long spilled out. Everyone had his own personal dissatisfaction, made worse by the fact that they were all so tired from constantly working: there had been 200 one night gigs in 1972 and 250 days of 1973 were spent on the road, but that was just an excuse for their falling-out. [35] The thorny problem of composer credits was unresolved and they were growing tired of seeing John treated as the star whilst they were often ignored. They quickly agreed that it was time to end the relationship. The decision left them without an album to satisfy their contract with Columbia. Two concerts were recorded in New York's Central Park from which a live third album was created, *Between Nothingness and Eternity* recorded on 5 August 1973 and released at the end of the year. The master tapes of the original third album were forgotten.

The addition of the gong to Billy's kit is especially noticeable on this album: he uses it on all the tracks and particularly at the very beginning and end of the album. The presentation of the three tracks is well considered and is part of what makes this album very special. Overall, there is a steady progression of tension and development of relationship between the musicians and the listener that works itself up into complete and utter disbelief by the end, what has been called "shock and awe" in other contexts.

The album opens with a track called *Trilogy* that, as you might expect, is comprised of three elements: *The Sunlit Path*, *La Mère de la Mer* and *Tomorrow's Story not the Same*. Billy's gong sets the scene that introduces a fade-in from John who lays down a woven tapestry of tones ahead of us. At 1.33 Billy's drums bring in the band for a very long phrase that swirls up, down and around the seven-beat base, ignoring the set timing pattern but each repetition of the phrase spread over three measures of seven. At around 2.00 a dialogue begins between guitar and electric piano. At 3.40 there's a final playing of the theme before we are led straight into the second phase of the trilogy. Violin and bass are playing a new theme as John provides an underlay and Jan makes bird noises. There seems to be no rhythm at all for this bridging piece. Suddenly, at 6.12 we're into the main chapter of the story with a robust theme repeated over a fourteen-beat time. Jerry leads through this piece of fire. At eight minutes the guitar begins another dialogue with the keyboard, each instrument alternating every fourteen-beat bar. By 8.30 it's clear they are deliberately accelerating and adding increasing intensity to their lines. It becomes a trial of strength and neither is going to back down. Billy pounds away behind and Jerry doodles at first, but soon he and Rick come in with the main theme repeated behind the soloists. The duel ends in stalemate at 10.55 and a gentle burbling phrase cycles in the foreground until a final flourish with the theme to end tidily at 12 minutes.

The second track is *Sister Andrea*, written by Jan Hammer and the only piece on the three albums not written by John. At first, it seems crude in comparison – just a basic 4/4 tune. How could he compete with McLaughlin the master composer? A kind of Deep Purple intro makes it sound like just another rock tune, repeated a few times. At 1.12 it falls out of time and floats into a guitar solo of real quality with just the keyboard behind. This is no piece of ten-second pop-piffle but a seriously developed and intense piece of master guitar work that cuts like a high energy laser. At 3.10 a drum roll brings the band back in with the rock 4/4 as John continues to shred concrete. There's a short orchestrated ensemble before Jerry takes a solo and at last Rick is heard clearly as he adds creative electric bass lines behind the violin. At 5.55 a new section begins with a wholly darker edge. Again, there's a repeated line made up of two similar phrases played by guitar and bass repetitively. Jerry vamps behind a Hammer solo on synthesiser with plenty of note-bending. Again, the pace and volume are gradually being wound ever upwards, assisted by Cobham's insistent drumming. At 8.00 there's a slightly awkward entry into the coda that is stretched out to 8.22 when the gong brings the proceedings to a close.

The final track is utterly awesome. The title *Dream* is of no consequence compared to the extraordinary exhibition of playing that is in store. Such is the complexity of the music that it has had musicologists arguing for years. For example, Kolosky includes an analysis by Kevin Michael [36] and, although I don't intend to disagree with him too much, it is clear that both of us found this hard work. It seems that there is a fairly common basis throughout of fifteen beats, although they are played at greatly varying times. Sometimes you can comfortably count five – which is much easier than counting fifteen, especially when the music is flying at mach speed. The dream begins with a slow fifteen in a very atmospheric opening section. The bass repetitively plays a long phrase, but counting through it isn't easy because there are some long notes. It's an acoustic strings sound that sets a beautiful twilight scene and gets everyone in the mood. The soloists sound like little mosquitoes buzzing around in the growing darkness. The pace of John's playing is mesmerising. At 2.17 Jerry joins in and moves away into a dream of his own making that parallels John's. For a while, the two men are flying around together as Rick provides continuity. At 3.41 the two instruments join briefly and Jan begins his own flight, though his focus is in a different direction for a time. By 4.40, all differences are reconciled and at 4.50 the drums lead the musicians into a new section of purposeful mayhem. By 5.10 Hammer still leads the pack. Cobham is driving harder and harder and builds a wall of percussion behind. Just listen to this amazing drumming from 6.00 to 6.35 when the theme returns for several repeats with the full band until there's a pause. This develops into a new section of musings between just the guitar and electric piano, sometimes ignoring each other, sometimes coming together as if by magic. The duet ends at 8.00 from which point the band enters a ferocious period of group mania where it's easier to count in fives because the speed is so dazzlingly fast. It all comes to an end at 9.15 with a new section, again in fifteens, but loaded in a completely different way that defies belief. It's a violin lead with the band in support. Once again, the instructions are to accelerate intensely and unremittingly in a way that seems as if it can never end. False endings are reached around 11.50 but from 12.00 onwards it's a period of suspended belief in reality. Everything culminates at 12.35 when Billy and John commence one of the most astonishing duets on record, playing incomprehensibly fast and in a time that defies calculation. The two men demonstrate complete musical telepathy as they are completely together throughout. It's a tour de force from both men that simply goes on and on, and on. By 16.00 we think it's all over, but then the bass joins in at last and the relentless pace continues once again as John gathers some breathing space. Hammer starts to add his weight but John is still bleeding notes onto the stage until at 17.00 everyone gets into the ring, working together, not in opposition. At 17.30 the band takes a saucy wink at the poor rockers left in the dirt: a burst of jocular rock rhythm creeps in and adds a tiny bit of humour to the immensely serious devastation. Finally at 17.50 the theme returns indicating that an ending may be in sight, but there are still three minutes to go! The tension is kept tight until John's solo finally ends at 18.30. A brilliantly designed ending lets us all down gradually as we abseil down from the mountain top and feel the exhilarating breeze in our faces. A repeated six-note bass theme acts as the rope down which the three soloists slide in complete confidence until the safety of the ground is reached at 20.50 and Billy's gong says all is done.

When I began this book, I was not a fan of the Mahavishnu Orchestra. I had collected the records and listened to them periodically, but not with sufficient concentration to have even slightly appreciated their contributions. As a jazzer, it was far too easy for me to dismiss it as tainted rock music and of no interest to me. That, of course, is partly why so many people came to hate jazz-fusion. The heavy use of electric guitar and the strange sound of an electric violin were too much to bear. They could only hear the rock elements and dismissed Mahavishnu out-of-hand as having no value to the jazz community. However, as I sit down to write this review in January 2007, I have just completed my reviews of the band's two previous albums and surprised myself by concluding that they both should be awarded five stars. I never dreamed that I would do the same for this third album. I have tried hard not to award stars too liberally, but I realise that with this band I have no choice but to accept it as being at the top of the jazz-fusion tree. I have written how it is impossible to appreciate what the audiences felt at those gigs some 35 years ago, yet I arrived at the end of this live album quite unable to speak or write! I can honestly say that I do not remember being affected by an album in this way before. It was not totally new to my ears, yet when I really listened to it I was stunned! When I first acquired Kolosky's book and saw that he had subtitled it "The greatest band that ever was" how could I do any other than just nod my head knowingly and say that, well, the comment was clearly wishful thinking? Now that I have taken the time study these three albums carefully over some fifteen hours or so, I can see that Kolosky has a point.

The Mahavishnu Orchestra: *The Lost Trident Sessions* – Rec. 1973, Rel. 1998 (****)

Staff changed at the Trident recording studios where Mahavishnu Orchestra worked, and the 1973 tapes of what was intended to be the third Mahavishnu Orchestra album were effectively lost until, one day in 1998, they were rediscovered and released as – wait for it - *The Lost Trident Sessions*, recorded 25-29 June 1973. All of the music from the live album is here, in a different order and in the kind of abbreviated form we might expect for studio recordings. At only (!) eleven minutes - half the length of the live version – *Dream* might seem emaciated but all the components are present. Nothing can compare with the live version, but this is still very good.

One very positive point about the record is the extra clarity. For example, in *La Mère de la Mer*, you are more aware of it as an impressionistic sketch, with sea, sun, sky and even the sound of birds captured better in the recording studio setting. Clarity doesn't matter much with the heavier rock music sections, and in

Tomorrow's Story not the Same the end section is especially well articulated. *Sister Andrea* is very good, with a superb synthesiser solo from its writer. Unfortunately, the ending shows signs of being unfinished at this stage. *I Wonder* has a most peculiar, other-worldly feel about it and when we realise it is written in 13/8, a very strange metre, everything becomes clear. *Steppings Tones* was written by Rick Laird. It is in a fast 5/8 with a plodding bass line like the Giant chasing Jack from the beanstalk. By now we have grown used to the long developments and a return to short three-minute tracks seems like we are getting snatches of ideas. *John's Song #2* must have been an untitled piece the band was working on. It seems like a piece of group improvisation, although at four minutes the piece comes together with a dark theme as Jerry begins a hard drive through the foreground. At 5.25, a final burst of theme brings it to an end on a resonant synthesiser drone. Naturally, the album was unfinished as a work of art, but the recording is well worth having for, although the music from *Nothingness* is all here, it is in a different form and there are three additional tracks, sufficiently well finished to be of interest to listeners who enjoy this music.

Musicians like guitarist Larry Coryell, a friend of McLaughlin who probably thought he was just as a good a player, could not help but be influenced by the success of the Mahavishnu Orchestra. Coryell's first album as leader, *Spaces* (1970) is often touted as an early jazz-fusion album, which is not correct. It's true that he had been fortunate in moving in all the right circles and was able to hire McLaughlin, Cobham, Corea and Vitous for his album, but the music has only brief flashes of rock-influenced sounds. The rest is either swing-based mainstream or retrospective music. Although the album is played with electric instruments (except for the very much anti-fusion Vitous), it shows very little sign of being in the new genre and leans more towards the free-form harmonies and constructs than the jazz-rock claimed for it.

It took longer for Coryell to demonstrate that he had absorbed the changes to jazz-rock. Coryell was much influenced by the music of Mahavishnu, as he showed on *Introducing Eleventh House* (1974). He hired Randy Brecker to take on Jerry Goodman's role and the album opens with Alphonse Mouzon, drummer from the first Weather Report album, doing his best to emulate Billy Cobham on *Birdfingers*. This track, along with two other compositions by Coryell, *Low-Lee-Tah* and *ISM-Ejericio* is clearly influenced by the 'electric modal' sounds of the Mahavishnu Orchestra, though it also has several funk-based tracks written by Mouzon and keyboardist Mike Mandel. Coryell was struggling to compete in the same league as McLaughlin.

John McLaughlin says "Jazz is about collective improvisation – interactive improvisation where you structure in order to get to another place collectively." Mahavishnu Orchestra (MO) was McLaughlin's band. He wanted to lead from the front by presenting the musicians with all of the music. He had chosen the best guys available for the stuff he wanted to play, but musicians of such quality naturally have minds of their own: they all wanted to contribute, and they did. The problem was that McLaughlin's name was always attached to the compositions and, in time, this had a destabilising influence on the band.

At first, they were all caught up on the wave of success. They rode it high and with huge amounts of confidence and zest. For the jazz puritans, the Mahavishnu Orchestra was their worst nightmare. It was loud, electric and the very antithesis of what they felt jazz was all about. Above all, it was very, very popular. It was music like this that helped to give fusion such a bad name in jazz circles. For everyone else, it was a revelation.

John McLaughlin and Carlos Santana: *Love, Devotion, Surrender* – 1972 (**)

During the early 1970s, John's devotion to guru Chinmoy was about as serious as it would have been to Sheffield Wednesday Football Club had he been born within spitting distance of the River Don. Whatever was the nature of the magic that affected him, it was undeniably successful in converting hard-line rockers, with most of the vices that went with the description, into well-behaved spiritual personae. By 1972, the magic had worked just as well on the world famous million-seller Carlos Santana as it had on John. Chinmoy had bestowed on Carlos the name of Devadip.

Santana was a big fan of jazz, even if he did not necessarily consider himself to be a jazz musician. He liked Miles Davis, Wayne Shorter and John Coltrane, and had been impressed by the Mahavishnu Orchestra, so it was written in the stars that the two men would meet. Santana was an order of magnitude more famous than McLaughlin and a guitar heavyweight to compete with Clapton, Beck and Page. It was part of the grand scheme of things that even the most outwardly modest musicians with aspirations of greatness would secretly burn inside with a fierce passion to out-perform their rivals in their bid to be the Undisputed Champion of the World (on guitar). It was therefore necessary to conduct a kind of gladiatorial axe combat in order to satisfy protagonists as to their level of power with the instrument and anyone who declined the invitation to joust would have been forever thought of as chicken.

What may not have been expected from their meeting was that the Mexican would become similarly attracted to McLaughlin's guru. So, when the two men (with the full agreement of the Columbia executives) agreed to make a joint album together, it was strongly tinged with their eastern affiliations and the somewhat over-the-top declarations of love, devotion and surrender that went with them. The album's cover picture shows the two men dressed as ushers to the Pearly Gates. That is off-putting enough to potential purchasers of the album, but wallets must have been firmly pocketed when the album was turned over to reveal titles such as *A Love Supreme*, *Naima*, *The Life Divine*, *Meditation* and *Let Us Go Into the House of the Lord*. This was surely too much for punters who could just as easily splash out on a couple of Frank Zappa albums? Jazz cognoscenti who would have spotted that the first two tracks were John Coltrane cover numbers, would have seen the names of McLaughlin and Santana alongside quasi-religious music. That was surely too much to bear?

Once the philosophical trappings had been cast aside, the music proved rather more accessible, but the packaging for what was supposed to be the ultimate guitar duel of its time was enough to put any serious rocker right off his muesli. As a result, the album did not sell. With an organisation like Columbia at their backs, this could have made it to the charts, but it was destined to fare almost as badly as a similar Battle of Titans involving Allan Holdsworth and Frank Gambale on an album called *Truth in Shredding* (1990). That, at least, could be explained by its having been made by a small, impotent record company.

The first track was little more than a nod to Coltrane. They play a much-simplified version of his great composition using the key focus of B, first as the background for a series of competing guitar licks and then as the means to chant the music's title like a mantra. *Naima* was the first surprise on the album. A Coltrane ballad written for his wife, both men played it sensitively as a duet for two acoustic guitars. *The Life Divine* takes inspiration from the first Coltrane hymn, adopting a similar chanting format over which to perform guitar gymnastics, this time over a variable chordal pattern. The effect was very similar.

Let Us Go Into the House of the Lord is nothing more than an extended jam over a simple two-chord theme. That's not to say it's worthless, for it will surely appeal to many listeners. It is not cutting edge music, however, even when viewed as a performer's platform, and such pieces inevitably become simply dull with endless repetition of simple structures when compared to the wonderful richness of other work by both these artists. All that results is the inevitable conclusion that this album was thrown together with very little forethought. The ending, gratuitously spun out to maximise the effect of two masters of the wailing guitar, is simply an exercise in over-indulgence.

The final track *Meditation* lasts for barely two and a half minutes. A guitar-piano duet, we are left to wonder who the musicians were. Apparently McLaughlin fingered the piano, whilst Santana played the tune like a student at Sunday school. [37]

Even today, this album may be of great interest to nostalgic students of rock music, but in the context of the other albums I am discussing, it's hard to see this as anything more than a curiosity. The other difficulty that always arises is that of distinguishing one guitarist from another. Of course, most practised listeners will be able to separate Santana's slightly harder leather-jacket tone and western-based improvisations from McLaughlin's smoother lounge-suit tone with more wide ranging harmonies. Nevertheless, those who produce such albums should always bear in mind the listeners' need to be clear about who is who. Neither did the album's packaging and concept help its credibility, but these were two men with a seriousness about their lives that tended to blind them to the realities of mere mortals who had other, more basic ways of earning a living. Paul Stump points out that it's difficult to take seriously a man you know to come from Yorkshire who comes out at a gig, clasps his hands together in front of him, bows and says, "Greetings, O people of Glasgow." [38] You can imagine what the Scots must have thought of that!

The Mahavishnu Orchestra: *Apocalypse* – 1974 (***)

After the first Mahavishnu Band folded at their last gig in Detroit on 30 December 1973, McLaughlin was extremely upset and could easily have decided to end the use of the band's name whilst it was at the pinnacle of its success. The market conditions could not have been more favourable at this time. Rolling Stone magazine labelled 1974 as the *Year of Jazz-Rock*, a title due in no small part to the success of the Mahavishnu Orchestra. John would have been mad to end the band here and he clearly had no intention of doing so. He set about hiring a new set of musicians to reconstitute a different Mahavishnu Orchestra.

Jean-Luc Ponty was the son of a violin teacher. Not surprisingly, from an early age he received a thorough education on the violin, ending his formal studies at the Paris Conservatory. By the mid-1960s he, like John, was attracted to jazz and the music of Miles Davis and John Coltrane. He recorded with Stéphane Grappelli and Stuff Smith. In 1967 he visited the USA for the Monterey Jazz Festival and then made an appearance on the album *Hot Rats* (1969) by Frank Zappa, with whom he made several more albums. In 1969 he was invited to team up with George Duke, who was at that time an acoustic pianist. Together they made *Live at Donte's* (1969) and at this gig George was persuaded to take up the electric piano for the first time. He, of course, went on to become a major jazz-fusion artist. Soon afterwards, the two men recorded *The Jean-Luc Ponty Experience with the George Duke Trio* (1969). John had originally thought of asking Jean-Luc to join the original Mahavishnu Orchestra in 1971. Ponty was still resident in France, moving permanently to the USA only in 1973. It would have been an expensive appointment, even after employment and immigration issues had been overcome; John chose Jerry Goodman instead. Now Ponty was his first choice and Jean-Luc did not hesitate to join what he saw as a leading band. [39]

Michael Walden was a young novice drummer when the Mahavishnu himself called to invite him to join the new Orchestra. He couldn't believe it. He was already a big fan of the band and it was a dream to be chosen to replace the world's best drummer. Walden had already been interested in following guru Sri Chinmoy's leadership and became more involved at John's invitation. As a result he later adopted the forename Narada. Walden would prove to be an excellent replacement for Billy Cobham, but would later choose a path out of playing and into a very lucrative production career with artists like Whitney Houston, Aretha Franklin, Mariah Carey, Starship and Al Jarreau. He was successful at that too. In 1987 he was awarded the title of "Producer of the Year", he won "Album of the Year" in 1993 for the movie soundtrack to *The Bodyguard* and the "Song of the Year" in 1985 for Aretha Franklin's *Freeway of Love*. He was also named as one of the "Top Ten Producers with the Most Number One Hits" by *Billboard* magazine.

When John met Michael (before Harry met Sally) he was part of a small nucleus of very proficient musicians, of whom another was Ralphe Armstrong. A bass player with more of a funky electric background than Rick Laird, Ralphe was a rare player of the fretless electric bass. He was also a teenager with no pedigree and, like Michael, was completely untried in a highly competitive professional music environment.

John chose Gayle Moran to play keyboards and sing. A woman he became romantically attached to for a time, Gayle later married Chick Corea. Compared to the band of musical heavyweights he had assembled in 1971, these were all surprising choices. It was almost as if McLaughlin was making a point by selecting people who would not disagree with him. As Kolosky observed, John couldn't bear to fall out with anyone, but he needed to get his own way if the second band was to stand a chance of replicating the success achieved by the first.

Plans were quickly laid for the recording of a new album. Perhaps the most surprising decision John made was to combine his band with a full size symphony orchestra. He invited the young conductor Michael Tilson Thomas to take on his next project, and, on the album, Thomas directed the London Symphony Orchestra. English jazz composer/ arranger Michael Gibbs was hired to write the score for the many musicians that were now involved. John wanted George Martin, the famous producer for the Beatles, to produce the record.

Martin later said it was the most difficult record he had ever produced. Yet, still that was not enough. McLaughlin wanted his own band to contain both strings and horn players. A number of additional players are personally identified in the credits. Marsha Westbrook, Carol Shive and Phillip Hirschi make up a string trio, although they were not allowed to play because of disagreements over Musicians' Union issues. However, the new Mahavishnu Orchestra was indeed expanded to include all these players who then went on the road throughout 1974.

Fans picking up the new disc, eager with anticipation of a follow-up to the earlier three stunning Mahavishnu Orchestra records must have been very disappointed. Here they found a fusion of a different kind – one in which McLaughlin seemed to be abandoning his forays into the electric jungle in favour of an acoustic golf course. What was almost treasonable to the fans was to do it alongside acoustic violins and other strings playing classical arrangements. Ugh! Such sounds were indigestible to fans of rock music that was now becoming heavier and more pervasive in the wider music scene because of the very approach McLaughlin had pioneered only one or two years previously.

The opening track is *Power of Love* a strong and beautiful arrangement of an acoustic guitar theme in an orchestral setting. There's no jazz here and the theme does little except run downhill, and then rewind itself back up, only to run downhill again. It is hardly the groundbreaking stuff the fans had become used to.

Vision is a Naked Sword begins with possibly one of the loudest cymbal swirls on record before Walden introduces a composition, written in 11/8 with much orchestral drama obtained from repetition of a repeated phrase across a wide range of exotic chords. Walden carries on drumming over the orchestra, impressively flexing his chops, as if this is a new concerto for kit and orchestra, complete with cadenza at 3.55. At 4.20, the new band finally appears, improvising its way into existence. At 6.55, John begins a section of fast bluesy solo that finally acknowledges the band's links to jazz. It takes a full minute to get going, by which time Ponty takes the lead until 9.35 when he gives way to John and a guitar/drum duet. Bass and keyboards come back in from 11.12 to fill out the theme John continues to play. At 11.50 violin and guitar play a short unison section before the orchestra returns with the main theme at 12.00. At 12.51 the band takes over, sliding around on the range of keys as if it were an ice rink. The violin takes the lead until a final guitar flourish rounds it all off at 14.21. It's close to the style and format of Band One, but with the addition of a symphony orchestra.

Smile of the Beyond is well sung by Gayle Moran, accompanied by the full orchestra, with words by Mahalakshmi being the only thing on the record not composed by John. The song has western harmonies, but there is a persistent colour that reaches beyond our mortal existence. At the halfway point, the song would normally be over, but the band comes in with an up-tempo tune that cycles over 22 beats (4 x 4 plus 1 x 6). The style of McLaughlin's compositions once again takes on a familiar shape with, this time, a descending repeated phrase. The singing continues as John improvises continuously. Then, at 6.10 the middle section is over and the original accompanied vocal returns. Overall, it's a beautiful song that leaves a good feeling behind.

The orchestra again leads off on *Wings of Karma* leaving jazz fans wondering why they purchased this disc instead of something from the racks of classical CDs. Stump describes it as a "Gibbs-arranged pastiche of the Stravinsky era". [40] There's some relief for them at 2.10 when the band takes on a great electric jazz vibe with guitar and violin in sync. At 2.50 the piece transforms into a strong McLaughlin solo with Ponty taking it on from 3.30. It's all over by 4.35 when the orchestra returns to complete the sketch.

As its title implies, *Hymn to Him* begins with a strong religious/ spiritual feeling and slowly evolves into a more genuine fusion of acoustic strings with electric violin and guitar. The drums and bass appear from 2.45 and a minute later John begins a lovely soulful electric solo. From 4.52 a bridging section begins that leads at 5.10 into a much fierier tempo with Walden at last beginning to sound as if he's trying to emulate his illustrious predecessor. McLaughlin, remembering at last to play like the fans expect, leads from the front with a blistering attack on the tune he has been slowly developing. A loud crescendo develops, centred around Walden, and then at 7.15 the orchestra returns for a short link to an excellent funky section at 8.00 when, with the drums, the bass and keyboard at last make a recognisable jazz contribution. At last here's a McLaughlin piece that actually swings: it was a long wait! At 10.10, a neat little guitar/violin duet starts up and my feet are irresistibly tapping for the first time. Hey! Isn't this what jazz is supposed to be about? At 11.11 Ponty begins to earns his dough and makes bread with a great solo, but it's not without some great support from the rhythm section. At 13.30 the orchestra is spliced in for some fireworks as guitar and violin take turns with the lead. Somehow the orchestra isn't deemed capable of playing over rock music: ne'er the twain shall meet, until at 15.20 there's a melding of musics and a long, grand climax is constructed until around 16.50 when the tension is gently eased. From 17.05 John and Jean slowly knead out their ideas in the embrace of the orchestra towards a gentle and inspiring conclusion that just doesn't let go. It's a really great ending that will leave most listeners on a high.

Compared to the music of *Inner Mounting Flame* and *Birds of Fire*, this is not groundbreaking stuff. However, there were not many jazz or rock musicians who had tried anything quite like this ambitious project at this time. There is, of course, fusion here, but the fusion is not an intimate one. Much of the music is not so much fused as spliced, and the ensemble playing of the two orchestras is kept mostly separate. This fusion could not be described as sophisticated, although the tones and images are mostly interesting and pleasant, often beautiful. The music should be inspirational to many listeners who are eclectic in taste, but those expecting to hear familiar jazz music will be disappointed.

It certainly does not feel like an album from a new Mahavishnu Orchestra, but rather an album of new music from John McLaughlin assisted by a large number of hired hands. As a musician with a shiny CV and a lot of expectation, Ponty must have been the most disappointed with his role in this album. Compared to the prominent role that Jerry Goodman created for himself, Ponty seems to have been pushed into the background.

The album seems inappropriately titled when I think of the end of the world occurring in cataclysmic horror – visions of the movie *Apocalypse Now* come to mind. I guess it depends on how you perceive the end of the world. (I should point out that Mahavishnu Orchestra albums are named after poems written by Sri Chinmoy and selected by John. Presumably, he derived inspiration for each album's content from these poems.) This album is quite the reverse of an apocalypse with much beauty and love engraved onto its surface. However, the music probably was apocalyptic for those expecting the fire and brimstone of Band One. There is always a lag in time as fans catch up with something new, especially because of the lead-time prior to release of records. By the time many of them caught up with the phenomenon that was the Mahavishnu Orchestra, the euphoria was over. The band had fragmented and reconstituted into something entirely different. It must have come as a considerable shock to many, but it was always unfair to expect McLaughlin to continue along the same lines. He had to move on and this was a good try at developing a new approach. What few would have predicted was the move into jazz-rock-classical fusion.

Throughout 1974, Band Two continued to tour extensively, with its own strings and horns trying to simulate the orchestral contributions, but the mission was now different and the band could not command the same kinds of audiences it had done before. Once you reach the top of any mountain, the only way is down. Many saw it that way: for example, Cook described *Apocalypse* as "drearily pretentious". [41]

The Mahavishnu Orchestra: *Visions of the Emerald Beyond* – 1975 (***)

For most of 1974, the Mahavishnu Orchestra was a quintessential quintet supplemented by a regular string trio of Steven Kindler, Carol Shive (violins) and Phillip Hirschi (cello), and also a horn 'section' of Bob Knapp (trumpet) and Russel Tubbs (saxophone). The band continued to tour and played music from both the *Apocalypse* album and what would become the new album, *Visions of the Emerald Beyond* (1975).

The opening bars of *Eternity's Breath* strive to redress the balance that had been tipped away from rock (and, to some extent, jazz too) in *Apocalypse* by returning the focus of the band to the jazz-rock arena. Even if the old days could not be revived, this music, with the addition of an increasing amount of vocals, was rather more to the liking of the early 70s fusioneers – though still anathema to the jazz purists! After a rousing introduction with a timeless reverberation of anticipatory motifs, the expectation is fulfilled as the full-blown rock anthem returns at 1.20 - and it's as heavy as it has ever been. Part 2 begins with a sound that is date-stamped with the period – something we can rarely attach to McLaughlin's music. The keyboard sound, supplemented with a new-found horn section is very 70-ish, even set in the odd 5/4 metre. Redemption is attempted by means of the mesmerising guitar and violin solos, but, even if it wasn't then, the piece is now inescapably trapped in its time-zone.

Lila's Dance is a thrilling return to the format of early McLaughlin compositions. It begins with the long theme politely expressed on acoustic piano. After just once through, the band fades in with a backwash played in a complex 10/8 time with Walden interpreting the ten beats in a beautifully syncopated language as expertly as his hero Billy Cobham would have done. At 2.20 the rock music starts, with John playing a phased electric solo to Armstrong's bass accompaniment. When Walden comes in his drumming is stunningly impressive. The music is now in 20/8, and the change from 10/8 to 20/8 parallels the complex time structure that was adopted on Band One's *Dance of the Maya*. It was good then and it's good now. John plays another withering solo until an ensemble rock section with horns begins at 3.51. At 4.35 the first theme returns to indicate the coda section that, in turn leads to a repetition of the piano introduction. This is a great track.

Can't Stand Your Funk is like a little two-minute cartoon that makes a side-swipe at one of the main elements of the 80s jazz-fusion period. It's made comical by being written in another of John's favoured odd tempos - 5/4. The piece concludes with a classic McLaughlin burst that demands our attention. In any case, far from being a put-down for funk, it's actually the reverse, just as the

Scissor Sisters lied when they said they didn't feel like dancing! The proof was when this track was the one chosen for release as a single. Perhaps it's a musical thumbed nose at Herbie Hancock who was now on the scene in a big way? No. John is showing that he's just as capable of playing funk as anyone else: he just chooses not to do it very often. It's a short piece of fun. I'm sure Herbie loved it!

From this point on the album, the tracks are presented thick and fast in a series of distinctly separate pieces, yet run together into what sounds and feels like a suite, even if the themes expressed in the titles are somewhat disjointed. *Pastoral*, is aptly named as the string trio, with a sprinkling of John's acoustic guitar, play against a chorus of birdsong. Sadly, it's rather uninspiring and serves merely to fill space. *Faith* follows on quickly with acoustic guitar backed by a strong drum presence. The theme is another of John's ever-rising doodles that climaxes at 1.05 and leads into a solo rock vamp that John uses to introduce a short blast of band frolics. Well, the final seconds reveal that at least Gayle seemed to enjoy herself. Next comes a song composed by Walden – *Cosmic Strut*. Clearly the apprentice had been learning his trade from the master, choosing to write it in 9/8. The music struts its funky stuff with the kind of sound that would become stock in trade for many bands later, with extra colours added from the horns. This runs straight into *If I Could See*, a short, rather insignificant linking piece centred on a vocal line from Gayle that swirls around like extraterrestrial dust. *Be Happy* is a simple order that follows straight on, with the usual menu of high-octane solos from Jean-Luc and Mahavishnu, played frantically in 14/8. There's nothing more here than an extended improvisation over a rock theme, but it's quite effective.

Earth Ship offers temporary high orbit respite as we relax to the sound of a gentle flute solo from Bob Knapp, overlapped by a theme expressed by the usual violin/guitar duet in unison. The relaxed theme must be effective for we nod off gently and suddenly open our eyes to watch the mythical winged horse *Pegasus* fly past the cabin window. *Opus 1* breaks the news that it's just a dream and time to come back down to Earth. John lets rip for the first two and a half minutes of *On the Way Home to Earth* with a final blast from a newly acquired guitar synthesiser. Then the full band turns up the power of the thrusters. Walden and Armstrong are at the controls for an Earth landing as John wistfully says goodbye to the Universe and submits to the gravitational field that draws him back to American soil. It's a soft, landing, but we know he's sorry to be home. He'd rather be back up there, flying.

This is an album with literal and metaphorical highs and lows. At the time, McLaughlin thought of it as one of his best albums. [42] In my opinion, the change in style from a small collection of long pieces to an uncomfortably large collection of short (and sometimes insignificant) pieces diminishes the value of what might have been a more successful album. It seems that this was a deliberate plan. *Pegasus* was originally an improvisation by Jean-Luc within a bigger McLaughlin composition but Ponty had expected to receive a composer credit for it. When he found that it had been listed on the album cover as another McLaughlin composition, he was very angry, the more so because Walden had been given a credit for *Cosmic Strut*. It was the deciding moment for him to leave the band.

Presented in a more considered way, as he had done on previous albums, this music could have come across as the themed project he perhaps intended. Nevertheless, that's an artistic viewpoint derived from study of the paper package. The album is certainly a most enjoyable experience when played in its entirety in a quiet room, without interruption.

The Mahavishnu Orchestra: *Inner Worlds* – 1976 (**)

The album *Inner Worlds* (1976) would be the last album of the decade from the Mahavishnu Orchestra, although in the 1980s there would be another revival. For now, McLaughlin instigated yet more change to both the structure of the band and its musical direction, which was becoming as hard to pin down as the patterns of time in the early music. Jean-Luc Ponty had arrived in 1974; George Duke recognised him as the world's best electric violin [43] so he could be forgiven for perhaps expecting to emulate Jerry Goodman. Nevertheless, he failed to do so. After little more than a year in the band, Ponty moved on, disenchanted with what he saw as a diminutive role. He had felt pressure from John and the others to follow Sri Chinmoy, but he had no interest and began to feel like an outsider. Nicholson quotes Ponty as saying that he had anticipated staying a long time: he had apparently found a musical soul-mate in McLaughlin. Then, in a burst of Gallic over-reaction, he pulls all his criticisms out of his pockets, and ends by describing the band as "like a car that could only function at 100 miles per hour. Crazy!" [44] It would seem that the disagreement with John over *Pegasus* could have been trivial in other circumstances, but in the overall context it proved to be the final straw.

It's hard for us to appreciate the differences today between the Mahavishnu Orchestra as we hear it on record and the one that played night after night on tour. The legacy stored on discs is a very poor reflection of what the band was really like as a working entity, not just on the stage, but during the many hours they spent together on the tour bus. This is especially true of *Inner Worlds* which did not at all reflect what gig audiences were getting. For the immediate gigs, Steve Kindler took Ponty's role, and by all accounts made a fantastic contribution. But violin did not appear on *Inner Worlds* or in McLaughlin's electronic bands in future, so the violin element had been removed from the music and the core of the band reduced from a quintet to a quartet, still supplemented with strings, brass and woodwind. At one point, a stunning female saxophonist, Jean Bell, took the platforms as the MO supported the Jeff Beck Band on tour.

By the time of the recording of *Inner Worlds*, the peripheral musicians had gone – an economy measure and sop to an increasingly restive recording company perhaps? Gayle Moran had left John for Chick Corea and was replaced by Stu Goldberg. Narada Michael Walden and Ralphe Armstrong remained, but the band's music took another turn, away from the 'third stream' fusion with classical music and back towards the jazz-rock, but this time with a new, enhanced commercial element. This, of course, went down badly with the cognoscenti. Stump, a McLaughlin fan, accused the Orchestra of giving way to populist tendencies, as if that in itself was a bad thing! [45]

So, just six months after the recording of *Visions*, and, just days after John had recorded an album of acoustic music with a group of Indian musicians that we shall shortly know as Shakti, the band travelled to a French Chateau to record *Inner Worlds* (1976) during the course of a couple of weeks in July and August 1975. The one member of the band who would have felt most at home there, Frenchman Ponty, was absent. Furthermore, the party was not a happy one. Ponty's disaffection had created more bad feelings amongst the band and, in any case, John knew that this incarnation of the Mahavishnu Orchestra was over. It was a feeling he remembered well from a few years earlier and it was with some difficulty that the band tried to hold it together for the recordings. Needless to say, it shows on the album, which contains numerous signs of dissent and lack of musical cohesion.

For the first time in the life of the Mahavishnu Orchestra, there were signs that McLaughlin was not the dominating force. It was as if he didn't care any more. He had already mapped out his new musical direction with his recording of Shakti. Meanwhile, Walden had already shown himself to be a strong musical presence. Now he became a more important influence within the band. He began to demonstrate an interest in being more than just a drummer by expanding his contributions into playing the piano, a wider range of percussion and singing what were increasingly sounding like pop songs that he had 'co-written' with McLaughlin. John had allowed him to contribute one song on the *Visions* album. Now McLaughlin was definitely loosening his grip as the album's tunes appeared with numerous different composers – Walden contributed to four of them. What was perhaps the most surprising thing of all was the inclusion of a track called *River of My Heart*, composed by Walden and Anderson and on which McLaughlin didn't even play. The walls of Jericho were surely in severe disassembly at this point.

Even though John seemed to have committed himself to an acoustic future, he continued to experiment with some of the new electronic toys available for guitarists who wanted more than just the usual sounds. Thus the opener *All in the Family* featured John in duet with himself, substituting for the violin by setting the sound of his rock guitar off against a new guitar synthesiser. The opening has Walden demonstrating his drum licks as if, like the substitute in a soccer team, selected in place of Cobham, he still needs to prove he's good enough. Once the piece is in full flow, a promising theme bursts out, but the music really goes nowhere after that and the song is little more than a controlled freak-out.

The second track is another reflection of John's interest in Coltrane, fuelled by the more general album theme in which the world's deep fascination with the TV pictures from the moon was impacting upon musical output of many artists. (We should remember the widespread use of themes of outer space at this period in music history: Chick Corea, Herbie Hancock and Weather Report were all using these ideas as themes not only for tracks but entire albums.)

Miles Davis had named one of his own pieces after McLaughlin. Now John was getting his own back with *Miles Out*, a title deliberately intended to have a double meaning, and just one of a number of compositions named with Davis in mind. It was indeed, so far out as to be classifiable in the 'like Coltrane at his weird stage' category, but played with his new electronic gadgets. From about 1.15, a simple funk vibe is established and feet start to tap expectantly, but it's a false dawn. As we have found so many times before, the essence of the composition is almost non-existent, and just like Dave Holland's contribution to Bitches Brew, the role of the bass is merely to repeat the same short phrase endlessly as if played by a machine. A few years later, it would be. As with most experiments, they rarely work first time, and this track is awful. McLaughlin is at his most abstract here.

The third track is *In My Life*, a sweet ballad sung by Walden, who also accompanies himself on piano, having relegated the professional keyboardist Goldberg to the role of backing vocals – not a good way to welcome a newcomer into the band. Whether you like songs like this or not, it is surely entirely inappropriate to play machine-gun guitar solos and McLaughlin's choice of solo style is poor. *Gita* is another vocal tune, far less inspired than the previous one, and in which the vocal is subsidiary to John trying out his latest synthesiser sound. Thanks to the excessive reverberation, the music is a mush of sounds, with no delineation of significant musical contribution. *Morning Calls* is little more than John unnecessarily showing off his versatility. Here he does a bad impression of the sound of the Scottish bagpipes. Walden plays a drone on the organ, whilst McLaughlin noodles around with a Scottish tune. It's harmless, and pointless. *The Way of the Pilgrim* is Walden's composition, and at last we are presented with something of substance. The piece is a funky jazz-rock composition in which all the players are at last in an environment they can stretch out in. It's not innovative, although it does represent much of the more popular style that those of us who lived through the 1980s will recognise. McLaughlin at last plays a 'normal' sounding Gibson Les Paul that will please those who like the sound of traditional electric guitar.

In *River of My Heart* Walden, with just Armstrong alone, pulls out all the stops to create the kind of number that Whitney Houston might have recorded. Of course, her career did not really begin until 1985 when Clive Davis, then boss of Arista Records placed her in the spotlight. In any case, it is clear that Walden's musical contribution would be far greater in 'conventional' areas of the music business than in this dying backwater of jazz-fusion, although, for him at least, this was an essential learning experience.

Planetary Citizen is a funky party, written and led by Ralphe Armstrong, but today the lyrics are trite and, at times, the music is entirely typical of the *Starsky and Hutch* style that I have written about in my study of Herbie Hancock. The piece is thankfully short, for it has little to offer. On the other hand, *Lotus Feet* is a good track from McLaughlin and is the continuation in a more Western form of the piece begun on the first Shakti album. It has a memorable and unusual melody that itself is not necessarily Indian, although it has Eastern inflections. It makes a far better statement than the volumes of naff lyrics that precede it.

Inner Worlds is in two parts, though that hardly matters, for it represents a return to the unbridled noise of the opening tracks. You could be forgiven for thinking that this is John's reaction to the other part of the band that clearly wants to move into a style of commercial jazz-pop music that is digestible to millions. But this is the world of the machine, as described perfectly in the movie *Matrix* and although the music could have made a great soundtrack for that film, this Inner World is the real one that not many of us would choose to live in.

Some 'last albums' have the words stamped on the cover: this does too. As a soloist himself, McLaughlin seems to be using the disc as a practice session and an opportunity to play with his toys, rather than to deliver considered music, but there's also an uncomfortable polarisation as McLaughlin distances himself from his colleagues. On one hand, he almost disappears into electronics and the weird improvisational world of free-jazz. On the other he almost gives up on his mates as they head off into the commercial pop music business. He can't even be bothered to play on one of the tracks and gives up a large amount of the album's space to music composed (and almost certainly directed) by his young friends. They, in turn, see their futures mapped out rosily in the funky world that was now rapidly developing out of the jazz-fusion experiments of the previous five years. For these reasons, it is unlikely that many listeners will like this entire album: the wide variation in polarity is just too great for average ears. Fans and others who are studying the Mahavishnu bands' output will acquire this album more as a collectible curiosity than as a treasure, and may, like me, feel that John was letting go at this point. 1975 was a bad vintage for the McLaughlin brand.

Shakti with John McLaughlin – 1975 (**)

Shortly after McLaughlin's arrival in the US he enrolled in a College course to study the music of north India – Hindustani music. Then, one day in 1971, he met an uncle and nephew with the name Shankar. The elder man, Raghavan, was a percussion player, whilst his young nephew was a virtuoso violin player. McLaughlin, who we have seen had since childhood possessed a deep predisposition to the sound of the violin, was immediately attracted to the young Shankar's playing. Later that year, in California, John met a tabla (Indian drum) player called Zakir Hussain, who coincidentally just happened to be friends with the Shankars. The components of a new band had now been assembled, but it took several years to come to fruition because of the frenetic schedule of the Mahavishnu Orchestra. It was ironic that in order to make the clean break from the MO, it seemed necessary for John to drop his use of the name Mahavishnu, even whilst he was cementing himself within an Indian band. But the move was essential for John's long-term well being. Shakti, as it would eventually be named, was very much a part-time band that played at any convenient opportunity, removing John from the harsh, competitive, uncompromising world of the critics that he hated and depositing him in a fresh musical environment that few westerners dared to tread. Here he was among friends.

McLaughlin was not the first to experiment in the fusion of jazz with Indian music. The first occurred when British jazz saxophone player Joe Harriott joined forces with Indian-born violin and sitar player John Mayer to form a double quintet from five jazzers and five Indian musicians. An album was recorded called *Indo-Jazz Suite* (1968) and by the time of two albums *Indo-Jazz Fusions I* (1967) and *II* (1968) the band had become well known - in the UK, at least. (Interestingly, the bass player for the jazz combo was none other than Rick Laird.) The use of the word 'fusion' is itself especially noteworthy because it had not so far been used in any significant musical context, let alone applied to jazz-rock. Sadly, John Mayer broke up the band in 1973 when Harriott died suddenly. With its British base, John would have known the participants well at a time when he was about to depart for the USA, even if he had not yet decided to study the music seriously.

By 1975, John had already experimented extensively with Indian stringed instruments such as the vina (or veena) and the sitar. These were instruments that had the closest lineage to the guitar, yet were very difficult to play to the standard that McLaughlin would have wanted. Wisely, he chose not to play them in public, but to apply his great skills to the playing of Indian-style music on the guitar. This led him to commission from guitar manufacturers, Gibson, a specially made 13-string 'guitar' in which seven drone strings were stretched at an angle across the sound hole where the usual six strings resonated the air of the sound box. A picture of this unique instrument adorns the cover of Shakti's first album. In this way, a guitar was created that was as close to a sitar as it was possible to get. One of those responsible for the construction of this guitar was Abraham Wechter who later became McLaughlin's personal guitar maker.

Armed with his unique new instrument, John immersed himself in the development of novel tunings, adapting his own style of playing to the form of the Indian raga. In Indian classical music, 'raga' is the name that is used to describe literally the colour or mood of the music. There are many similarities to the term 'mode' in Western music. The most obvious are, of course, the major and minor modes, with the major traditionally being associated with lighter, happy moods, and the minor with sober, sadder ones. I have already described in outline some aspects of the use of other modes in jazz in my study of Miles Davis, and a more detailed description of that and the theory of Indian music are beyond my scope.

In a sense, the blues is a raga too, and McLaughlin even devised new ways to fuse the blues with the raga. Many found strange McLaughlin's willingness to express his activities at length to journalists in difficult, technical jargon. Stump, however, recognising McLaughlin as one of the foremost jazz-fusioneers (along with Miles Davis) saw this new activity as another manifestation of John's spontaneous desire to "hybridise first, then play, then intellectualise." [46]

By 1975, Shakti had been in informal existence for almost four years, but the year began very badly with the Mahavishnu Orchestra in its second spell of disintegration, and with John disenchanted with Sri Chinmoy and intent on dropping his Mahavishnu forename. John was artistically and spiritually messed up. For months, he didn't play at all. He severed ties with all things that were painful to him, including to his wife, Eve, who wished to maintain her discipleship of Chinmoy. John turned towards Shakti for salvation.

On 5 July 1975, John's entirely acoustic band recorded an album of Indian music at the South Hampton College on Long Island, New York, much to the disdain of Columbia executives who must have regarded their star electric jazz-rock guitarist as committing a form of professional suicide. It's worth commenting that today, Columbia (now part of Sony) is delighted to earn the revenues from marketing the album (and all the others from the McLaughlin catalogue) in the Jazz Legacy series of CDs, a label that by definition accords McLaughlin the status of a Contemporary Master! However, we should not fool ourselves. This is strictly Indian music and was never intended to be jazz, unlike the music on the *Indo-Jazz Fusions* albums. Even in today's multicultural western societies, for many listeners there is still a large barrier between them and the sounds of Indian music. It was one thing for John to enjoy the casual musical relationship with his Indian friends at gigs, but quite another to enter a recording studio with the aim of releasing albums of Indian music to the world. It was a certainty that McLaughlin was imposing a serious limit on the size of his market by such a career move, yet in 1975 it probably seemed the only route out of his personal hiatus.

The juxtaposition of jazz with Indian music may seem strange at first. However, there are several shared properties that make Indian music attractive to jazzers. As with all musics of ancient origin, when there was no question of expressing music by written notation, music was strongly based either on improvisation or on the careful passing of defined methods, styles and constructs from teacher to pupil. Improvisation is one of the most significant, for the need to improvise is strong in both forms of music. So also is the acceptance of very long musical forms. Jazz has always strongly resisted the demands of the music and broadcast industry for a product of three minutes duration and the acceptance of very long pieces as normal had been possible since the days of John Coltrane. Of course, it was only really possible with the arrival of the twelve-inch (25.4 cm) diameter long playing vinyl record (LP) which played at 33.3 rpm and characteristically had a maximum of thirty minutes music on one side, but was more usually twenty. Of course, long musical performances are most appropriate in live concerts and the option to squeeze a recording onto a disc, whether vinyl LP or plastic CD, sometimes necessitates editing.

The third commonality was the acceptance of new forms and harmonies in the jazz sphere, an advance again inspired by the likes of Coltrane and Ornette Coleman. Still further similarity can be found in the use of the drone, a strong focus on a single tone or chord centre that results in a given musical culture, not necessarily from any decisions about style, but from the very way the music is created on instruments of certain design. The fact that Western music has been so characterised by multi-chordal harmonies is very much a result of the more advanced designs of musical instruments such as the piano. I have elsewhere made many comments regarding the use of single chord music that were commonly adopted by Miles Davis and later by Joe Zawinul.

Thus, from the first track *Joy*, we find McLaughlin playing his 13-string guitar, a musician from a Western background and playing a Western instrument, who is immersing himself in the musical style of not just another genre but another human culture. As we might expect, his tone lacks the sophistication of western music and is raw and earthy. The music is based very much on repetition and therefore not associated with any kind of process of advancement - why should it be? In that sense, it is clearly virtuosic and empathic, full of energy and vitality in the same way that jazz can be, and can be described as 'mood music'. This, of course is clearly represented by the title, *Joy*, and by the title of track three, *What Need Have I For This - What Need Have I For That - I Am Dancing at the Feet of my Lord - All is Bliss - All is Bliss*. Let's just call it *Bliss*.

Lotus Feet is a simple improvised piece with first McLaughlin and then Shankar creating music that, we now know, is the precursor to a rather more accessible piece that appears on the final album of the second Mahavishnu Orchestra, *Inner Worlds* (1976). Frustratingly, the music fades out just as the Western version begins at around 4.44. *Lotus Feet* is perhaps the best known piece from John's Indian repertoire.

The half-hour long *Bliss* is something of a marathon for the inexperienced listener, although this is quite normal in Indian music. Notable in this long piece is some astonishing guitar playing at 14.45. Then, from around 19.45 there is an extended tabla solo from Zakir Hussain (with some support from the other percussionists). The tonal focus is clear from the tabla, for which there is no clear equivalent in Western music other than the timpani found in the symphony orchestra. Long percussion solos will become a feature of Shakti performances, and this one arouses much approval from the audience and the piece finishes soon afterwards.

The editor of *Downbeat* magazine insisted on drawing parallels between this and Coltrane's work, in particular, the relationship of Hussain with McLaughlin, and that of drummer Elvin Jones with Coltrane. [47] But don't be fooled: this is Indian music, not jazz. The question as to what is Indian music and what is not will occupy some of the discussion that follows.

Shakti: *A Handful of Beauty* – 1976 (***)

By 1976, John was recovering his spiritual composure having moved to a new home in a different part of New York, yet he chose the make this second Shakti album back at the place that must have held somewhat painful memories – the Trident Studios in London, UK.

When it begins, *La Danse du Bonheur* (*The Dance of Joy*) is played at a pace faster than I can dance. But first there is an introduction of vocal percussion, a clever feature employed occasionally over the years for example, in *Get Down and Sruti* on *Natural Elements* (1977) and in *Blues for L.W.* on the album *Live at the Royal Festival Hall* (1990). The music keeps its single chord focus and the early part allows Shankar to really develop a great violin solo, showing us how good he is at playing notes almost beyond the frequency of human hearing. (You should put your dog in the other room at this point!)

Lady L is written by Shankar and therefore much more Indian, even though I get the feeling that it is written for one of John's new girlfriends, Katia Labèque. The first section of the 12-minute track, *India*, is one in which John demonstrates his special guitar. The guitar is featured in close-up on the album cover and at last you can get an idea of the 'scalloped' fingerboard – the rounded hollows between the high fret bars are clearly visible. These allow the bending of the notes that is part of the Indian style. The head of the seven resonating strings can also be seen in close-up. John plays here in his most practised Indian style, using the sculpted frets to bend the notes as much as he can, whilst beating the drone strings at intervals in between. It's effective and accomplished playing, although I suspect that it never quite hits the mark of true authenticity. Of course, the doubts are at once dispelled when Shankar takes the lead and the music has variety, great rhythm and lots of colour.

Kriti is a traditional song from South India and is an example of Karnatic music. The music is bright, uplifting and played at great speed, much of it with guitar and violin in unison. *Isis* is the longest track at 15.13 and is another piece credited jointly to McLaughlin and Shankar. The first part is another haunting melody based around two alternating chords on John's guitar and dedicated to a woman – this time an Egyptian goddess whose karma spread through many cultures. John plays one of his extended solos in his inimitable, fiery style. Then there is a long solo feature by Zakir Hussain, and anyone who has seen him perform live will know that he is as capable of stunning listeners with his virtuosity on the tabla as any western drummer playing a full set of drums. The solo played here lasts around six minutes, but he is well capable of playing solos far longer than that.

Two Sisters is an interesting piece, full of poignancy and longing. Here are two beautiful sisters, so full of joy and love, but which should I choose? I could so easily love them both. An easier choice to make, perhaps, than later when there are seven! I guess it's a bad case of the *Monogamy Blues*. Another piece by John, you should easily be able to hear that *Two Sisters* is, indeed, a blues with Indian intonations and is therefore a fusion in its own right. It's the best example so far of such work. As we examine the music more closely, we find that, despite going to great lengths to acquire a special guitar and to play Indian music on it, John's own compositions are usually western-sounding; Shankar's, on the other hand, are undeniably from the east. This will become even more noticeable in the next album.

Shakti: *Natural Elements* – 1977 (****)

The third and last instalment of the Shakti adventure was fulfilled with the album *Natural Elements*, recorded in Geneva, Switzerland in July 1977. It is the most western of the three albums and a veritable delight for lovers of acoustic guitar, although you do need to be able to enjoy Indian spices too. As a teenage guitar student, I was entranced by the many new dimensions that the sound of the 12-string acoustic guitar offered over its diminutive 6-string sibling. The insertion of sixths, ninths and major sevenths into the usual chord shapes in the recipe of sound made the dish boil with delights. With recordings such as these, John is achieving very similar effects. Here he revels in the amazingly rich sounds he can create with his special Abe Wechter guitar and every track is strongly coloured with its resonant harp-like tones, which he achieved only after years of practice and experimentation with techniques and tunings. It is worth remembering that this album does not advertise itself as being Indian music – perhaps deliberately, and it is not. With three of the four musicians coming from the Indian musical culture, it is inevitable that it will take on many of the characteristics of Indian music, but with McLaughlin in the driving seat, it is very much a fusion of east and west. This forty-minute album can be enjoyed at its most basic level simply for the luscious acoustic-fest that it is, but when you take into account the endless hours of work expended in arriving at the end-product, it is clearly far more than just another album.

Track one is *Mind Ecology* in which McLaughlin and Shankar stretch out over a fast, even breathless, but very energetic base of percussion. A continued drone is used throughout, set up by T. H. Vinayakram playing a juice (Jew's) harp. John reinforces the drone with regular strokes of the resonance strings of his 13-string guitar, specially tuned for the occasion, as the percussionists drive themselves to apoplexy. It's a thrilling ride and a real highlight of the album. From time to time, the guitar and violin join in the frantic pace like ragamuffins leaping onto the running board of a speeding Toyota Land Cruiser, only to jump back off and roll in the dust, smiling at their own mischief. And all the time John's Wechter special sings its arrogant detached theme.

Face to Face continues with more acoustic honey, dripping from the strings of John's instrument. After a brief timeless introduction, a rather less frantic – though still energetic – pulse drives the music forward. It's a sound that leans more towards western tonalities because of the use of some simple chord changes and when John solos, it's with many of the same phrases he used under his electric alias. But all the while, Shankar's violin and the incessant pulsing of the tabla and timbales imparts Indian colours and textures in this true fusion of musical styles.

Come On Baby, Dance With Me is the one track written exclusively by Laksminarayana Shankar and it is the most Indian track of the collection. A short, energetic celebration of joy, this is a sapphire amongst the diamonds.

The opening minute of *The Daffodil and the Eagle* is a clear example of John's intention to infuse some natural elements from the blues into this music. The slow theme that begins the track is a clear blend of blues-inflected note-bending style of the western guitar into the eastern context and the early violin part could even be from a Country and Western gig. The catchy theme played during the first minute is left behind when the piece shifts into a higher gear from 1.05, from which point the tune is a mishmash of phrases and themes that leap about in tempo and borrow from bars as far apart as Delhi, Dublin or Nashville.

Happiness is Being Together might as well be in Kingston Jamaica, for the music has the style of a Caribbean calypso and by now it should be quite clear that this album was never intended to be a record of just Indian music. Either side of the two-minute mark, there are even some western vocals reminiscent of Crosby Stills Nash and Young. In contrast, *Bridge of Sighs* takes on a worried theme, as its name indicates. For me, though, this is more focused on the old grey cement of that famous bridge than it is on the beauty of the waters that flow beneath it.

John's early guitar theme for *Get Down and Sruti* is a sophisticated animal, far grander than the rest on this disc. This is DNA not daffodils. It's about being married, not just the wedding. Perhaps he didn't see it that way, for the music doesn't build on that, and moves away into simpler territory. At the end of the piece there's another section of vocal percussion. It's a strange, slightly schizophrenic piece. In contrast, *Peace of Mind* is an exquisite way to bring this lovely album to a close and is an excellent piece for hearing the magnificent instrument John is playing – his strumming of the drone strings interspersed between his wonderful melodies. The title of this one matches the music perfectly, and as the last notes die away, it's one of those occasions when all but the hardest listeners utter a hugely contented "Ahhh…!"

If there is a criticism to make, I have to say that the veracity of the listening experience is undermined somewhat by the need to double-track John's playing, albeit in places, on tracks 4 and 5, for example. The problem arises because the violin in Shankar's hands, at least, is not a good accompanying instrument. Thus, when John plays a solo with his normal picked style the single notes sound bare with just the percussion for accompaniment, hence the need to overdub himself playing chords in the background. This, of course, does not matter a jot to someone listening simply for pleasure, but when we analyse the artistic achievement of the album, it is inevitably slightly diminished by not being as natural as the title suggests. However, this nit-picking should not deter anyone from buying and enjoying this very good album. I hesitated to award four stars, but the vision of this album is wonderful. Those of you who like eclectic sounds will love this. Let's be honest, this is not jazz, but rather an Indian-flavoured record of great acoustic guitar music that should have appeared in the racks of contemporary folk music alongside the likes of John Martyn. This is John McLaughlin's patent application for a world music genre, filed at a time before few people could have conceived it, and certainly before Joe Zawinul began to claim it for himself.

John McLaughlin: *Johnny McLaughlin, Electric Guitarist* – 1978 (***)

Despite McLaughlin's spiritual sojourn with Shakti, during which time he rejuvenated his musical soul and licked his Mahavishnu-inflicted wounds, the commercial realities would not go away. He was contracted to Columbia, a commercial outfit that must make a profit, but which had never predicted profits to be made from Shakti, despite the fact that the overheads for running a band like Shakti were a tiny fraction of the massive expense of the MO. By 1977, McLaughlin needed to undergo another oscillation from acoustic to electric phase.

The album *Electric Guitarist* (1978) is a musical autobiography, a fact about which there is little doubt from the moment you pick it up. The album cover bears a delightful photograph of John as a handsome schoolboy, adjacent to a genuine business card from his early days in music. The name Mahavishnu is notable for its absence and we assume that the album is being presented as a marker to realign himself with the jazz mainstream. There are no reports of a divorce from Sri Chinmoy, and his music was still appearing with Chinmoy's name attached to the publishing rights. However, a discreet and polite distancing had taken place. John never openly rejects his adopted Indian name, but he makes no attempt to promote his eastern face for some years to come and this album contains just about everything else from his portfolio to date.

The album begins with a Mahavishnu Orchestra refresher, tellingly titled *New York on My Mind*, and is a look back to the halcyon days of the early 70s in the clubs of the Big Apple when the band bowled people over like ten pins. Amazingly, John managed to hire both Billy and Jerry to play alongside himself and Stu Goldberg; Jan was still mad with him and refused the invitation to play.

As for the music, well, it could easily have been taken from one of the sessions of the first band.

The second trip is a reminiscence of John's *Friendship* with Carlos Santana. The theme is instantly melodic and memorable, leaning uncomfortably towards pop music, but the piece soon adopts a good Latin rhythm through the support of expert percussionists Alyrio Lima and Armando Peraza. Narada Michael Walden plays drums, Neil Jason bass and Tom Coster organ. It's pleasant listening that is inoffensive to most tastes, but Santana deserved to be given something grittier to play and what could have been an opportunity for me to rediscover my salivary gland just makes my mouth dry.

McLaughlin chose to present his love of R&B by hiring the new saxophone star, David Sanborn, to play his piece *Every Tear from Every Eye*, but although the roots are obviously in R&B, the piece takes a sophisticated approach that is impressively emotional without being over-technical. Possibly inspired by the deep emotion John was feeling at the time, it is a highlight of the album. Tony Smith plays drums and the self-effacing Patrice Rushen adds some rich textures on her Fender Rhodes electric piano whilst always staying true to the aims of the piece.

John's continuous love of Coltrane's music is refreshed with *Do You Hear the Voices that You Left Behind?* This is a forceful high-tempo piece of mainstream jazz quartet music that John plays with Chick Corea, Stanley Clarke and Jack de Johnette. It's not so much an echo as a direct take on Coltrane's best-known piece *Giant Steps*, although McLaughlin makes it rather easier by leaving out some of the changes. Nevertheless, this is another highlight of the album, despite its distance from jazz-fusion.

Unless it's a mistake, the indication on the sleeve notes is that the track *Are You the One? Are You the One?* was not recorded at the same time as the others. Hence, it could easily have been pulled from the archive of Lifetime recordings labelled 'unused (but still dreadful)'. A trio with Jack Bruce and Tony Williams, it is typical of the kind of shudderingly bad material they recorded around 1969-71. I am astonished that some ten years later McLaughlin had not yet realised how bad this stuff was. The album is ruined by its presence, but I suppose that, if you write a sensibly accurate autobiography, you have to own up to your bad habits.

John's many practice sessions in duet with his friend Billy Cobham just prior to the formation of the first Mahavishnu Orchestra are represented by the penultimate track *Phenomenon: Compulsion* and this is presented pretty much as one of their heavy duty jams, with lots of guitar effects that weren't available first time around. There is both theme and structure to the piece, but it's the sheer energy of the duo that impresses most.

The final track, *My Foolish Heart*, would seem to be a comment on his personal life which was reportedly suffering a few hardships. The solo electric guitar piece is gentle, reflective and beautiful in a way that McLaughlin was beginning to make his own. As a supremely creative musician, John did not often resort to cover numbers except for pieces that had a special place in his heart. Consequently, this is a special interpretation from a master guitarist and leading jazz musician that, like a Turner painting, embraces a huge swathe of emotions and experiences, expressed as colours within its modest frame.

The music on this disc certainly spans much of John's career so far, but without the Indian music. In one sense that is good because it is very representative of what he was about in the first decade of his career. However, a mixed bag of material like this is likely to get a similarly mixed response from its listeners, most not liking all of it. To be enthusiastic about a quarter to a third of the music on a CD is not a good reason for buying it, but if you are new to McLaughlin and want to know what kind of music he was responsible for, this is a good place to start. There was a lot more to come later, however, with many new sounds yet to invent.

One Truth Band: *Electric Dreams* – 1979 (***)

The direction in which McLaughlin had started to travel on *Electric Guitarist* was largely followed also on *Electric Dreams*. He had decided to concentrate on jazz for the time being, although continuing to imbue his music with eastern elements whenever it was appropriate. To this end, he hired his Indian friend L. Shankar to continue to add the sound of the violin, although the instrument is not present on all tracks. Otherwise, the band he had drawn together on the earlier album was the same here: Stu Goldberg, Fernando Sanders Tony Smith and Alyrio Lima. Even David Sanborn made a return guest appearance on the final track. No longer being retrospective, this music was more unified with ladles of jazz, blues, soul and a soupcon of flavours of Vienna and the Punjab.

Guardian Angels is a short opener with John playing acoustic twelve-string guitar against Shankar's violin. The music is in two equal parts that simply flow timelessly from beginning to end. During the second, he plays the single long melody in unison with Shankar and another overdubbed track acts as accompaniment. Listen for the delightful little motif at the end: it could be an echo of George Harrison or many others from the pantheon of pop guitarists. As it stands, it's a beautiful cameo piece, and it would seem that this is only the introduction to a longer piece that he would record with his guitar trio on *Friday*

Night at San Francisco (1980).

Miles Davis is an opportunity to get his own back on Davis for naming a piece on his *Bitches Brew* album after John. It's not especially representative of Davis's music, although the inspiration is there and there is a brief musical reference at 3.48 to Miles in the form of the theme from *It's About That Time*. In fact the piece has many echoes of Pastorius and Weather Report, with electric guitar superimposed. A serious rock vibe kicks in at 3.32 and this is maintained until the music fades at 4.50 and leaves me wanting more.

Electric Dreams, Electric Sighs marks a return to the complexity of the early Orchestra days. The music begins with a gentle waltz-time ballad led by John on a slightly muffled electric guitar that renders the piece quite hymnal. But it keeps changing its harmonic direction as the chord sequence twists like an asp in your grasp. Then at 1.55 a new section begins and takes about thirty seconds to settle down into a metre that could be defined mathematically as a languid 11/8 but is more comfortable as a cycle of 22-beats. Smith's drumbeat, supported by Sanders' electric bass, feels like it ought to be a solid 4/4, but the half-beat that results feels awkward. It creates a real edge and you wonder who might be the first to make a mistake with an entry or an emphasised beat. The music becomes ever more tense as Shankar's slithery violin takes charge. Then at 4.24 the gear changes up again as Goldberg takes his turn. Finally, John plays banjo, a remarkable choice of instrument in the circumstances, but one that is, strangely, not at all out of place. From 5.50 John returns to electric guitar that now is starting to scream, as I do for the joy the piece has finally roused in me. This piece just seems to keep going around and around, tightening its hold with each twenty-two beat cycle until I just beg for more. Once again, the ending is tantalising. If ever a piece could go on and on past its fade, this is it.

If you found the metre of the previous track hard to comprehend, the next is even more difficult. The remarkable track *Desire and the Comforter* begins with a fast gentle percussive rhythm behind some apparently unrelated sequences of lush, loosely related chords and a gorgeously plaintive electric bass solo that's right in the front of the mix. At 1.45, the mood changes entirely and, after a brief section of funky fours, from 2.00 the metre becomes dominated by a pulsing rock rhythm that comes out in cycles of 10/4 metre that is split unequally into 13/8 and 7/8. With Shankar's violin prominent, this is a throwback to the days of MO1. As the cycle continues, each of the lead instruments shares the soloing until 4.08 when the rapid time of the opening bars becomes the dominant speed and John shifts into his rapid guitar solo mode. At 6.12 the funky fours become the final vehicle and the band turns the music into a party atmosphere before the music fades at 7.30.

Love and Understanding begins with a succulent Indian-style violin melody, and, if it had continued for the whole of the piece, I would have been very content. At 1.36 the music shifts away from the restful Indian landscape into a more traditional vocal ballad well sung by Fernando Sanders and reminiscent of Michael Sembello's contributions to David Sanborn's album *As We Speak* (1982). The music moves between being a gentle ballad and a spunkier kind of soul with McLaughlin and Shankar playing in unison. Later, when John takes over on lead guitar his sound is rich and unhurried, a real contrast to his more common style.

Singing Earth is another brief interlude that is a kind of cameo of the view from a flying saucer that buzzes our planet to see what's going on and decides that no changes to our software are necessary. It seems pointless but is at least inoffensive and does not disturb the vibe of the album, which, by now, is burning.

The flames are fanned still further by the frantic pace of *The Dark Prince*, another allusion to Miles – christened Prince of Darkness by Wayne Shorter. In his early days there were times when his live band might have played as fast as this. Here, the pace is around 400 beats per minute and throughout it Fernando Saunders keeps up a steady six beats per second or thereabouts, whilst John plays twice as fast! It is a display of technical ability, but the music is strangely unexciting as it stays on its tight time-track in its swing-time mainstream format. Despite the incredible technical ability on display, it's exactly this kind of track that leaves critics like Cook unimpressed. [41]

With all the music on the album written by John, except for a forty second flourish by Goldberg, McLaughlin is still getting his inspiration from his soul, rather than earthly sources. *The Unknown Dissident*, however, is a rare statement of political protest at some undefined event that presumably has roused his passions. It's a little out of context, with what has gone before, and the use of an English police siren to introduce the piece is strange. As far as I know, the English don't shoot political prisoners, even if they admitted that they do actually have some. As for the music, it's a soulful rant against oppression, something that neither McLaughlin nor Sanborn is known for. All assignations aside, the music is a beautiful platform for David Sanborn to play in the style for which he is best known – a passionate, lyrical soulful style with his razor-edged tone leading this very good electric band. A generation of young saxophone players grew up trying to play like this! Played in a slow, 2-beat soul rhythm at 40 bpm, you can also hear it as six-to-the-bar, and John, just being John, throws in the occasional seven-beat bar. Oh Boy!

McLaughlin's return to considered jazz was welcomed by most observers and this album is an uncontroversial addition to the main body of his work. Anthony Braxton, jazz composer, musician, and early collaborator with Chick Corea, once observed that Westerners lose sight of the true nature of creativity because of our need to compartmentalise the musical forms we listen to. My opinion is that it's due to our privileged accessibility to such a large quantity of music. How could we ever make informed choices about what to buy if everything was lumped together without any kind of classification? One thing is clear, however, as McLaughlin says with this record: there is only One Truth – music is Universal. It's just that this stuff is, once again, dreamily electric.

John McLaughlin, Jaco Pastorius, Tony Williams: *Trio of Doom* – rec. 1979, rel. 2007 (***)

In 2007, Sony Legacy released a CD of some unique recordings that, until then, had been the subject of folklore for many jazz enthusiasts. On 3 May 1979, the US State Department surprisingly sponsored a music event in Havana Cuba, a country ruled by Fidel Castro, a Communist and infamous *bête noir* in the USA since the early 1960s and the time of the Cuban missile crisis that so nearly precipitated the Third World War. Known officially as *Havana Jam* (and unofficially as *The Bay of Gigs*), a number of pop and jazz acts attended the three-night festival, including Stan Getz and Billy Joel, and a one-off grouping of John McLaughlin, Jaco Pastorius and Tony Williams that Jaco named the Trio of Doom. About twenty-five minutes of the programme was allocated to this dream team that was for many fans their jazz version of Cream or the Jimi Hendrix Experience.

The men arrived in Havana, each with a composition under his arm and not much practice under his belt. John took *Dark Prince*, Jaco took *Continuum*, Tony took *Para Oriente*, and Columbia took their tape recorders. Each piece was played, as planned, although not at great length, and the time slot was filled out with some solo drumming and a second piece that John and Tony had played together in Lifetime, *Are You the One, Are You the One?* In the end, the expectation far outweighed the result and, for various reasons, the tapes were disappointing, especially to John who said they could be released "over my dead body". [48] In particular, Jaco had entered his period of long mental decline and his behaviour had become extremely unpredictable. John, who had got to the top of his profession through strong personal discipline on stage, couldn't deal with Jaco's behavioural issues and was furious with him. Nevertheless, a week or so later, when they were all back in New York, the Trio went into the Columbia Studios and recorded the same material under better, more controlled conditions. It is said that, as a result of the argument over the release of the live recordings, Columbia actually released the studio recording of Dark Prince with some audience overdubs on *Havana Jam* (1979). [48] That was the end of the matter.

The band never played again; Jaco died in 1987 and Tony in 1997.

Thus, the 2007 release is important from a historical point of view for it presents an accurate account of a famous event in the history of jazz. John's long-time technical friend, Marcus Wippersberg, used his skills to restore and improve the tapes of both the live and the studio recordings, all of which are included on the CD. All the facets of the musicianship and style of these three greatest jazzers are on display and from that point of view there are absolutely no surprises on the album, except for the rose-tinted comments by John about his memories of the gig.

Al diMeola, John McLaughlin, Paco de Lucia: *Friday Night in San Francisco* - 1980 (***)

By 1978, McLaughlin had arrived at a low point of his career. Not only was his music not receiving the acclaim he felt it deserved, but he was receiving poor support from Columbia, largely because of his work with Shakti, which the company considered uncommercial. It would be a little longer before matters would come to a head. Some say he was fired by CBS, others that John took matters into his own hands and forced the company to release him. Either way, McLaughlin needed a completely new focus and took the bold step to leave the United States to live in France where he knew the atmosphere was entirely different and where he could essentially start afresh. He was continuing to enjoy playing acoustic guitar, especially as he had made the transition from steel to nylon strings, getting closer to the Spanish style of playing he admired so much. The time was right to form some new musical relationships and to move his career into new territory.

Paco de Lucia was born in 1947 in Algeçiras, Spain. He was invited to the USA in 1976 by Al diMeola and the two guitarists recorded an album *Elegant Gypsy* (1977). Sometime in 1978 John invited Paco to his Paris apartment for dinner and a new musical relationship was born. Almost at once, it was planned to form a trio with Larry Coryell and to record and tour together. They embarked on a world tour during the winter of 1978 to the spring of 1979. There was no album to promote the tour, but the event was a smash hit with the public who were largely unaware of Coryell's addiction to drugs. There was one official video recording of the trio on Valentine's night, 1979 at London's Royal Albert Hall before it disbanded. Coryell's patent unreliability demanded that a change be made, but he would be a hard act to follow. Amazingly, another guitar virtuoso was found in Al DiMeola and it was this trio that recorded an album of the most successful pieces from their repertoire in the Warfield Theatre, San Francisco on the night of Friday 3 December 1980 at the end of a second triumphal world tour.

The contents represent, of course, an acoustic guitar extravaganza, based largely on music of Spanish influence. Analysis of the music is difficult and, in the view of the musicians who shrink from categorisation, pointless anyway; Stump calls it "adulterated Flamenco", which is probably the best short description. [49] It is almost never jazz, although there is plenty of improvisation in the Spanish guitar tradition. Clearly, the styles invoked during the playing reflect the origins of each player, with McLaughlin being the most eclectic and de Lucia the most Spanish. Even so, it is difficult to accurately identify the players of many sections except where they range into rock, blues and even pop. The difficulty for listeners wanting to do more than just listen to the amazing playing is in figuring out who is playing with whom and whereabouts they are in the mix. That also, of course, depends on which way your speakers are connected or which way round you wear your headphones.

Oddly, for something promoted as a guitar trio, the album is more duets than trio. Track one is a medley of Al's *Mediterranean Sundance* and Paco's *Rio Ancho*. The former is a super melody, embellished over the first five minutes by means of an alternating solo-over-chordal-accompaniment format. The seamless join into *Rio Ancho* is made at around five minutes. The piece is clearly Flamenco-inspired, based on a rotating sequence of four descending chords in the chromatic sequence E, D, C, B. For the next six minutes or so it proceeds to offer an extended series of improvisations of startling ingenuity and energy. McLaughlin sits out that one, but duets with Al on track two for Chick Corea's brilliant composition, *Short Tales from the Black Forest*. This is a splendid piece, transforming from a duet to a duel from three minutes, especially when the two men have fun with Henry Mancini's theme to the *Pink Panther* from 4.12 onwards, break into rock chords at 5.00, Chuck Berry emulation at 5.40 and a blues solo from McLaughlin at 6.10.

With Al now sitting out, John and Paco play track three, *Frevo Rasgado*. The final two tracks are trio pieces. Track four is Al's composition *Fantasia Suite*, a piece notable at 3.35 for a progression to the highest notes playable on a normally tuned guitar. Track five is John's *Guardian Angel*, a piece that, strangely, does not sound as if it was recorded live at the time it was supposed to have been. Both tracks are further complicated for the ear when played by the trio and with the style of each player sounding very similar to the untrained listener.

Friday Night was enormously successful, cementing the successes already achieved by the earlier tour with Coryell. Stump attributes this success to the bad reaction at the end of the 1970s against electric music. [50] Apparently audiences were wooed by the reversion to music that sounded as if it had been created by humans instead of electronics. It seemed that McLaughlin's decision to abandon electric guitar for the time being would pay dividends.

John McLaughlin: *Belo Horizonte* – 1981 (***)

Belo Horizonte was recorded in a few days during June and July 1981 at the top Ramses recording studio in Paris. John formed a small group that consisted of his new girlfriend, classical pianist Katia Labèque and François Couturier on keyboards, John Paul Celea on bass and Tommy Campbell on drums. The Labèque sisters – Katia and Marielle – had already become well known in Europe for their classical piano duets. Both Labèque sisters were graduates of the Paris Conservatoire and Katia's career in classical music was hardly touched by her dalliance with McLaughlin's jazz. Jean-Paul Celea was a classically trained acoustic bass player. In 1978, he met François and the two men played alongside many leading French jazz musicians. Campbell was the odd man out. Tommy, a superb American jazz drummer and Berklee graduate, went on to have a distinguished career working with Sonny Rollins, Dizzy Gillespie, Manhattan Transfer and Clifford Jordan, as well as more recently Robin Eubanks.

As one who always tries to find visual imagery in music, I cannot help but be puzzled by the first two tracks. *La Baleine* is a title that means 'whale' in French, yet the introduction to *Belo Horizonte* is surely the call of the whale superimposed over the sound of the sea? Meanwhile, *Belo Horizonte* is named after the first planned Brazilian city, capital of the state of Minas Gerais, yet the second piece, *La Baleine*, unmistakably has the rhythm of the samba. OK, mistakes are often made on album sleeves, and mistakes in listings are more common than you might think: secretaries and graphic artists don't work in recording studios with busy musicians. However, the piece named as *Belo Horizonte* is the piece with the same name that opens *Que Allegria*. Stump says the opening to *Belo Horizonte* represents the Amazon rainforest, but I don't buy that. Perhaps it's as simple as saying that the sound effect was attached to the wrong piece at a late stage. It's a very curious juxtaposition. Perhaps we should just get on and enjoy the music.

There is no doubt whatever that this is an album of pure joy. John loves his new life in France and has a new love in France. This particular French woman, Katia, has understandably revitalised his musical outlook. Electric guitar is a thing of the past and the album has a luxuriant, fresh, crisp acoustic sound. Although it does use synthesisers, the sounds are entirely compatible with the bright sunny day, blue skies and crisp white clothing depicted in the album's artwork. John looks and sounds like a man who is head-over-heels in love. The music is in standard European harmonies and has no unusual metres that might alter the album's locus. We could absolutely not call this a jazz-fusion record so we shall have to put that side of our interest on hold for a while.

Belo Horizonte is almost indecently fast, and it seems even John thought so in retrospect, for he slowed it down significantly when he re-recorded it in 1990. The melody is played in unison with Katia playing a flute sound on synthesiser, which adds to the acoustic feel. She also contributes a lively and accomplished solo synthesiser flourish that sounds well improvised for someone who specialises in written music. Couturier adds some nice sophistication with his electric piano and Celea is pushed hard to keep up on acoustic bass (and does so admirably) as the piece steams its way through a fairly standard format to a rewarding end.

La Baleine is as sophisticated a samba as the music frequently is. It's also very appealing and bears all the hallmarks of quality hotel foyer music. I use that phrase not in detriment, however, for whilst Stump and others decry the devastation that cool jazz has wreaked upon the genre, I could not disagree more. It is this very kind of sound that builds the bridges between the average listener and the jazz musicians, enabling them to make an honest living from their chosen career. That is a very good thing in my book. Just as this music would probably not have been possible without Stan Getz and Charlie Byrd in the 1960s, so also was it probably the inspiration and enabler for much of the music of the 1980s and 90s – good music, by the likes of artists such as Lee Ritenour, Dave Grusin, Bob James and many others. These musicians have had more than their fair share of derision from jazz purists when all they set out to do is entertain. Here McLaughlin is showing the way forward and it was good enough for him then. It's not cutting edge stuff, but it is very pleasant music that has a valued place in our culture.

The short piece *Very Early* is another of John's periodic reflections to one of his early heroes, Bill Evans, although this piece, a duet in waltz time presumably recorded with himself, is so short as to be somewhat pointless. However, it is a very satisfying interlude and did point towards a project that John would embark upon more than a decade later when he would record an entire album of music very similar to this, *Time Remembered* (1993).

One Melody begins as a guitar-drum duet with the clearly very talented Tommy Campbell. Perhaps it would have been more aptly named *One Key* because, after a beautiful *rubato* introduction, it becomes a drone in A. Apart from some ensemble bursts, the only other obvious element is percussion played by Jean Pierre Drouet who comes in with congas from around 2.48. A great insert runs from 3.24 to 3.37 with Celea bowing the bass with fine resonance. There are a several short bursts of Indian-inspired phrases, at least two of which have echoes of John's days with Jerry Goodman on violin. This is a rather rambling piece that nevertheless makes an impact on the album and improves with listening.

From the monochordal composition of *One Melody* John shifts to the other end of the spectrum for *Stardust on Your Sleeve*, a very sophisticated construction melodically, but one that can simply be enjoyed for what it is. The band is comprised of Couturier, Celea, Campbell, now joined by François Jeanneau on soprano sax. The music could easily have been a collaboration with Miles Davis's saxophonist Bill Evans, who was only now working to bring Miles out of his retirement. But the sound is very definitely that of Evans, both in playing and composition, as a very fine melody, with some of the same kind of music that would appear on the Egan/Gottlieb/Evans collaboration *Elements* (1982). Everything about this music smacks of love, honour and respect for humanity.

Augustin Dumay, another premier league classical musician, plays violin on *Waltz for Katia*, a pleasant piece clearly created in the classical style, albeit with jazz rhythm attached. This is not 'Third Stream' music in the sense that it was intended for the elements are merely bolted together, and when the rhythm briefly becomes overt swing fours at 2.24, it's a dead give-away. (Katia and Augustin don't play during that bit.)

Zamfir is named after Gheorghe Zamfir, a Rumanian musician and flute virtuoso. Consequently, the music is pastoral and soulful. The piece opens with an acoustic bass solo by Celea. At 1.02 the band starts and Couturier plays a synth solo that sounds like a flute. Celea continues to solo as the piece evolves in a continuing pastoral mood. Later, McLaughlin develops the mood with a delicious baritone sound that is languid and sensual through to the faded ending.

The last track is *Manitas d'Oro* (Golden Hands), a Spanish guitar duet with Paco de Lucia, no doubt written with the great Flamenco guitarist Manitas de Plata (b1921) in mind as well as John's friend Paco. John was already starting to put in a lot of work in this style of music and it would become a major part of his career repertoire that I report in other sections.

In this album, McLaughlin is leaving behind all the baggage he had collected from the 1970s and starting with a clean sheet – new country, new friends, whilst exploring his love affairs with three shapely bodies, two of which were guitars made by Abraham Wechter and Richard Schneider. Some great albums are created as a result of an intense experience with chemical substances. If this one was created as a result of love for a woman, I'll vote for this every time. But then I'm just an old romantic!

John McLaughlin: *Music Spoken Here* – 1982 (***)

In the summer of 1982, McLaughlin revisited the Ramses studio with the intention of repeating the days of delight he had experienced the year before. Since 1981, with the powerful Warners record company at his back, he was in an environment he obviously felt entirely comfortable with. Surrounded by his friends and technical staff he trusted, he could continue the good work he began twelve months earlier. However, things were not entirely the same as last year. No longer was he the dizzy, head-over-heels-in-love schoolboy; now he was the dominant male, strutting his stuff. The context for *Music Spoken Here* was promoted on the album sleeve thus: sexy male musician (bare-chested John) exhibiting his independence by trying to fit a square peg into a round hole. The title was saying, "I'm the musician around here; who are you?" His experiences with the critics had clearly not abated.

The music was different too. The same musicians were present, although there were fewer than in 1981 as John limited himself to the nucleus of his band: Labèque, Couturier, Celea and Campbell. However, instead of the joyful box of designer chocolates that was *Belo Horizonte*, here was the musician's toolbox with each artefact chosen for its functionality. About half were made in Spain. The yin-yang of 1981 was now replaced with his more usual paternalistic mood, and the dominance of acoustic over electric vibe was distinctly diminished. John was also showing signs of the amount of time he had been spending with his acoustic guitar trio playing strongly Spanish-flavoured music. The first, *Aspan*, is Spanish – nay, Moorish - at times. It is melodic, yet earnest music, with John delivering his usual strong lines on acoustic guitar and Katia adding a lot of extra colour from her synthesiser.

Blues for L.W. is a curious construction. L.W. represents Lech Walesa, the Polish miner who led his country out of the strictures of Communism and became the country's President in 1990. He did spend most of 1982 in prison, so that, at least, was justification for his blues tribute from McLaughlin. However, since he wasn't dead, or even close to it, it seems odd that John should use the opening section of this piece to depict a funeral. I guess, after my problem over *La Baleine* and *Belo Horizonte*, I should have learned not to take John's music and titling too literally. At 0.58, for no obvious reason, he uses the fanfare taken from its fleeting appearance in Gil Evans' arrangement of *Blues for Pablo* on Miles Davis's great album *Miles Ahead* (1957). John himself said on his album *Thieves and Poets* (2003) that he 'borrows' from other musicians. Stolen or not, it's beautiful music. Then, at 2.50, the funeral becomes a wake by breaking into swing fours. Persuaded by John to try her shapely hand at jazz, Katia bravely takes an extended solo, and demonstrates the fantastic dexterity we would expect from a premier classical pianist. Sadly, despite being verbally encouraged by John, she demonstrates the gulf between jazzers and those who rely totally on paper dots; her improvisational skills are restricted to the kind of random selection that novices employ. This track would later appear on John's trio album recorded with Trilok Gurtu and Kai Eckhardt at the Royal Festival Hall, London.

The Translators is a mysterious piece that may refer to the title of the album in which John implies that he is talking to people who do not speak his language – critics perhaps? This music is the soothing intercourse that takes place between those with little to share by way of understanding when they have the benefit of intermediaries. And in the true style of good negotiators, this music can't ruffle any feathers. At just over two minutes long, it's effective, but short. But then, how long is a piece of string?

In *Honky Tonk Haven* John shifts his position from strong sunlight to the ambiguous shadows of illegal activities, suggested by the electronic ambience of the piece, and confirmed by the final wailing of police sirens. Katia returns to the safer territory of delivering complex arpeggios, whilst John's electric guitar sounds unusually strange after so much work on his acoustic box.

Viene Clareando is a short section of Spanish music played by John on two guitars, played as a light aperitif for the altogether more serious fare of *David*, which also appears on *Passion Grace and Fire* (1983). I feel you need to be much more seriously interested in ethnic Spanish music than I am to derive the full benefit from this piece. Filled with skill and intensity, the music is at one moment slow and timeless, and then suddenly becomes zestful and determined, with an intensity greater than you'd easily find in modern Spanish popular culture. Celea's fluid bass playing is especially noticeable here.

The taste of Spain is beginning to become the dominant flavour as John injects *Negative Ions* into the atmosphere. It's defiantly electric and futuristic, and throughout the 1980s defined what most people thought of as sexy, male technology. I can't stop myself associating the opening synthesiser theme with business training videos that aimed to communicate enthusiasm and excitement amongst their viewers. That doesn't mean that this has dated, however – unlike a lot of music of this type. This piece still sounds vibrant and forward-looking, and is testament to John's mature vision of what he was trying to achieve.

Brise de Coeur means 'broken hearted' and it not difficult to imagine the vibe for this beautiful duet between John and Katia, now on piano. As a more formal written piece, it allows her to display her true skills in an environment that is more appropriate to her background. Oddly, however, it never threatens to moisten the eyes of this old sentimentalist. *Lôro*, meanwhile, is a light and playful piece and a fine way to bow out from the album. Indeed, taken with *Belo Horizonte*, this pair of Franco-Spanish albums makes a good part of a music collection. There's a huge variety of music here and anyone with an eclectic taste will enjoy listening to them. On the reverse of the sleeve to this album, John (still bare-chested) is trying to work out how long is a piece of string? I'm sure he knows the answer, but just wants to leave us guessing.

John McLaughlin, Al diMeola, Paco de Lucia: *Passion Grace and Fire* - 1983 (**)

The album *Passion, Grace and Fire* was recorded by the trio in late 1982 and was different from *Friday Night* for a number of reasons. This was a studio album with all of the seriousness that results from prior planning and none of the light-hearted spontaneity that gushes from the live recording. All of the six tracks were trio pieces with an equitable distribution of two tracks from each of the three composers.

Both McLaughlin's compositions are taken from his last album with Katia Labèque. *Aspan* is the better of the two, with the three similarly matched guitars difficult to separate at the best of times. Perhaps the most remarkable moments are when all three players fire off their supersonic broadsides with impeccable accuracy at the very end. It's hard to imagine such playing being matched anywhere else.

All of the technicalities are present on the album, including many fireworks, and surprisingly some signal conditioning of Al's steel string guitar, which makes identification a little easier on, for example, his own piece *Orient Blue Suite* (it was incorrectly titled *Orient Blue* on some editions). The second track on the album, it is a suite in two parts, the first a lively dance in 6/8. The second part commences at 2.33. It has a strong logical melody and lots of shifts of mood and tempo, through to a faded end with lots of hand-claps. Once again, McLaughlin and de Lucia sound very similar on nylon strings, although John's style is invariably punchier and louder in the mix, John to the left and Paco in the centre. The next two tracks are by Paco, the unashamedly Spanish *Chiquito*, which has sections of both two and three guitars, and *Sichia* which sets out with a rhythm that feels more Brazilian than Spanish, though it settles down into a lively, melodic fiesta piece with lots of percussive action. The second McLaughlin piece is the Spanish-influenced *David*, which might seem better placed on this album than on *Music Spoken Here*, but it is none the more exciting because its construction from clumsy groups of disjointed chords simply does not fire imaginations. Every time you think it will lift you up into the clouds, it just loosens its grip without warning and heads off in another direction - an example of complicated composition for the sake of it. I can't help feeling that John is rudely trying to be more Spanish than Paco with this music. *Passion, Grace and Fire* is diMeola's second piece and is clearly intended to display all those qualities even if grace is the first sacrifice to be made in such a competitive environment. There is certainly no shortage of passion or fire on this album, but I suspect that unless you are well tuned into this style of guitar extravaganza, you may find it actually dull without the crowd pleasers that were such a joy on the *Friday Night* album. Neither of these albums is jazz, despite the musicians' protestations that much of the trio's music was improvised.

Mahavishnu Orchestra: *Mahavishnu* – 1984 (****)

In 1983, John made the difficult decision to reform a band under the title of Mahavishnu. There is some confusion about exactly what the band was called. The band was promoted as "John McLaughlin and Mahavishnu" on the next album, *Adventures in Radioland*. Strictly speaking, it may not have been a new version of the Mahavishnu Orchestra, yet it was natural for fans to think of it that way and those responsible for marketing the band's gigs and albums became confused. John himself referred to the band as "the third version of MO" and on the latest available release of the album, the album title is *Mahavishnu* and the band is indeed named as the Mahavishnu Orchestra.

Whatever the details, the formal association of John with a band called Mahavishnu was a big risk to take. There was every chance that he would alienate all those listeners for whom the name was synonymous with the greatest thing they had ever heard. Just as had occurred with the transition from MO1 to MO2, these fans of the eighties would almost certainly be disappointed because the band could not have the original personnel and could not reproduce music that compared in any way with the fantastic sounds of ten years before. The need to take the risk may have outweighed the perceived magnitude of the risk itself. Chick Corea would similarly try to reproduce his Return to Forever success with his Elektric Band in 1986. It worked for him. Even if he was happy with it, John's career was disappointing many, not least Warner Bros., his record company. Sales were disappointing and his scattergun approach to his work did not help focus the minds of those who were likely to buy his records. Even Miles had come out of retirement and was pulling in the crowds. Perhaps a revitalised Mahavishnu band could recover some of the euphoria of the early 70s?

John chose some of the best musicians that he could possibly have hired. He had always remained close to Billy Cobham, who remained his first choice drummer, but he made a strategic decision to change the sound of the band by having a saxophone instead of a violin. John adopted Miles's strategy of hiring the cream of the young players. Davis's saxman, Bill Evans, had proven himself beyond measure. What's more, having just left Miles he was now available and was hired. So too were the great keyboardist Mitchel Forman and the stunning young electric bass player, Jonas Hellborg. Born in 1958 in Gothenburg Sweden, Hellborg stopped the show at the 1981 Montreux Jazz Festival, where he impressed many jazzers, including Michael Brecker with a short but mesmerising solo performance. Brecker introduced him to John, and Jonas passed on some of his tapes. Two years later, he got a call from John asking him to join a revised band called Mahavishnu. Hellborg, who had worshipped the band since he was a kid, was overwhelmed. It was the big break he was looking for. Hellborg's stage presence was as captivating as John's had been at the early Mahavishnu concerts of 1971, with Hellborg's shaven head, shades and animated movements exaggerated by his use of a large double-necked bass. His presence on the album, *Mahavishnu* (1984), recorded in April and May of that year cemented a brilliant artistic achievement for him and put him on the road to consistent future success.

Many, on the other hand, considered the album a flop. Worse still, McLaughlin was vilified like he had rarely been before. Reminiscent of the description "disco schlock" applied to Herbie's work of 1978-81, *Mahavishnu* was described as "a shambles with a smile", "a well-intentioned wreck." [51] It was the ultimate irony that the man with a large share of the responsibility for the wave of hatred that accompanied the creation of jazz fusion, was now being attacked by his own side because he was not making jazz-fusion that was as good as he did then! The paradoxes and contradictions would have made a good Scotsman buy a round of beer. The record company must have been displeased too: the disc disappeared from the commercial radar for many years and is very difficult to find in 2007. This is a terrible result of the commercial aspects of the music business. The public and, more importantly, the critics, were not prepared to accept this "ill-timed and ill-favoured reincarnation." [52] Nostalgia rules OK.

Mahavishnu is a clear example of just how perverted the music business can get. Here was a great album, completely exploded because of the previous history of the band's leader. Clearly, the decision to revive the much-loved MO had been the wrong one; a band called *Colin's Donkey* might have had more success. The music is seriously focussed on jazz-fusion, with keyboards and bass all electric, and McLaughlin more electric and digital than he is on other albums. Here was another problem for him: in moving on, and playing with a new sound, he was not the fabulous electric guitarist his fans (Kolosky being one) expected. John was now an experimentalist fond of playing a Synclavier II 'digital guitar'. This kind of sound seriously disappoints fans of the electric guitar, mostly because it is hard to distinguish the sounds it creates from those of a keyboard.

Let's examine the music that proved so controversial. *Radio-Activity* is a title with double meaning. In this context, it pointedly refers to the drive to penetrate the mass media by getting airplay, something that had eluded John almost entirely throughout his career. It is a great fusion track with Cobham in brilliant mood. By around thirty seconds he is driving the rhythm beautifully as John sets up some chordal backwash prior to the main theme. There are a lot of musical tones and textures floating around in the vacuum of the electromagnetic spectrum and these lead slowly into a deep vocoder-like sound at 1.43 that gradually rises in pitch so that it is clearly not a vocoder. As the energy builds, John starts to sound like a psychologically disturbed violin whose mental state is somewhat schizo. At around 3.30, Evans at last arrives on the scene and plays soprano over a staccato guitar synth line. Evans always plays harmonically with great verve and energy. Nuclear criticality is reached as Cobham and Hellborg withdraw their control rods. Finally, at 5.10, a last-ditch blast from Cobham sets up a lively finale. His drumming becomes seriously invasive as the stream of energy from spontaneous atomic decay heats the surroundings to molten temperatures.

The fantastic start is immediately transformed in *Nostalgia*, an exquisitely atmospheric sound that immediately transports listeners to the banks of the Ganges. The mist swirls gently over the cool, clear water as the sun's rays gather strength in the early dawn. John's electronic sounds paint the most beautiful pictures in our minds as we just lie back and let this music sweep through our consciousness. Bill's soprano sax complements the sound perfectly and the bass, keys and drums all come together at 1.40 to pick us up and carry us off to wherever we want to be. The music is a wonderfully impressionistic sound painting filled with peace and joy and the lovely warmth of the nostalgia we all feel from time to time. Nothing else is required.

Next is *Nightriders*, a superb funky piece that gets everyone going except the musically dead. John comes through with some juicy guitar playing that is almost normal, but squeezed through an electric filter like apple juice through muslin. Bill plays a mean tenor sax as Mitchel Forman, dubbed the "strafer" by Bill, lays down the funk with his thick synthesised chords. Hellborg and Cobham make a typically invincible duo throughout. The only disappointment for me is that, being based around a drone, I keep expecting it to move up a gear, in which case my veins would surely have exploded. Sadly, it never does, but that's a small criticism.

East Side, West Side is a stunning piece of high octane jazz-fusion. After a rapid burst of machine-gun fire from John and Bill played as an intro in unison, the piece begins with a real theme – for a change! It lasts until fifty seconds when it then moves into a high velocity set of improvisations based around 172 beats per minute, but with most of the playing performed at four times that speed. In other words, John and Bill are playing at 688 notes per minute with extended phrases at more than ten notes per second. We expect fast playing from McLaughlin, the man who has made explosive fast guitar work his trademark. However, you should listen seriously to Bill Evans's tenor sax playing after the brief restatement of the theme at 1.58. From 2.23 this involves very fast and beautifully melodically constructed phrases that span as much as five bars and eighty-odd consecutive strategically placed notes instead of the random blasts that many other tenor players would have produced! That's truly exceptional playing by any standards. Later, he and John play the traditional jazz game known as 'fours' which is essentially where they alternate every four bars, but soon move on to 'twos' to turn up the energy of the music even more, if that were possible.

Clarendon Hills is the only track written by Bill Evans, and this is very characteristic of his compositional style at this period of his career. Bill writes extremely considered melodies using conventional harmonies and overlays them with his beautiful vibrato-less soprano saxophone melodies. In this case, John does the same for the early part of the piece. Then at two minutes, Cobham comes in to set up a super, solid backbeat and soon Forman is laying down his extensive sheets of chordal backings. A doubling of speed at 2.36 gives the piece a boost in energy before coming almost to a stop at 3.04. The whole mood of the music now changes. A repeated motif juxtaposed with a set of slowly evolving chords creates a truly beautiful spine-tingling vibe. Bill creates a mouth-watering atmospheric backwash over which he plays his weepy melodies. Then the music takes off at 4.24 once again for a final charge towards the finish and Billy turns up his after-burners. The final denouement retraces the steps of that wispy repeated theme and Bill wrings every gram of sadness and emotion out of his saxophone. It's a stunning piece. Enjoy.

Track six, *Jazz*, is John doffing his cap to Weather Report with the whole sound of this short piece an echo of a band he knew well. The Weather Report mood continues on *The Unbeliever*, a sullen, unsettling piece that is more about a feeling and a sensibility than it is about notes written on manuscript paper. The sequence is dreamlike and other-worldly, but it's a disjointed and disturbed world that we would all like to leave at the earliest opportunity. Then comes *Pacific Express*, another fast piece that takes a minute to leave the platform and then surely speeds like a train towards its destination. After the theme, Jonas takes a solo from 1.50, followed by a tenor exposition of the theme that begins smooth and luscious, but finishes with some rough edges. Then Billy gets a great solo opportunity before John comes in with another very fast solo that could easily be a keyboard sound. Except for the curious addition of the robotic voice in parts of this piece, *Pacific Express* could have been a component of the album of music Jan Hammer would write for *Miami Vice* in 1985. They gave him awards for that, as well as a great deal of money.

The final track, *When Blue Turns to Gold* deviates from the direction of the rest of the album. Unable to resist his eastern urges, John dumps his new band in favour of other friends. Katia Labèque begins with a flourish of acoustic piano and then the piece transforms into a last encounter with the wonderful, colourful sounds of India, as expressed by H. P. Chaurasia playing Indian flute and Zakir Hussain on percussion. This track is a gentle way to play out the album and at only just over three minutes in length doesn't detract from the overall feeling that this was a special album to listen to.

There are some who say that *Mahavishnu* was a cynical and commercial ploy to put McLaughlin's flagging career back on track. [53] There is no doubt that this album is commercial, but, as I have said now many times, why is it so bad if it sounds good? One of the sterner critics of this band's output was writer Paul Stump who lacerates the music as "phoney bombast" derivative of what Miles was doing at the same time with his albums *Star People* (1983) and *Decoy* (1984). It seems that when artists such as McLaughlin who prove themselves capable of operating at the cutting edge then decide not to do so, their resulting output must, by definition, be trash. What's worse is that all the other musicians are inevitably tarred with the same brush, which is clearly ridiculous in this case. McLaughlin's use of the Synclavier was as destructive for critics like Stump as the vocoder was for Herbie Hancock, and one of their biggest difficulties with the music was that they couldn't easily write about his playing because they couldn't distinguish it from the sound of the keyboard. Apparently, instead of being a master guitarist, he sounded like a novice synthesiser player. That's also patently untrue, but it's not hard to understand such reasoning and to conclude that the album did McLaughlin no favours. Stump records it as John's "most outstanding musical failure." [54]

Clearly, if you listen to this expecting the fireworks of the earlier versions of the Mahavishnu Orchestra, you will be disappointed. Listeners should simply accept this music as coming from Colin's Donkey. There's no law that says this should be an album of electric guitar music, although there are some glorious such moments on the funky track *Nightriders*. The rest is all about the new electronic sound of the eighties, with John playing guitar-synthesised music for much of the time. Paul Stump makes the point that Pat Metheny succeeded where McLaughlin failed by playing Synclavier and still sounding like a guitarist. [55] It is certainly true that with Mitchel Forman's heavy duty electric keyboard sounds predominating beneath, it is often difficult to distinguish what is played on keyboard and what is played on guitar, but what the heck! It's not a problem for me because I love the sounds for what they are: richly layered, spectral and energetic. Bill Evans' saxophone playing is utterly organic. This is not a record dominated by saxophone, for the whole package is coherent to such an extent that it is the music that matters more than any individual contribution. For once, McLaughlin is not left, right and centre of the disc. Its electronics ooze with hue, especially in the impressionistic passages. The music is new, extremely dynamic in places, utterly beautiful in others. Even if John was trying to follow Miles's lead, what was wrong with that? McLaughlin has never tried to hide his complete admiration for everything that Miles Davis stood for, and at this point in Miles's career, Miles too was as commercially focussed as at any point since he began to play.

Mahavishnu is different from any of John's previous albums, and that is a very positive feature of most of his work. Whenever you pick up a McLaughlin album, you're never sure what you will hear on it. In this case, the music is also very accessible – something that exclusivists always hate. Like Zawinul, John's music was dispensing with much of the traditional jazz form. He was also laying back from the very complex time signatures he had used before, but he was making up for that with new tonal colours and textures. The music may not have been absolutely cutting edge, but it was setting the standard for many other accessible and enjoyable jazz-fusion albums for the rest of the 1980s. Hellborg is superb – always there, rarely obvious. Forman too is solid and essential to the whole package, but Billy Cobham is at his very best on *Mahavishnu* and the album is a joy on that basis alone. Sadly, Billy was missing from the next album and should not have been. Somewhere along the line, there was a crossing of wires. As Billy readied himself for the band's 1984 tour to promote the new record, there was confusion about how he was going to ship his equipment. Before he was able to resolve the issue, he discovered that the tour was going ahead without him. Danny Gottlieb, who had been playing in Pat Metheny's band and was already loosely attached to McLaughlin, was formally hired for the drum seat, but was always second best. Billy was very angry and there was a rift between the two musicians for years afterwards.

So, was it wise to reinvent the Mahavishnu Orchestra? Probably not. Nicholson, for example, polite compared to some commentators, described the band as "surprisingly lackluster." [56] To change the personnel and the musical style was always going to alienate some, but John had tried forming bands with other names and still not achieved commercial success. What else could he do? To my mind, Colin's Donkey would have been a far better name. However, for the time being at least, McLaughlin carried on, full steam ahead.

John McLaughlin and Mahavishnu: *Adventures in Radioland* – 1986 (****)

The drive to boost sales continued with Mahavishnu's next album, *Adventures in Radioland* (1986), a pointed title that told DJs to play this music "if you dare". Snappy titles were now the name of the game, and the music leaned in the same direction. Yet again, however, the album was different from its predecessor. John was not using the Synclavier as much, returning to his more singular electric beast, the Gibson Les Paul Special. There was also another big change on drums. Not only was the mighty Bill absent, but his successor, Dan Gottlieb, had mischievously adopted a set of electronic drums, another feature of 1980s jazz-fusion that seems to spontaneously ignite the fires of critical tongues. Simmons? How dare he!

The opening song was *The Wait*, written by Jim Beard who must have been hovering in the wings at this point. Mitch Forman was about to leave the band because he had already promised to do a tour with Wayne Shorter. Forman plays on this album, but was replaced by Beard for the tour that followed. At first, the music is true to its title and the electronic drums intermittently punctuate the pensive mood from the sax and keys, making it feel like something big is about to happen at any moment. John takes over in a similar vein, idling pensively. At 1.45, the rhythm properly starts. We're still waiting but not for long as the piece really kicks off at 2.04. Forman is loud and John winds it up to compensate, sounding like only Rocker John can as he flails his Gibson appropriately. At 3.22 he lies back a little and lets Bill in at 3.42. Evans proceeds to perform some good tenor sax licks in a short solo that leads at 4.36 back to the pensive intro. Whatever we were waiting for was well worth it.

The splitting of *Just Ideas* from the next track *Jozy* is an interesting example of how John may have avoided committing the same mistake that he did with Jean-Luc Ponty's *Pegasus* on *Visions of the Emerald Beyond* (1975). This time, Forman's music is credited to him but acts as an introduction to John's *Jozy*. It's beautiful music that can be enjoyed simply for its own sake. Bill plays the plaintiff melody on soprano sax with John on Synclavier in mellow unison. It's just lovely.

Jozy follows straight on, a piece dedicated to Joe Zawinul that encapsulates a lot of what Joe was about. Jonas and Dan use a neat sustained monochord keyboard backing to establish a super cool vibe. Bill and John continue the sharp-edged tune in unison and the ensemble work is well honed with keys and drums making occasional, precisely timed interventions. At 2.20, John takes on a solo with the sound of Joe's keyboard mimicked on guitar synth. Later, with *Thieves and Poets* (2003) John would say that he 'steals' from the sounds of those who influence him. He is surely doing this at this point with both Joe's sound and his style of composition, which is mostly linear with hints of verses and choruses. It's not quite the continuous drone that Joe liked to use frequently, but the echoes of Zawinul are strong and the music is cool and mean.

At last, titles were beginning to take on an importance of their own. *Half Man – Half Cookie* may mean nothing at all, but it's fun! Written by Bill Evans, this is a strongly electronic tune with Bill playing sharp percussive keyboards, as he often did for Miles. His raw, robotic sound is complemented by Dan's silicon kit and a similarly artificial bass line. John is the only player seemingly normal as he plays a melody on his Gibson. By the third minute, the piece has collapsed into a brilliantly chaotic mayhem with many overdubs of sax, guitar and synthesiser breaking out like convicts from a kindergarten. The piece finally ends in some sort of order, the way it began. This piece is an indicator of the kind of music that Bill Evans was deeply into at this point on his brilliant album, *The Alternative Man* (1985).

Florianapolis is a piece jointly composed by John and Mitch. After a catchy melodic theme for the first 33 seconds, it's a jolly jumble of changes that would keep any musician on his toes as John unpredictably leaps about on his acoustic keyboard like a musical flea on heat. This forms a complex main theme that you really do pick up after a few times through. At 1.25 Bill is on board and humming on soprano to a grand Latin buzz. At 1.55, the song repeats its themes, and from 2.07 you can just take delight in the beautiful way the band plays this ensemble material, slick and very professional at every turn. Next John brilliantly takes on an extended solo that is one of his career trademarks and the level of technical achievement should never be understated. The themes return at four minutes before the piece ends with a great 'trombone' solo, either from John on Synclavier or Mitch on keys – who knows? I don't really care. This music is lively, uplifting and great fun to listen to. By the 1990s there were many other bands - Spyrogyra was one - playing in this style and making a great success of it, but its embedding into the style that became 'smooth jazz' was the kiss of death with the jazz puritans and John got flak for this too.

Gotta Dance is a fascinating experiment in electronic construction that benefits from careful listening at high volume. A lot goes on inside its four-minute length. A burbling undercurrent of electronics introduces John's clean acoustic melody at 0.45. This turns into a catchy soprano sax melody played in unison with guitar at 1.07. The music seems to have locked into its relaxed groove, but then at 1.42, an ungainly male with an urge to dance beats his way into the room and thrashes around with arms and legs flailing. Now that's not dancing. There's a snatch of a swing band on the radio just before the idiot's uncontrolled fist knocks the radio off its stand. At 2.51, calm returns and just what led to the intrusion is uncertain, but it's a fascinating piece of music.

The Wall Will Fall begins with a heavy rock theme, surprisingly set in 6/8 metre like a tiger in a tutu. Here, fusion means exactly what it says. This menacing masculine theme is grafted onto a furiously fast piece of jazz-fusion. These two themes alternate throughout until, like a truck striking a Ferrari, the car is completely overwhelmed by the sheer mass and power of the leviathan. The early rock theme seems harmless enough and the unmatchable pace of the jazz indicates a no-contest situation. There are no weird metres here, just good old-fashioned jazz-fusion. When the truck catches up again at 1.57, it's with a more threatening intent and John's guitar synth sounds really mean. Bill's saxophone is just too fast for it at 2.57 and speeds away into the distance. At times, even his nimble fingers are stretched to maintain the pace set by the rhythm section. Trouble is: traffic lights. Up trundles the truck at 4.15 and keeps right on. Now that's no contest!

Appropriately, the track *Reincarnation* is one of several that find another life in the as yet undetermined future. The music here is intended to be a beautiful evocation of a wonderful religious belief. It is played, more or less, as a duet between Hellborg's bass and John's synthesiser, with atmospheric additions from Danny and Mitch, and finds its own level of success. Like a shot of heroin, once you have listened to the extended version of this on *Qué Allegría* (1992), there's no going back. Disappointingly, Hellborg has been one of the least noticeable players up to now, but this makes up for it.

Mitch Match is a fine contribution from Forman that, like *The Wall*, grafts two rhythmic forms into an exciting and enjoyable piece. The first is a fast melodic theme based around the backbeat but strongly disguised and embellished by Dan Gottlieb's clever drumming. At 0.42 there's a nice chorus that acts as a focus – something we've almost grown used to living without in McLaughlin music. Then the music quickly moves forward with another unique guitar synth sound from McLaughlin that is a cross between a whistle and Chaurasia's flute. Mitch's keyboards push along from behind John's solo until at 1.47 it transforms into a more conventional swing rhythm. This continues until 3.14 when the original theme returns. Finally, the very effective chorus finds an extra use as a neat, crisp way to end what was a rewarding listen.

John returns to acoustic guitar for *20th Century Ltd* and, in a display of virtuosity unparalleled on any other of his records, he lets rip with music that I can only describe as sheets of chords. The backing of keyboard spikes acts as rather irrelevant punctuation marks on this remarkable outburst. This piece serves simply as a reminder of just what a great guitarist he is, even having just made a record that is dominated by electronic gadgetry and - some would say -

gimmicks.

Adventures in Radioland is similarly constructed to *Mahavishnu*. It is a great album for listening to for pleasure and well represents the status of jazz-fusion in the mid-1980s. Like its 1984 predecessor, this is a very good jazz-fusion record and discs like these are the very reason I wanted to write this book. Most listeners who like jazz-fusion will enjoy playing these two records, although I would discourage you from using them simply as background music. Anyone can hear how the feel of the music in the mid-1980s is different from what it was when the whole scene began at the end of the 1960s. Being very much a combination of jazz and rock with technology as a fundamental building block, the musicians' main medium was crude at first. Synthesisers were still experimental (and very temperamental) beasts in the early 1970s. We should never underestimate just how difficult it was to make mature sounds from these very complicated and user-hostile devices. They required endless patience and a great deal of skill and knowledge from potential users – hence the reason why album sleeves listed names of people credited with "programming". Specialists who knew how to get the best from these devices were very valuable. John was one of the few musicians who took the trouble to do it himself; Herbie Hancock and Joe Zawinul were two others.

We had to wait until the 1980s for the technology to deliver other silicon children, including drum machines, sequencers and the microcomputers that encapsulated and controlled the entire process of making good electronic music. Records such as these were refining some techniques, yet still exploring others. As McLaughlin demonstrates here, there were plenty of new, unexplored sounds. Finally, let's not forget the embryonic compact disc that was in gestation as these records were being conceived. This entire musical and technological environment was as exciting at this point as it had ever been and from the listener's viewpoint, much of the jazz-fusion of the 1980s (and early 90s) was then (and is still) very good.

But Stump drips in vitriol. This "toe-curling" record was his "weakest album" and, despite being lost for words, he managed to find enough to be able to describe it as a "parlous mess... the most catastrophic failure of John McLaughlin's career." The "horrid" Simmons drums represented the "musical bankruptcy of the decade." [57] Like Herbie Hancock, McLaughlin had met his musical Waterloo by just doing what great musicians do – trying something different. The crime – if that was one – was to try to earn a living from it.

John McLaughlin: *The Mediterranean Concerto for Guitar and Orchestra* – 1990 (****)

The latter part of the post-Radioland 1980s was a low spot in McLaughlin's career; there was an untypical four-year gap in his discography. At a time when he should have been in top gear, cruising the musical highways to endless applause, it seemed that his scatter-gun approach to his career had backfired on him. His many directions had turned into no direction. No proper band, no recording company for soothing corporate personality cultivation, no significant fan-base. His self-imposed exile to France did not help, as all other musicians who tried it found. To exist at the pinnacle of the music business it was necessary to live in New York, LA, or possibly London. John was prepared to travel and did so in a variety of musical combinations, but all of which changed personnel too quickly and did not sit tightly focussed like witch-hazel on a lay-line. He filled in his time in many different ways, such as making occasional cameo appearances on albums by his ex-sidemen, a kind of throw-back to those now distant days touring the recording studios in London before his career took off. He even took a role as a guitarist in the movie *Round Midnight* (1987). His relationship with the record-buying public was not helped by his style of playing that always sounded like a flamenco guitarist trapped in a sonic time warp. His playing was brilliant, of course, but when every solo sounds, to untrained ears, like another piece of flamenco, well, you can only digest so much energy and ethnicity before it's time to move on to something more relaxing. Then, as with a number of other jazzers who had the necessary skills, like Chick Corea and Joe Zawinul, John found himself having a 'classical period'.

It all began back in 1981, after a concert at the Hollywood Bowl. John was having dinner with Ernest Fleischmann, Executive Director of the Los Angeles Philharmonic Orchestra. Fleischmann asked John if he would return to the bowl to play the *Concierto de Aranjuez* by Rodrigo, probably the best known piece of serious classical music for guitar. John agreed with the tongue-in-cheek condition that he could also play a *Concerto* of his own. To John's surprise, Fleischmann was delighted to make him the offer. So it was some three years later when, on Thanksgiving Day, 1984, John played the premier performance of his *Concerto for Guitar and Orchestra – The Mediterranean*. Miles Davis came to the gig with Burt Bacharach.

One of John's earliest recollections was from the age of about six, hearing the choir at the end of Beethoven's *Ninth Symphony* and being affected by it. There was plenty of classical music in his family context and it consequently became a part of his musical sub-conscious. He had been given the opportunity of flirting with classical music for his album *Apocalypse* (1974) and had enjoyed it very much, even if it had proved to be an ambiguous event in his career. Then, in the late 1970s he had come across the two Labèque sisters and had fallen in love with Katia who was deeply immersed in classical music.

McLaughlin's guitar *Concerto* is a very 'normal' piece of classical composition, complete with some admirable cadenza sections at the end of his movements. Of course, as a jazzer, it is always hard to entirely ignore his rhythmic roots and in places he adds some brief sections of music with the more obvious beat of the twentieth century. I believe it makes a very valid addition to the limited repertoire of music for classical guitar and orchestra. The music is delightful, full of the French and Spanish Mediterranean colours we would expect. The first movement is varied and accomplished, although my disc seems to lose the guitar amongst the orchestra during some of the louder sections, which are very stirring. The second movement is a fifteen-minute examination of the sadder, reflective nature of life and is as beautiful as anything McLaughlin has written. It does have a more energetic section towards the end. The final movement is intended to be animated and, although I thought the melodies were rather more mediocre here, the music is never dull and ends on a very high point that leaves the listener feeling that the previous thirty-five minutes were well spent. This major work proves what an exceptionally versatile musician he is and I feel confident it will excite and satisfy any lover of classical music.

It's true that he was significantly assisted by the very good orchestration of Michael Gibbs, and the renewal of his relationship with LSO conductor Michael Tilson Thomas was another good decision. It was another four years after the premier that the recording was made, in England in the summer of 1988, and the disc was finally released in 1990, along with a collection of *Duos for guitar and piano*, recorded around the same time with Katia. John said that his inspiration for the *Concerto* was, of course, only natural given that his home in Monaco looked out over the Mediterranean. [58] We cannot fail to notice the selection of music for the pieces with Katia: *Brise de Coeur* taken from *Music Spoken Here* (1982), *Two Sisters*, which first appeared on *A Handful of Beauty* (1976). The piece entitled *Zakir* is a beautiful ballad that is used here for the first time, but also appears on *Remember Shakti* (1998).

John McLaughlin Trio: *Live at the Royal Festival Hall* – 1990 (****)

In 1988, John McLaughlin formed a new trio with Indian percussionist, Trilok Gurtu and Berklee graduate Jeff Berlin on electric bass. After a year of touring, with only modest success, the John McLaughlin Trio replaced Berlin with a young bass player, again from Berklee Music College, Kai Eckhardt. Perhaps it was the fact that the momentum had been building, or perhaps it was a sudden gelling of musical personae, but a transformation in the band's fortunes was soon noticeable. By the autumn of 1989 McLaughlin was back on track with a superb new jazz group playing top-notch electro-acoustic jazz. On 27 November 1989, John played a gig at the Royal Festival Hall on London's South Bank of the Thames and the show was beautifully recorded for us to enjoy. The John McLaughlin Trio played a set of mostly acoustic music, with the assistance of some sophisticated electronics called a Photon MIDI interface manufactured by the company Phi Tech, a box of tricks fed by two transducers made for him by Larry Fishman. The first was a classical guitar transducer feeding a mini pre-amp in the base of the guitar. Then a bridge transducer was fed tiny microprocessors by the pre-amp. The signal thus produced went to the Photon guitar synth and was switched on and off by means of a foot switch. In this way, John was able to play only his acoustic guitar, made especially for him by master craftsman Abraham Wechter, but was able to create more than just the sound of the plain acoustic. Unlike a standard electric guitar, each of his six strings produced a signal that could be manipulated. Now, only the flick of a footswitch away was access to an array of powerful new sounds, such as the ability to play chords and listen to them reverberate into infinity whilst he played on.

All this is evident on the trio's recording, which is so superbly balanced that you can hear everything the musicians play. The record is much edited and the sequence is different from the one that night, which is a great pity. The album begins with Miles Davis's *Blue in Green* from his greatest album, *Kind of Blue*. It's a beautiful opener that swings in and out of mainstream, classical, Spanish and folk guitar styles with ease, yet still gives scope for some lovely solos. No electronics here.

For once, it's nice to hear some spoken intros between the pieces, but John forgets to say that Mitch Forman's lovely tune *Just Ideas* precedes his own cool song *Jozy* for Joe Z. Both were tracks from *Adventures in Radioland* (1986), the former written as an introduction to the latter. The transition takes place at 1.50 as Trilok plays some effects reminiscent of Joe's Austrian winter in wartime. The cool, slow, funky rhythm soon gives the game away and this piece is played with panache with the help of some interesting electronics to make the atmospherics even more interesting. At 2.47 John plays one of his meanest chords and then kicks his foot switch so that the chord is held in suspended animation whilst he continues to play over the top. This is just the start of his superb use of the Photon circuitry to enhance his sound to a new level.

Another track from the *Radioland* album is *Florianapolis*, now in an extended form that gives much scope for some creative musical displays during a glorious fourteen and a half minutes. At first it's simple acoustic trio music, with John loosely playing his theme with great vigour. Eckhardt's accompaniment is chordal at first, but takes the theme too from time to time and is far more than just electric bass playing. As he did in *Blue in Green* John likes to drop the established rhythm from time to time, to allow the three of them to improvise more freely. At 6.32, Eckhardt takes a short bass solo and than at 7.12 John takes back the lead, now with some superb sounds that dodge the interface between electronic and acoustic sound. It's pretty much a free improvisation at this point and hard to imagine that it's all just one man playing. The wonderful sounds continue for over five minutes with each musician tossing in ideas that seem as if everything is pre-planned. No, it's just that they know each other so well by now they are in complete sympathy with each other's musical directions. By 12.45, they pull each other back towards the theme and at 13.12 there's a last bass flourish that might lead them in an entirely new direction. Instead, it's used as a coda through which Trilok takes the lead and the piece ends in triumph at 14.50.

Gurtu wrote *Pasha's Love*, a very complex piece that combines many elements and styles played both fast and energetically, as well as slowly and passionately, with many changes of tempo along the way. *Mother Tongues* begins with echoes of the many languages of music. The sounds envelop listeners and surely evoke a mass of different emotions depending upon each listener's background. At 2.17 a deep-seated electric blues swing kicks in as the digitised guitar is invited into action. At 4.42 John returns to solo acoustic and the music develops into a very percussive folk music type of rhythm as Trilok now adds some electronic percussion sounds. Eckhardt's bass takes the lead and soon moves the piece into new areas of extreme funk. At seven minutes it sounds like the piece is over and the audience spontaneously applauds, but it's just another transition that allows the ingenious Gurtu to embark on an extended improvisation to a pair of guitar chords, constantly repeated, probably with the aid of the guitar synth. The solo ends at 16.20 whereupon the trio's brief reprise of the theme leads into a lively coda and a gentle finale to the concert at 18.37.

As an encore, the trio plays *Blues for L.W.* a song written in support of Lech Walesa who, as I said above, was part of a protracted struggle against communism in Poland. Far from being the simple blues format we might expect, this one is much more densely written. The first three and a half minutes are constructed once again from the timeless trio playing the three men have specialised in. Then it breaks loose for a lively section of swing before moving into some scat-sung vocal percussion, starting with Trilok and ending with all three chipping in. "He's the one!" they declare. However, I suspect that at least two of the three men were referring to JM, not LW. It's a nice piece of humour at the end of what must have been a stunning gig.

The album is based on the lush sound of a Spanish acoustic guitar with gentle and occasional imposition of electronic overlays that enhance the aural experience without dominating it. The acoustic sound is the one that best fits John's fiercely Spanish style of attack and is beautifully balanced by Eckhardt's electronic bass sound, so different from the acoustic string bass that would normally have been used in such a combination. Gurtu adds so much more than just drums, with his wide range of percussive effects and is surely as much of a star of percussion in the 1990s that Nana Vasconcelos was in the previous decade. Yet Gurtu was a drummer too, and an amazing one at that, which was obvious to anyone attending the gigs. Some even went as far as to proclaim him the best drummer in the world and he began to win poll after poll in *Downbeat*, an accolade that is hard to surpass.

This recording is the only disc we have to represent years of such marvellous gigs by the Trio in this style, largely because there was not a record company at the time with sufficient faith in McLaughlin to sponsor it. Subsequently John picked up a recording contract under the Verve umbrella and this music now has that company's imprint. Perhaps one day the entire recording of this gig will appear? I wish…

John McLaughlin Trio: *Qué Allegría* – 1992 (***)

In the autumn of 1990, Kai Eckhardt followed Jeff Berlin into the sunset and was replaced by Dominique Di Piazza, the third player in succession to show just how big an influence Jaco Pastorius had been to young bassists in the 1980s. The fact that there were now so many players performing at such a high level and in a way that had not been seen on bass until Jaco, was testament to the man's influence. Bass was no longer the "plunk, plunk" beat provider in the background but a concert-level solo instrument in its own right with virtuosi musicians to devote their lives to playing it.

Trilok Gurtu continued to devote himself loyally to John's music and the Trio performed regularly to very favourable reviews. John's music too continued at the same very high level, predominantly acoustic and to exceptionally high sound quality thanks to Wechter's guitars, but also with the often seamless invocation of the digital synthesiser that gave him the extra width and tonal range.

Belo Horizonte opens the album, a piece that was now over ten years old, but had now been rejuvenated with John's enthusiasm for the new Trio. Anyone familiar with the original version will be surprised at the leisurely pace adopted by this version at first, but soon you realise that its difference is its strength. Although the original theme is, of course, outlined at the start and finish, this version is very much used as a vehicle for improvisations by the Trio, John,

Trilok and not least the superb Di Piazza who shines brightly on bass as an excellent replacement for Eckhardt. The gentle start is more than compensated for by the final energetic flourish that leads to an exciting climax, and the piece is capped perfectly by the most beautifully resonant final chord from John. This piece is a triumph.

Baba is a composition by Trilok Gurtu. It begins with a completely different atmosphere, reflective and sober, opened by a thoughtful introduction from John with the help of some gentle electronics. At 1.05 a plodding Jaco-ish bass line leads over some hand drums and John plays an electronic theme until 2.25 when he starts up a superb walking blues tune with Trilok now drumming normally. After some of the deep complexity of John's music, it's a real treat to listen to an uncomplicated but entirely fresh blues like this.

Reincarnation has Kai Eckhardt briefly back in the bass seat and with John continuing his quest to legitimise the music of *Adventures in Radioland* that had received such a critical mauling back in 1986. It's an Indian-style blues for the first four minutes, as if John is painting a picture of both an Indian and an American, trapped in their mortality. Then, at 4.23, the full impact of the Hindu philosophy becomes clear as the music becomes swathed in tones of the utmost beauty. It really tries to capture the unquantifiable qualities of something mere westerners and many other mortals besides can have little idea about. If this is what lies ahead for me, I can sleep easy for the rest of my life. The final chord is a spoiler, a disappointment that casts that inevitable seed of doubt. Even if John is wrong about reincarnation, this is still utterly superb music.

It's back to life on Earth with *1 Nite Stand*. Eckhardt is present again as the piece sets out its stall. It's a brilliant distillation of the music of 50s and 60s middle America, with echoes of rock 'n' roll and blue jeans and high school proms. John's electronic guitar sound is the essence of Chuck Berry without ever being him. And played alongside the sophisticated bass and drums of his very non-American friends, especially during a great slap-bass solo from Jonas, it remains very much a jazz piece. John has been criticised for not swinging as much as other jazzers, but this piece really rocks!

Marie is a two-minute solo musical cameo from Dominique that allows him to present himself to the public as a bass player of some importance. His skill is surely excellent. The music is followed by *Hijacked*, a slightly impenetrable piece that ought to keep up the wonderful momentum of this album, but doesn't. The album starts to slide downhill from here, like a warm juggernaut parked on a hill with the brakes improperly engaged.

Mila Repa begins with an improvisation by Trilok that introduces a very slow contemplative guitar melody that is memorable, if uninspiring. Then a beautiful middle section takes the piece to an entirely new level and a feeling of anticipation of something special doesn't materialise. The early theme returns and the piece fades slowly out like a sunset on a cloudy day.

The title track is a disappointment compared to some of the music that has preceded it. Inserted here is the same scat-sung percussion interlude that appeared on *Blues for L. W.* Stump [59] points out that this idea was based on a tradition in Indian music called Khayal, which he interprets as meaning 'nonsense syllables'. Most of us, of course, are not aware of that. As a novelty at a gig, it's fine, but it does feel a bit tasteless as a centrepiece of the title track on a quality jazz album.

By now, it seems that the album is destined not to maintain the very high quality of the first half and this is confirmed by the final track, *3 Willows*, which is one of the least memorable tacks in the McLaughlin portfolio. I am suddenly aware that I have not heard any ensemble bass playing since *Hijacked* and wonder if I have missed something? My expectation that *Qué Allegría* would be the studio half of a superb pigeon pair is unfulfilled: the live album is by far the better of the two.

After a series of gigs to promote the album, the members of the Trio went their own separate ways. Trilok had been with John for over four years and the two men would partner each other again in the future, but now Trilok had his own projects to explore. John, too, had plenty more up his sleeve.

John McLaughlin: *Time Remembered* – 1993 (**)

In the sleeve notes to his album *Time Remembered* [60] McLaughlin says that he had been a fan of Bill Evans since he was a teenager and had first heard him play on Miles Davis's albums of the late 1950s. He says how he had always wanted to record an album such as this and describes how he conceived the music as being played entirely on guitars. He identified the Aighetta guitar quartet to provide his support. Clearly much work was involved in creating the charts for non-improvising musicians and John was fortunate enough to be able to delegate the work to his student Yan Maresz who would also play acoustic bass guitar. The result is a collection of undeniably beautiful but uniform, plodding, bland songs. As so often happens with McLaughlin, the music never swings and you might never guess that Evans was a great jazz musician. The music is perfectly performed, but so homogeneous in texture and tone that you would never know there are six guitars in action, let alone be able to identify the soloist, except for his typical, but this time occasional, fiery dashes.

Beautiful as it is, this is not a jazz record and jazz fans will be disappointed. McLaughlin fans will be disappointed because he has been blended almost into obscurity. Even fans of the guitar will be disappointed because it is so difficult to pick out the playing of any particular guitar. Unassisted by the arrangements, the songs float about in the breeze, overwhelmingly peaceful, but never pinned down enough to grasp the melodies. Overall, this is music to die to. The occasions when the group sounds like harpists, as in the best track, *My Bells*, are perfect for passing on to the fully stocked guitar shop in the sky. I'll ask my wife to take note of that for my funeral.

The Free Spirits: *Tokyo Live* – 1994 (***)

In 1993, McLaughlin formed a new band called The Free Spirits, again playing electric guitar with Dennis Chambers on drums and Joey DeFrancesco on Hammond organ. Chambers (b1960) was brought up in the informal school of music and was apparently gigging in nightclubs around his hometown of Baltimore at the age of six! [61] His first major gig, however, was with the Parliament/Funkadelic band in 1978. Chambers became well-known for his amazing technique, as well as his musicianship and, though his physical stature reminds some people of Mr T from the TV Series *The A Team*, his playing can be both extremely powerful and supremely sensitive. Dennis's career has been focussed most strongly in the jazz-fusion arena and has included gigs with musicians such as Bill Evans, Mike Stern and John Scofield, as well as Steely Dan and Carlos Santana.

Like Chambers, Joey DeFrancesco (b1971) has played keyboards since a very early age. Born into a strongly musical family, his father and grandfather were both B3 organists, so it was no surprise that Joey chose to continue the family tradition, gigging with his father from the age of six and solo from the age of ten. At seventeen he recorded on *Amandla* (1988) with Miles Davis, and it was inevitable that his great ability would be noticed by B3-lover McLaughlin. DeFrancesco was voted top B3 organist in the 2003 *Downbeat* Critics Poll.

It's clear that this was a fun project for John. Weird metres and complex constructions are mostly missing on the album *Tokyo Live*, captured at the Blue Note Tokyo Jazz Club in mid-December 1993. The band is well named and this trio runs through a set of John's numbers (the only exception being Miles's *No Blues*) as if they are entertaining kids at a holiday camp. The opener is John's *1 Nite Stand*, one of the great tracks from *Qué Allegría* (1992) and it's just as much fun here. DeFrancesco's organ is a real highlight as the piece as the band flies through this great blues. *Hi-jacked* is taken from the same album and wasn't impressive then, but it's presented here in a more accessible format with the strange head followed by a straightforward, animated jazz improvisation.

The third track is *When Love is Far Away*, a ballad with Chambers sitting out and DeFrancesco playing the delicate melody on trumpet with great sensitivity. Next comes *Little Miss Valley*, a blues based on a 16-bar cycle that continues the theme of having a great time, rather than playing difficult pieces that require a lot of concentration. In contrast, *Juju at the Crossroads* begins with a sprightly melody that announces itself as a very tricky little number that will keep everyone on his toes. However, the three men hold together with precision throughout the harmonic obstacle course. Once that's out of the way, it's a hell-for-leather dash through the solos, first with John, and then with Joey, whose nimble finger-work is truly amazing. Far from a steeplechase, this is athletics suitably for an Olympic sprint final. *Vuhovar* (sic) was clearly written in sympathy for the poor people of the Croatian town of Vukovar who in November 1991 suffered a massacre of their loved ones during the Balkan troubles. After an introduction that is suitably respectful, the rest of the piece lightens somewhat and does its best to entertain, whilst never losing track of the serious event that inspired it. Miles's tune *No Blues* is no surprise amongst all the other McLaughlin compositions and the altered twelve-bar blues is easily knocked off in masterful fashion by these fine musicians.

An English movie critic, Mark Kermode is well known for his style of broadcasting in which he occasionally gets off on a rant and finds himself speaking so fast he doesn't finish a sentence before moving on to the next. When viewers and listeners complain, his response is, "Well just keep up!" I think this is a good example of his brain working faster than he can physically speak. John McLaughlin's mind clearly works in a similarly fast way – possibly faster than he can physically play. The last track, *Mattinale*, is based around a speed – in 4/4 common time - of approximately 380 beats per minute. He plays quite a lot of the piece at 760 beats per minute – which is more than 12 notes per second! The introduction to the piece is a slow, contemplative, very ethereal melody, which most players would be content to develop at the intrinsically slow pace established from the start. Again, McLaughlin's style is to constantly introduce rapid phrases that are so fast that, on this occasion at least, he actually does not succeed in delineating the notes properly. His response to any criticism we might make would probably be the same as Kermode's, yet he has indeed received criticism for this style of playing, which derives from the Flamenco guitar tradition. There's a long tradition in jazz for playing at breakneck speed – what musicians call 'showing off their chops', and is a way of demonstrating a musician's prowess. McLaughlin's habit of playing fast in what sometimes feel like very inappropriate places is unusual and can be annoying. It is here.

Of course, the other players do indeed keep up. DeFrancesco's playing is stunningly pacey for a twenty-two-year-old, especially since his bass lines are a pretty good substitute for another human being stood alongside. Chambers is good, but his real abilities are never on display on this record, let alone on this track. Such music ought to be very impressive, but the melodic construction is of the kind that just washes over most heads. It's not modal, yet the changes are unpredictable and feel illogical. Consequently, when it is finished after 20 minutes, there's a feeling of excitement – even breathlessness at the breakneck speed – but no deep satisfaction. This album is pure jazz of the highest quality played by musicians who are amongst the best in the world. What better recommendation could there be? The recording illustrates superbly well what it must have been like to attend a club gig by a McLaughlin Trio. This record is not about attacking the frontiers of jazz - it's about securing them.

John McLaughlin: *After the Rain* – 1994 (***)

Any musician fortunate enough to have Elvin Jones agree to play in his band is obliged to pay homage to John Coltrane and McLaughlin was no exception in this album. Jones was Coltrane's drummer of choice for the last years of his life from 1960-66 and this experience enabled Jones to move the art of drumming forward another notch and become regarded as one of the greatest jazz drummers before the two men became estranged by Coltrane's crazy excesses. With Joey DeFrancesco completing the trio, here is a very good album that will satisfy most casual listeners. It was recorded on the Verve label, a subsidiary of Universal Music.

The nods to Coltrane abound. The title track *Take the Coltrane* is by Ellington with a little joke in the title referring to his own *Take the 'A' Train*, of course. One of the pieces for which Coltrane was most famous is the unlikely *My Favourite Things*, which he used as a vehicle for his work on soprano saxophone. No surprises here as the trio play it as straight as Coltrane's horn. *Sing Me Softly of the Blues* is a delicious composition by Paul (or Carla?) Bley that does what it says in the title. *Encuentros* is a delightful McLaughlin composition in 6/8. *Naima* is another well-known Coltrane composition played beautifully here. John's *Tones for Elvin Jones* gives a humorous nod to a Chick Corea title. Then follow two more Coltrane songs: *Crescent* and *After the Rain*. Sandwiched between the two is Santamaria's *Afro Blue*.

The only people likely to be disappointed by this album are those listeners used to McLaughlin's trailblazing guitar fireworks, of which there are none here. However, you will find a very pleasurable collection of fine quality, considered tuneful jazz. What's wrong with that?

John McLaughlin: *The Promise* – 1996 (****)

Artists who have a claim to any kind of career in music always produce an album of *Greatest Hits*, sometimes a most unseemly short time after the start of their career. These albums are characterised by cheap productions with no sleeve notes and no musicians named on the albums. Worse still, the *Greatest Hits* aren't. However, it is undeniable that such albums serve a useful purpose in extending the artist's career. With his album, *The Promise* (1996), John came up with an entirely new take on the *Greatest Hits* model. Here was an album of all new material with himself in all of his most recent musical environments. The result is a delightful eclectic patchwork of music stitched into an almost unbroken braid with threads of short spoken and musical cameos.

Track one is *Django*, a piece written by John Lewis, leader of the Modern Jazz Quartet. McLaughlin here uses the opportunity to play alongside rock guitar master, Jeff Beck, who is also a serious jazzer. The rhythm section is made up of Tony Hymas (keys) Pino Palladino (bass) and Mark Mondesir (drums). The song starts as a hymn of celebration to the great Belgian swing guitarist of the 30s and 40s, Django Rheinhardt. It's played as a waltz in a verse/chorus format with Jeff leading off. As a kind of nod to the rocker in their midst, the band plays the middle eight in rock fours, which might suggest that this was a McLaughlin arrangement – it was not. John takes the second solo, at which point it's interesting to compare the styles of the two men. The final pass has both contributing in parallel, although it's never played as a duel. The track is very good with a lot of variety, even if the three-to-four transition seems odd.

The second track is another homage, this time by John for bop-jazzer Thelonius Monk, although I can't remember Monk ever playing this fast and with this much swing. John's pals here are Joey deFrancesco and Dennis Chambers, who here gives the lie to anyone who thinks he is only about beef and funk. On *Thelonius Melodius*, Chambers is at his dazzlingly swingiest best on this track, delicately creative with every twist and turn. Joey's playing is the star-turn of the track with JM playing well, but second best to deFrancesco's brilliant Hammond B-3.

Track three is *Amy and Joseph*, a short piece of pseudo-orchestral music played as a beautiful rhapsody entirely by John using his acoustic guitar and a battery of electronic keyboard sounds. Yan Maresz deserves credit for arranging this gorgeous piece of music and I can't help wondering why McLaughlin didn't make more out of it. *No Return* could easily have been a track from a mid 1980s Miles Davis album, in fact it's a lot better than some tracks we would find there. Oddly, it's Joey deFrancesco who plays muted trumpet just like Miles – bum notes and all, whilst McLaughlin plays everything else. *El Ciego* is another recording of his trio with Al diMeola and Paco de Lucia, presumably recorded before they parted irritably. The track is substantial – over nine minutes long – and a good reminder of the heady days of Spanish acoustic concerts past. It is also too long, and seems to have little more to say after the halfway point. That's a shame because this aspect of John's career deserves more exposure to new ears.

It's noticeable that McLaughlin, as a creator of the jazz-fusion genre, has built some substantial edifices along the long path of his career. *Jazz Jungle* is one such milestone that indicates the current state of jazz-fusion in the mid-1990s. It is an earthquake of jazz-fusion. Not some carefully designed, crafted composition that requires nimble fingers but ranks little more than an inconvenient tremor: this is a full-blown scale ten cataclysm. The band of heavyweights is led by Dennis Chambers, a brilliant drummer with a physical stature to match his giant constitution. Jim Beard, James Genus and Don Alias make up the similarly expert rhythm section. Something of a stranger to the saxophone on record, John has here chosen tenor heavyweight Mike Brecker, and it certainly demands someone of his stamina to even begin to contemplate what McLaughlin had planned.

This music is almost fifteen minutes of hard-edged, macho jazz-fusion. Oddly, it sets the scene with a brief section of freeform jazz. You can almost feel the testosterone-fuelled musicians slavering to get started, a signal provided by the immediate and massive interjection of tectonic plate energy from Chambers. From that point on, there's no escape as the saxophone and guitar take turns to ride the shock wave of supercritical power. Along the way, listen out for two sections of utter geophysical chaos, the first from 9.40 when all semblance of the original landscape is crushed into dust. The second, even more devastating event comes at 13.25 when a Brecker crescendo signals the imminent arrival of the full-blown earthquake, which takes almost a minute to dissipate. There are few survivors.

The Wish has Trilok Gurtu and Zakir Hussain teamed up with Nishat Khan on Indian sitar. Once more, this is a superbly effective fusion of jazz with Indian music that is centred on a sweet memorable theme. As usual, it is atmospheric and calming, although there are some splendid moments of soaring musicianship. The final beautiful lingering chord is a blend of sounds that seems to contain a whole new world within it and leads straight into a short jam with John, Sting and his then drummer, the physically diminutive (but definitely no lightweight) Vinnie Colaiuta. It clearly is a jam, and the only comment I can make is that it's a pity they did not record something rather more serious. This is followed by half a minute in which John is creating a hip-hop vibe using his electronic toys. He calls it *Tokyo Decadence*.

Shin Jin Rui is a substantial piece of jazz-fusion, with the same band as for *Jazz Jungle* but played in total contrast to it. David Sanborn's alto sax substitutes for

Mike Brecker's tenor. After a languorous intro, there's a main theme with sax and guitar in unison, as they do a lot on this track. Jim Beard has a fine solo on electric piano, and after a reprise of the theme, Sanborn plays a solo that is quite restrained by his standards. There's a sonorous Don Alias percussion interlude, a mid-section of sax/guitar unison and then a similarly modest McLaughlin solo. The two main players take turns to lead the piece towards its faded end and we are left with a feeling of satisfaction, though perhaps a little surprise at the restraint they all showed.

Finally, John is joined by Philippe Loli and Yan Maresz for *The Peacocks*, a beautiful acoustic guitar trio of the kind found on *Time Remembered* (1993).

As a *Greatest Hits* album, this would have been a hit for any other musician. Once again, however, it seemed to pass the music world by. So let's get this straight. This disc contains over seventy minutes of music, the tracks of which are all different and span a wide range of styles. Inevitably there will be some that sound great and others that do not. As a résumé of what John McLaughlin is about, this CD is very good indeed and if you were going to check out McLaughlin the musician, this is a great place to start.

Paco de Lucia, Al Di Meola, John McLaughlin: *The Guitar Trio* – 1996 (**)

Recorded some thirteen years after *Passion Grace and Fire* (1983), the follow-up to the guitar super-trios of the early 1980s was a long time coming. True fans of the guitar will probably find this album fulfilling, but for those more interested in McLaughlin's career and, perhaps in finding another little pearl hidden amongst the diamonds are in for a disappointment with this revival disc.

La Estiba is written by Paco and inevitably Moorish, leading us to think that here is another collection of predictable - even dull – ethnic Spanish guitar studies. Well, almost – but not quite. *Beyond the Mirage* is the first sign that di Meola, at least, is intent on taking this tour bus off-road and down some new tracks. His warm, intimate sound is refreshing, even if the other two try to turn the bus around.

The start of *Midsummer Night* sounds like Al's bus has just left without us. This time it's John's party and the introductory noises indicate that everyone is having a good time. John's intricate theme is entirely characteristic of his style and this is a good, fun piece. *Manha de Carnaval* is a splendid, professional duet from John and Al, their perfectly matched nylon strings forming two inter-woven parts that result in an intimate rendition of this well-known standard. *Letter from India* is a most unexciting piece, written by John and played as a duet with Paco. Sadly, it does nothing to invoke the spirit of the title, largely because of Paco's inexperience in Indian music. In contrast, *Espiritu* is an interesting piece by di Meola who plays all the music himself. Playing as a duet, his solo is on his Hermanos Conde nylon strung Spanish guitar, whilst his accompaniment is on a steel stringed Ovation. *Le Monastere dans les Montagnes* is one of the few highlights on the album. Written by John, it is harmonically much more adventurous and keeps my attention well throughout. The music seems to be on the up by now, and the opening to *Azzura* is splendidly atmospheric with a crystalline clear blue water tone and a freer structure from Al's Ovation guitar. Unfortunately, at 2.22 the freer structure adopted by the introduction becomes formalised into a rambling series of episodic improvisations linked by a catchy melody, and an ending that is far removed from the dripping icicles of the start. The album ends with *Cardeosa*, a composition by de Lucia in which all three musicians canter through the countryside and, at length, disappear into the sunset like Patagonian rancheros.

This is a record about three individual musicians. They're not a band, although their playing is very homogeneous and McLaughlin, for a change, is notable for the back seat he occupies. If one musician succeeds in steering from the front it's di Meola, with his distinctive steel string sounds and his keenness to employ different harmonies. Stump records that a lot of sparkle had gone from the tripartite relationship by the time the three musicians completed their final tour together in 1996. [62] All I can say is that it is starting to show on this record. There's excellent performing, as we might expect, but no magic.

John McLaughlin: *Molom: A Legend of Mongolia* – 1996 (**)

In 1994 John wrote the music for a film made in France by Marie Jaoul de Poncheville called *Molom, A Legend of Mongolia*. Apart from a few tracks that are traditional folk songs sung by a choir and the *National Song* of Mongolia, all of the music was written and played by John, with percussion by Trilok Gurtu. The music is mostly what a listener might expect, a collection of musical cameos – often short - that can be cut and spliced where appropriate to accompany the imagery of the film, rather than specific, structured compositions. The sound is easy on the ears, delightful in parts, and rather more western than we might guess. One pleasant surprise is John's use of his melody for *Lotus Feet* as the *Boy's Theme*, track 3. Though the music may have worked very well for the film, its identity as stand-alone material to enjoy is somewhat diminished by the constantly churning melodies and colours that are ephemeral rather than substantive.

John McLaughlin: *The Heart of Things* – 1997 (****)

With *The Promise*, John seemed to be saying, "Here I am: This is what I've done. Where shall I go next?" Thankfully, his choice was back into jazz-fusion and the creation of two wonderful albums with a new band called The Heart of Things. The 1997 studio album was complemented with a live album and this pair of discs would set the standard for their time.

Perhaps having decided that he liked the sound of saxophone in his jazz-fusion repertoire, McLaughlin took the pot-roast that had come to the boil on *The Promise* and turned it into a full-scale banquet. He commissioned a completely new band to celebrate the occasion, although he retained the services of Dennis Chambers who now (along with Dave Weckl in Chick's Elektric Band) had moved the goalposts from the positions set out by Billy Cobham. McLaughlin had always had a close affiliation with drums. He liked percussion in his Indian settings, but on the whole was not so interested in percussion for his fusion music as long as he had a drummer that could satisfy him. That, of course, was easier said than done. John's fusion metres were the most complicated in the business with some 80-90% of the music not in the usual rock fours. Anyone with pretensions to holding the drum seat in John's band had to be entirely comfortable with the weirdest timings you could ever find. All that said, John did hire percussionist Victor Williams for his new band, whilst his saxophonist was Gary Thomas, a member of M-Base Collective from whose school Chambers had previously emerged. McLaughlin's chum Jim Beard was hired for keyboards and the young electric bassist Matthew Garrison, son of acoustic bassist Jimmy, completed the line-up, which became known as The Heart of Things. The 1997 music that appeared on the album of the same name was to become hard-core material for the inevitable long tour that went with it.

The first track on the album, *Acid Jazz*, is awesome. It begins with a synthesiser-led theme that gently swirls around our heads like the mist in a wood as the autumnal sun burns it away. As the last wisps of water vapour rise up through the golden boughs, the woods come alive with activity. Mac, Matt, Jim, Dennis and Victor create a harmonic splendour of sound, working together like the elements themselves in a fractal landscape of gorgeous music. Then at 1.30, there are some rich chords that resolve the scene perfectly, followed five seconds later by an entirely new beat, based in nine and sounding like an alternating five and a four. This is one of John's favoured odd metres and will occur again in other tracks. Chambers performs it as if he was born doing it. Though the beat is strong and urgent, there's a lazy backwash from the synth that adds a nice colour and then, over the top of everything, a short disjointed theme acts as a milestone throughout the journey of this extraordinary piece. As usual, it's played in unison by the guitar, synth and bass and repeated just to make sure you get it – no sign of Gary yet. But the relationship between this theme and the rhythm of the drums is quite superbly unrelated. Then at 2.25, a half speed pace is adopted and Gary Thomas comes in with a soprano saxophone solo that seems not to care about the band playing in syncopated sixes that dissolve into indefinable time for 24 beats and then return to sixes again. This format is repeated as Gary weaves a beautifully textured solo past all the obstacles. Perhaps my description sounds rather chaotic, yet this is some of the most sophisticated orchestrated music of the 1990s and it surely impressed everyone who heard it. When that's done, a new milestone is reached at 4.22 and it's a slightly more urgent six-beat that starts afresh from 4.45. A quizzical theme appears on saxophone and serves to introduce a new guitar/sax phrase at 5.40 that comes as a cry for help. After another milestone at 6.41, Chambers is now starting to burn at 6.52, his double-bass drums thumping furiously as McLaughlin begins one of his penetrating forays with just the drums to keep him in check. This time he keeps it short and at 7.50 there's a final reprise of the theme from which the short coda brings the piece to an end at 8.05.

With this track, McLaughlin is once again staking his claim at the head of the short queue of jazz-fusion bands. This piece is the brain to *Jazz Jungle's* brawn. Yes, it's a properly thought-out studio version, with all the sophistication that goes with it, but there will be looser, more inventive versions to come over the approaching months as the band take this on the road. You'll be able to hear what they made of it some eighteen months later on their *Live in Paris* album, detailed below.

John switches to acoustic guitar for the first part of track 2, *Seven Sisters*, another cleverly crafted piece of wonderful jazz-fusion music. Seven is clearly the theme of this music, for the early sections are in 7/4 metre. After a brief guitar intro the main theme is played in unison on keys and tenor sax with a timeless electric piano sound that perfectly fits the mood. The harmonies are rich and the chords flow seamlessly like waves lapping around the rocks along the seashore. It's a kind of verse and chorus structure. The chorus runs from 1.44 to 1.54 and is repeated to 2.04. Then an improvised section follows, still in 7s, John on electric guitar swapping leads with Gary. From three minutes, the music takes on a more serious air and a new section of tough written music, similar in style to Chick Corea's crafted compositions, starts at 3.22 with sevens temporarily abandoned in favour of fast metre-less rhythm. From 3.45 there's a period of calming, with Dennis using a series of cymbal strokes to bring the piece back to a calmer mood by 3.57. Jim Beard takes the lead now, through a section that includes a repeated two-note motif in the background that will appear again at the end. Jim solos over the changes of the early theme, and Dennis comes in front to string it up tight ready for a single run through the chorus at 5.18. The serious section returns. Then at 6.20 its time for an extended improvisation section, saxophone going first, now in 14s! Alternating with guitar at first, they are soon both in competition. By 8.30 Chambers has doubled his bass drum beat and the tension continues to build through to around 9.30 when the alternating two-note motif takes over for the final section, which fades out modestly at 10.17.

With a title like *Mr D.C.*, it's not hard to predict that the third track is focussed on the prowess of John's favoured drummer. Bearing in mind what he showed himself capable of on *Jazz Jungle*, we should be quaking in our boots in anticipation! For the first minute, he's like a steam engine with smoothly functioning pistons pumping comfortably under load. But unlike that symmetrical mechanical beast, this one's generating similar noises in another undetermined odd metre of John's. I think I'd have better success trying to guess the password to his e-mail than working out this metre. Effectively, it's timeless as John and Gary invent unmeasurable but clearly written phrases over the top of Dennis's pumping steel. From 1.04, Jim's synth leads the band in with a theme from 1.08 that's played twice and still focuses on Dennis's amazingly mysterious timekeeping. At 2.09 the piece takes up a rhythm of slow threes. Finally, this hair-raising piece settles down into a four beat rhythm from 2.37 onwards, first with a great bass solo from Garrison, then with John on guitar synth from 3.20. At 4.02 there's a short bridging section before Gary Thomas plays a duet on tenor sax with Dennis from 4.17 and John follows again from 4.50 with one of his fierce blasts of fractured quavers. Thomas switches to flute from 5.35 and duets with Jim. At 6.03 the music starts to wind down to an ending and a final flourish from Garrison at 6.28. At 6.37, there is a final reprise of the seriously complicated written first theme to conclude crisply on seven minutes.

Fallen Angels begins with a rapturous introduction containing lots of rich piano chords and luscious improvised saxophone lines. At two minutes a rhythm begins that sounds like slow swing but is actually a 9/4 (four plus five) metre. The mood becomes a complex shade of blue as the music cycles through a sequence of changes that are about as unfathomable as the existence of angels in disgrace. The main theme runs from 2.40 until 3.15 with a secondary theme from 3.21 to 3.48. Listen for the sound of angels crying from 4.00 to 4.28. Saxophone takes a solo from this point, then, at five minutes John's guitar synth briefly takes over from Thomas's smooth lines. The two men come together for a run through the both first and second themes from 5.38 to 6.33. After this, a period of contemplative improvisation leads through to the faded ending.

Healing Hands begins with a Victor Williams rhythm on percussion that indicates an African or Latin feel. When Dennis Chambers starts the drumming at 0.43, it becomes a rock-based 4/4 with a drone in A. Over this John plays a rather more synthetic sound on his midi-guitar than he generally uses. At 1.45, the main theme commences in F, and moves back to A via F#. My best description of this amazing melody is that it's like a caterpillar walking on tintacks, although that's a contradiction in scale. From 2.20 to 2.33 there's a brief drumming section from which point everything changes: the rhythm to 6/8, and the chords to a new sequence based in A as John solos with a bright synth sound. The fours return at four minutes and Gary Thomas takes over with a brilliant, cool solo focused on D that is on the edge of meeting the harmonic requirements of the changes. There's nothing very technical about what he does, but he makes every note count. A distilled version of the theme is back at 5.38 until 6.04 when the music turns a corner to a new key focus of C. The original theme in F returns from 6.53 to make a clean ending at 7.28.

The final track, *When Love is Far Away*, is a live McLaughlin acoustic solo and, beautiful as it is, it is entirely misplaced on this album of serious jazz-fusion. John's quality control was sadly amiss when he allowed this to be included on an otherwise fine album. Some of you may decide that I am being too critical on this point, but for me this album has a strong place in the history of jazz-fusion and this track detracts from that. Paul Stump criticises the album as a whole because McLaughlin is, he says, "side-lined" and "may as well be a guest". [63] Perhaps this is a fair comment from a fan of the guitar virtuoso who needs to be constantly reminded of the level at which John is capable of playing. In my view, the music is the winner on this album. There are no waxing stars on this album, except perhaps for Chambers, but it is a whole band performance that comes through, not a blaze of glory for any musician in particular. This album is all about the music – brilliant arrangements and written parts beautifully interspersed with short, solos. Chordal colour and harmony is at its richest on this album and some of the rhythms that underpin each track are as complex, yet subtle, as anything John has played elsewhere. All in all, the leader has succeeded superbly well in showing the world that there's plenty more that's new and exciting about jazz-fusion as a genre.

The Heart of Things: *Live in Paris* – 1998 (*****)

Towards the end of the tour, an exceptional live recording was made at *La Cigale* in Paris. The band was the same as for the studio recording except for the addition of Otmaro Ruiz instead of Jim Beard. Half of the titles were the same too, except that the pieces had evolved and were now receiving the live treatment.

All of the elements of the excellent piece *Seven Sisters* are present on this version at track one, but, as is usual, there's a significantly developed improvised section towards the end in which the tension is wound up gradually and then released equally gently for a beautifully calm clean ending.

Mother Tongues is a piece revived from John's time with the Trio and recorded on the album *Live at the Royal Festival Hall* (1990). It begins at once by deliberately trying to confuse us about the rhythm. John opens the piece with a riff that sounds like he's playing threes, but the drums injects confusion and for a while from 0.22 it sounds like it's in fours, but then from 0.30 Dennis seems to be playing fives, which is where it settles. It's a very clever ruse to make use of five being made up of two and three and by inserting pulses in different places we can be fooled into all sorts of beliefs. A nice theme appears along with a chorus from about 1.08. Garrison takes the first solo from 1.35. It's an utterly brilliant solo and demonstrates he too can play extremely fast lines, along with some chords from 2.30. Thomas takes over on tenor sax from 2.54 as Chambers and Co. turn it up a notch. The theme is back at 4.10. From 4.45 the whole thing evolves like a chrysalis into a bad caterpillar as the tempo is doubled up. First McLaughlin, then Ruiz takes turns to solo over the changes. From 6.40 the pace is breathless with Chambers' bass drumming taking on the characteristics of a pneumatic drill. This sharing vibe is continued over and over again, with each player's turn becoming ever shorter until 9.12 when both are vying for supremacy over the other. At 9.34 the signal is given for it to end and the pace immediately returns to the original. There's a brief interval of percussion at 10.08, which sounds as if an edit was made at this point; the five-beat theme reoccurs at 10.29. A gentle birdcall motif initiates the coda at 10.57 and there's a clean end at 12.44.

Fallen Angels begins with echoes of Weather Report's *A Remark You Made* in which the repeated pair of chords is used as a backwash over which to paint some colourful extemporisations. It takes nearly three and a half minutes to get to the main theme. However, once begun, the rest of the piece is played out much the same as in the studio version. As the music heads towards its conclusion, there's a gentle fade that lulls the listener almost into drowsiness, only to get a rude awakening at 9.45.

The longest track on this long album is *The Divide*. This is a very serious piece of music that is definitely not for the squeamish. Its title is an indicator that here is something that crosses boundaries. In fact, it treads a path deep into a new dimension of electronic music that few dare to tread, whilst retaining the usual elements of cutting edge jazz. The opening 1.17 is a section in which the band plays orchestrated music, John and Gary playing a written theme in unison that is as jagged as it gets, and roughly equivalent to looking into the mouth of a great white shark. Meanwhile, Otmaro plays a sequence of chromatic rising and falling chords that try to follow the steps of the lead instruments in a similarly angular fashion. At 1.17 the band becomes quiet in preparation for a long sax solo that begins at 1.25 sax. The chromatic chords continue beneath Thomas's carefully developed modal solo, whilst Dennis and Matthew maintain the precise rhythm that is in 4/4 throughout – at least something is easy about this piece!

The benefits of live gig recordings are clear here for the solo is much longer and more steadily developed than it would be in a studio recording. At 5.24 there's one short phrase culled from the first section that acts as the indicator for the band to enter the next phase. From here, the music takes on an entirely new dimension. It's a world in which new, previously unobserved silicon life forms come into existence. Whether they are allowed sustenance for growth or whether they are exterminated soon after birth is very much a lottery.

At 5.32 the band take up a drone focussed on C. John opens the door to the incubator, playing his midi guitar with an electronic sound that is a bit like a badly distorted guitar. Keys, bass and drums all work together behind him. At 7.10 there's a brief conversation with Otmaro's synthesiser, but the main thrust is to take the organism by the scruff of the neck and tighten the noose until it screams to be set free. By nine minutes the air is rapidly being expelled from this unwanted silicon organism. At 9.22 the signal to move on appears again and nine seconds later at 9.31 the ensemble play a part of the original written theme to regroup ready for the next experiment with artificial life, this time in Otmaro's hands.

At 10.12 a new creature is conceived and its assembly begins, the music once more a drone, but this time in A. It's a series of electronic squawks from John, Matthew and Otmaro that define the ingredients for the new creation. Dennis's rhythm restarts in fours once more at 10.45. At 11.20 the creature seems to be ready to leave its test tube and Otmaro gives it a close inspection. It seems to have some essential body parts in some odd places, but is certainly fully functional. At 12.05 the drums shift up a gear as Otmaro lets his creature loose in the lab. By 13.30 there seems to be nothing it can't do. The ensemble – without sax or guitar - is in full production and the clever creature is in danger of getting out of control. At 15.05 the creature is caged and the band winds down with a short bass feature. At 15.22 the synthesiser leads in with the chromatic chords and at 15.29 the sax and guitar reprise the original theme for the last time, the piece ending crisply at 16.25. Music like this takes a long time to approach. Its scope is immense. The harmonic structure of the written theme and Thomas's solo is modal, which is always difficult for most listeners. The two long improvised sections that follow at least have the commonality of a key focus. This leaves the listener free to follow the development of the improvisation. Finally, the electronic sounds are not to all tastes, but become more palatable with repetition. In summary, music like this leaves me in complete amazement! Just how high can high art get?

Tony is a composition clearly written to mark the death in 1997 of John's friend Tony Williams. An extended drum feature, it begins with a haunting refrain played solo on synthetic piano with some gentle percussion and a faint synthesiser accompaniment. A tenor saxophone entry just before the three-minute mark is rueful and builds to a crescendo at four minutes. Then, at 4.10, a drum roll creates a sense of expectation and at 4.32 Dennis begins to solo in 6/8 metre. It's a long section of magic that only drummers of his calibre can conjure up. The many rhythms he superimposes over the steady six beat is truly amazing, whilst constantly keeping the original starting rate of 145 beats per minute. If there was any doubt before, Chambers proves here that he is a major league drummer entirely qualified to be playing this homage to Tony Williams. The drum break continues until he ends it at 11.15 with the same drum roll he began it with. The whole band plays the piece out with the original soulful song that bids Tony a fond farewell from his friends.

Acid Jazz is the finale and it is played as you would expect at the end of a live gig when fireworks might be expected. As with *Seven Sisters*, the composed elements are present, but the introduction is different and there are some innovations in the intervening sections that make this a new piece. A greater degree of freedom is present than in the studio version, and there are more electronic effects added to the mix of improvisations. As the piece continues, the original themes are pushed farther into the background as other ideas developed over months of touring are worked on. At around seven minutes, there is a significant hallucinatory section as a lot of ideas swirl around in a haze of group improvisation. The theme reappears just once more at 9.28, used as a lead-in at 9.45 to a long section of seriously distorted improvised guitar that continues in 11/8 until 12.32. At this point the music breaks back to what could be four, five or six-beat rhythm in readiness for the final distorted melody of the theme. The ending is cataclysmic, and, like the bad guy who gets shot at the end of a movie, simply refuses to lie down and die.

It's hard to separate these two albums but the second one edges its elder sister into second place. At 78 minutes in length the value is excellent – all of it jazz-fusion to the very highest standard. The quality of the bandsmanship is very high indeed, with no single player dominating and each one impressing enormously. Some of the music is very hard listening, in particular, the modal piece *The Divide* is at the top of the scale of difficulty for most ears. Dennis Chambers' solo on *Tony* is stunning. Some listeners find such long solos boring, but this should be set against both the quality of the musicianship and the generous length of the album as a whole. The album sounds like a full set at a gig and there is no obvious editing, which is a real plus. Some listeners may be disappointed by the repetition of three tracks from the first album, but they are such good tracks and appear in a different guise so does that matter? It gets my rarely achieved five star award for being the best of its kind and one of those albums that simply keeps on getting better the more you listen to it.

Remember Shakti: *Remember Shakti* – 1998 (***)

The year 1997 was the fiftieth anniversary of the independence of the states of India and Pakistan from British rule. To celebrate, a British arts foundation sponsored McLaughlin to reform his Indian band Shakti and to play a short tour of the UK. The concerts were recorded and issued as a double CD. John was lucky enough to attract Zakir Hussain back into the band, but L. Shankar and his violin were no longer available. John invited the great bansuri flute player, Hari Prasad Chaurasia who had played as a guest on Mahavishnu's *When Blue Turns to Gold* (1984) to join him. On percussion, in place of Vikku Vinayakram, was his son, V. Selvaganesh, and so, to distinguish the band from the earlier version, John amended its name to Remember Shakti.

As a musical elder statesman of independent means, McLaughlin could at least do as he liked. World music was now established as a bona fide style of music and he no longer had a hungry record company at his back, demanding that he change course. The new band was able to record and tour in whatever way was most agreeable to its members and the three albums that were released over the next four or five years bear all the hallmarks of a group of musicians at ease with themselves and their music. As Jaques Denis pointed out, the albums seemed to come in threes, "like testimonials to what Shakti represented: Intelligence, Beauty and Power." [64]

The first track is *Chandrakauns*, an extended piece that lasts for 33.33 and is played by Hariprasad on bansuri flute, accompanied by Zakir and Uma Metha. Without John's electric tones, this is pure Indian music played by masters of their instruments and even more delightful in places for the interplay between Prasad and Hussain. The second track is *The Wish*, a piece written by John that he played with Zakir on *The Promise* (1996). John plays a long introduction on electric guitar, so it is not until around 6.20 that the familiar melodic theme breaks out. Nothing is hurried on this album, and if you don't like slow pace, don't buy this album. Next *Lotus Feet* makes a re-appearance, played, once again, at a delightfully calm pace and mostly featuring Hariprasad, although John makes a short solo on electric guitar. The harmonies here are sublime on this very popular McLaughlin composition. Just when you thought the music was laid back, you find yourself horizontal with *Mukti*, an exceptionally slow, spiritual piece of music. The bansuri flute weaves its hypnotic spells for the first four minutes. *Zakir* is written by John for his friend and adopted by Zakir on his own album for ECM, *Making Music* (1997).

At over two hours twelve minutes in length, this album represents good value for money and is a very good balance of east-west music – a real fusion of musics that is to a large extent driven by John's use of the electric guitar.

Remember Shakti: *The Believer* – 2000 (**)

McLaughlin appears on the cover with a standard Gibson electric guitar, which is something of a surprise and perhaps shows how even Indian music has become more westernised. The wonderful mandolin player U. Shrinivas now took over as the second lead instrument, although the photograph of him on the album cover shows him with a diminutive electric six-stringed instrument. Once again, V. Selvaganesh was on kanjira, ghatam and mridangam.

This album is a single CD, supplemented with a second CD of video material, all of it recorded during the European tour of 1999. The music of the opening track *5 in the Morning, 6 in the Afternoon*, is a true fusion of Indian music and jazz. The drone is regally electric and the quality of the recorded sound is as high as it gets. John's electric guitar is perfectly placed and he achieves the Indian effects he needs to retain the musical authenticity, whilst also creating music that western ears can find more accessible. The piece is conventionally structured with a head that is delightfully pleasing and which focuses and bridges the solos.

Remember Shakti: *Saturday Night in Bombay* – 2001 (**)

It was very appropriate that the sixth and last album of the Shakti series should be recorded in India. The album *Saturday Night in Bombay* is a clear parallel with John's Spanish ethnic milestone *Friday Night in San Francisco*, a signpost to just two of the extremities of musical genres straddled by this remarkable musician. Not surprisingly, perhaps, it is the most Indian and John takes an unusually low profile amongst a large cast of musicians. John's only composition is the brief *Luki* that opens the CD. A new sound to Shakti albums is the Hindustani slide guitar of Debashish Bhattacharya, which solos along with John's electric guitar. The second track is *Shringar*, a piece that lasts almost half an hour and features Shiv Kumar Sharma playing the santur, a 72-string hammered dulcimer-type instrument that derives from Iran. The piece is slow to develop, but is atmospheric and relaxing. *Giriraj Sudha* is mostly vocal music, written by Shrinivas and sung by Shankar Mahadevan, and will test your level of acceptance of eastern harmony and style to the full. Finally is Zakir Hussain's *Bell' Alla*, another long piece that allows him to include a significant solo of his own. Fans of Indian music will like this, I'm sure, but the album is one of the least significant of the six.

John McLaughlin: *Thieves and Poets* – 2003 (**)

Thieves and Poets is a three-part suite of Spanish-acoustic music written in the western classical style. The work for orchestra and guitar was commissioned in the 1990s for the Deutsche Kammerphilharmonie by its director Jürgen Nimbler and was orchestrated by Yan Maresz. McLaughlin describes the three movements as a process of change from the old world to the new: the first part is in the old world, the third part is in the new world and the second is the transition between them. There aren't many hints about what exactly that means, but McLaughlin records in the sleeve notes that touring and performing with the orchestra was "one of the greatest musical experiences of my life". [65] After two further revisions, separated by numerous years, the music had evolved into the form recorded here in June 2002 with the string players of the Pommeriggi Musicali di Milano and their conductor Renato Rivolta. The soloists, Viktoria Mullova (violin), Matt Haimovitz (cello) Paul Meyer (clarinet) Philippe Loli (guitar), Bruno Frumento (tympani) were recorded separately in a studio reconstruction. There is, of course, very little relationship with jazz here, although there are the constant echoes of John's entire musical lineage to found within its bar lines. It goes without saying that the output from this consummate professional is of the highest standard. The sound of the finished result is as good as anything produced by those who specialise in this style of music. It is astonishing to even contemplate that this was the brainchild of the greatest jazz-rock guitarist.

The second part of this album is a follow-up to the album of acoustic guitar music, *Time Remembered* (1993). This has all the same faults. That music was bland; this is worse. It's as if I have just passed away and I'm listening to the St. Peter's Heavenly Host Quintet. His choice of 'standards' is peculiar. The songs *My Foolish Heart, Stella by Starlight* and *My Romance* are undeniably standards, although they are delivered in such a way as to be unrecognisable, but where did *The Dolphin* jump out from? It's very hard to get through this turgid material that is, like the heavenly band's outfits, monochrome: entirely white – with a hint of green. On second thoughts, never mind the Pearly Gates club that John's just bought the franchise for. I'm going to advertise my ticket for sale on E-bay and instead book a table at Lucifer's Grill and Bar where, so they say, Jaco's Big Band is on an extended run.

John McLaughlin: *Industrial Zen* – 2006 (****)

In 2006, John amazed the record-buying public again with a new album of modern jazz-fusion. The band he chose for his tour was a knockout, with Gary

Husband brilliantly fulfilling the role on keyboards. Mark Mondesir was recruited to take on the challenge of drumming for this project, although Husband himself was an excellent drummer too. Both men have cited Billy Cobham and Jan Hammer as big influences in their musical development, which shows clearly in the way they approach this new incarnation of the Mahavishnu Orchestra. Young bassist Hadrian Feraud was also an excellent choice, especially in view of the opening track, *For Jaco*. Everything about this track is brilliant, and I have not come across music that has had such an effect on me since the title track to Bill Evans' album *Alternative Man* (1985), which has a lot in common with this. Coincidentally - or perhaps not – John's old sparring partner Evans himself is a guest on this track that is simply on fire, with John, Bill and Hadrian taking solos in that order. And as Feraud plays the track out in true Jaco style, even the final phrase at 5.00 is Jaco's, which John has lifted from *Continuum* on the album *Jaco Pastorius* (1976).

New Blues, Old Bruise is a fascinating piece with plenty of interest, a major focus being the use of a sampled close-harmony male choir on keyboard to complement John's deliberate and considered heavy rock sound. At 2.15 a transition to a much faster and higher pitched guitar is reminiscent of all those years of rock guitar greats. At 3.22 the piece falls out briefly, to return to the earlier guitar mode at 3.42. The piece ends with a mystical combination of choir and transcendental electronics that is fully in keeping with this seriously fusionist album.

Wayne's Way is a very good piece of electric Indian music, and another example of Indian jazz-fusion that McLaughlin has excelled at. Once again, John is employing the same kind of far-out metre he has always relied upon for his unique brand. The short phrases that make up the theme are set amongst musical expanses of geographical proportions - so long they are timeless. Another intriguing guest is the female soprano sax player Ada Rovatti, who adds a tone and texture that is refreshingly different from the instantly recognisable Evans. John's solo is second and characteristically punctual. From 4.30 the piece becomes manic, and Indian, if it was not recognisable as such before.

Just So, Only More So has Bill Evans riding bareback on his trademarked soprano sound. It's a pleasant ballad, until 2.36 when a forceful rhythm and a series of undulating phrases of differing lengths rocks and rolls across the landscape. By 7.15, the earlier balladic refrain has returned to complete this fascinating journey through musical hyperspace. *To Bop or Not to Be* continues the album's theme of churning, timeless electronic musical themes. This is a drone with John's metronomic solos constructed of modal sixteenth notes that never seem to form predictable sentences. The piece was dedicated to Michael Brecker who, at this time, had fallen seriously ill. *Dear Dalai Lama* begins with an address to the man himself, a Buddhist epistle of peace and love. Ada Rovatti plays a hauntingly beautiful tenor sax solo. At 4.13 the piece becomes fast and furious, led by Evans at first, and then by John's guitar synth. At 9.48 there is a sudden fracture and a return to the slow saxophone theme coupled to the choral synth sound used earlier.

Señor CS is intrinsically 12/8. Here is another quite remarkable, piece that is relatively straightforward in its construction, but so cleverly composed and played that it is timeless in both senses of the word. The extremely effective separation of the music from the formal time signature and the exclusive use of electronics make me feel as if I am floating around in musical cyberspace, supported on a magic carpet of pure spectral energy. This is McLaughlin at his best. I can listen to this music over and over again; it is continually novel and surprising and it is true 21st century jazz-fusion.

In complete contrast, *Mother Nature* is an Indian song commercialised in a kind of Bollywood style. After the brilliant opening of this album, there is a disappointing downward trend to the standard of music from track six onwards. John's apparent intention to make an eclectic collection of songs doesn't come off.

This is an album that could so easily have been awarded five stars, and for me it is the constant churning of musicians from one track to the next that is at fault. I am perfectly happy to accept an album that is artificially constructed in the studio, especially since it has the title *Industrial Zen*. Electronic music is clearly as close to artificiality as you can get, and it doesn't really matter where, when or how it was recorded, it is the result that counts. This could be dubbed an album of world music since most of the world's studios seem to have been used to make it. However, there is an inconsistency here that just takes away that 'stunned into silence' feeling when the last track fades away, and the last track itself is an unforgivable contribution. The use of Rovatti throughout would have been a preferable option, much as I like Bill Evans. Her playing throughout would have cemented the album as coming from one coherent, rehearsed and fully interactive band, rather than a mish-mash of temps. Nevertheless, this is nit-picking complaint.

John McLaughlin: *Floating Point* – 2008 (*****) [CD]; *Meeting of the Minds - The Making of Floating Point* – 2008 (*****) [DVD]

In 2007, John spent a period of time back in India and soon found that he was experiencing a period of unexpected creativity. He wrote a lot of music in a short time and even he seemed surprised that he soon had enough to fill a CD. It was therefore a spontaneous decision to record the music right there in Chennai (Madras) with some of the best Indian musicians he could get. Thus was born the *Floating Point* (2008) CD project, supplemented with a video recording of the five consecutive days (26-30 April) spent in the studio and published on an excellent DVD called *Meeting of the Minds - The Making of Floating Point* (2008).

In the DVD, John is unashamed to proclaim that he is a fusion musician, and qualifies the statement by saying that, whilst he has studied Indian music, he is still a Westerner. He explains that his music is fundamentally Western jazz music, but with constructions that allow Indian musicians to join in without compromising their own musical rules. As with other forms of folk music, classically trained Indian musicians play in modes (ragas) that do not include any significant chord changes in the way of Western music. This came about because of the way the instruments are constructed. John's approach is to use certain kinds of Western changes that best fit the Indian modes and so fuse the two forms of music. On the DVD, the point is made several times by the Indian musicians themselves, who understand perfectly the clash between the two styles and do their best to blend and mould their contributions into a harmonic whole. John says that he writes with specific players in mind and this adds further support to the musicians who might otherwise have felt uncomfortable in such a context. John makes the point that this music would not have been possible twenty years ago because the Indians simply could not have coped with it. However, their exposure to Western music is now such that they are quite at home with John's compositions – indeed, they positively flourish in his environments.

Listening to the album, it's as if John had heard my criticisms of *Industrial Zen*, for here he is playing in a single location with a coherent band – albeit with a slight daily change of personnel. The music is coherent in style too, formed from a blueprint of dynamic melodies in McLaughlin's usual quick-fire style, often spliced around some out-of-tempo atmospheric sections that delightfully break back into tempo with a solo from the guest and then John.

The core tracks were laid down with the help of Indian keyboardist Louiz Banks, drummer Ranjit Barot and percussionist Anandan Sivamani. Indian-born Banks admits that he has been in love with jazz ever since hearing Oscar Peterson, Chick Corea and Herbie Hancock. Banks doesn't get to shine on the DVD, but his beautiful pastiches provide the rich harmonic backgrounds without which the music would be much poorer. Much of his effort has clearly been put in before these sessions and he is ever-present in support as John directs each daily guest, coaxing the best out of each musician.

Barot is a busy drummer in the traditional Western style. His drumming is rock-solid, sometimes intrusive. He dominates a background with the solidity and polyrhythmic embrace to such an extent that you could describe him as an Indian Tony Williams, although he is rather too dominating in *Aggaji (for Alla Rakha)*. He has a remarkable feel for the complex rhythms that McLaughlin asks him to play. Even though playing in 10/8, on *The Voice*, for example, John makes it clear that he can use the bass drum whenever he likes; he should not get into a mechanical groove. That makes the music feel even less dependent upon the Western time signature than usual and contributes to the delightfully detached rhythm that is characteristic on most of these tracks. Barot's drumming is expertly supplemented by the inventive percussion of Anandan Sivamani and the two men together are strong enough to make the absence of bass on the DVD unnoticeable. No bass was used during the Chennai recordings - Hadrien Feraud made his superb contributions later back in the Mediastarz studio in Monaco.

The music for six of the eight tracks was recorded over five days, with a different guest musician on each day. Two musicians returned from John's past recordings, singer Shankar Mahadevan and Debashish Bhattacharya on slide guitar, both of whom joined John for *Saturday Night in Bombay* (2001). John has written *The Voice* especially for Mahadevan and spends some time explaining how he should sing his raga, and not be put off as John moves into others (keys, that is). He shows Mahadevan how the same notes are appropriate throughout. Shashank plays Indian bamboo flute for *Off the One*. He understands how the tonic note of the western scale is the root of the raga as McLaughlin's music takes liberties with his classical training. From his side, John points out how the modes of Miles and Coltrane are well suited to Indian musical forms.

Raju is a piece with Hindustani slide guitar played by Bhattacharya in which John reuses one of his classic 12/8 rhythms. Most western players would throw their hands up in despair if asked to play such complex rhythms but these experts spend a little time coming to terms with what is required and then move on to playing it. *Maharina* is a track with just the basic band and is an opportunity for Louiz and John to play off each other.

Niladri Kumar plays electric sitar for *Five Peace Band* that is placed last on the CD. He does an amazing job as he keeps up with John's lightning fast keyboard runs by means of remarkable finger acrobatics. Played loud, this track is sensational, with memorable, singable hooks and some slick jazz changes that Niladri negotiates as if he grew up doing it. Wisely, he explains how music is universal to everyone, whether from east or west, by virtue of the combination of the *sound* with the *lifestyle* that is attached to it. John judges that the virtual world is playing a big part in the fusion of world musics as much as the players do it in a physical sense. On the record, Feraud gets a significant bass solo that is disappointingly dulled in the mix, but after some brilliant all-round playing, the album ends on a real high as, for once, it reaches an orchestrated ending that leaves behind a wonderful feeling of exhilaration.

It is clear from watching the DVD how all of these Indian musicians are stars in their own right and the skill of their playing comes across far better than from listening to the CD alone. Amongst the real highlights is Naveen Kumar making the most wonderful sounds on Indian flute with just a single bamboo tube and a few finger holes. The piece entitled *1 4 U* could have come from Nelson Rangell's flute – and I mean that as a compliment. Just for once, John's melody is sufficiently approachable for it to sound truly joyous and Naveem's playing is truly inspired. He doesn't think about his improvisations beforehand, he says, preferring to play the notes that God provides for him at the time.

One of the most striking things about the DVD is the wonderful sound quality of the music, but of course it should be remembered that the source for the soundtrack could hardly have been better as a direct feed from the live recordings! With everything in digital these days, there's no reason for any loss of quality and there isn't. Yet, somehow, the music on the CD seems less vibrant after completion of the many overdubbing, mixing and mastering procedures. Although there is no single complete track on the DVD, I did not feel cheated and it certainly did make me want to get the CD, even if I had not already done so. The other point is that the video footage is strictly in the documentary style with no artistic obscuration. Thus, McLaughlin fans can luxuriate in being able to see his amazing finger-work at close quarters, as well as his Indian pals, of course. Another remarkable aspect is the method by which the most complex rhythms are communicated in such a short time to musicians who do not read western paper music. Thus, the "dak-a-dak-a-dak-a-dak-a" vocalising that has appeared in several places on earlier albums now takes on a new significance. Especially stunning is the way the musicians cope with the killer section of polyrhythms on *Inside Out*. With Rajesh's electric mandolin as the guest instrument, and Banks playing an excellent solo, this piece is a superb blend of styles, harmonies and melodies, all bound up in unfathomable rhythm.

John plays another of his beautiful custom guitars by Godin, and often employs it as a synthesiser for a lovely legato sound that takes the edge of his machine-gun runs. All in all, this is a five-star album and my nomination for the best Indo-jazz fusion album of all time. But Louiz Banks gets the last word: "Besides being one of the greatest virtuosos of the guitar, *this is a great human being* and such a creative person!" Well said, Louiz.

John McLaughlin and the 4th Dimension: *Live @ Belgrade* – 2008 (****) [DVD]

John McLaughlin and the 4th Dimension performing at the Barbican Hall, London, Saturday 31st May 2008.

At the time of John's 2008 European tour, there was a certain amount of confusion about just what the gigs were about. A lot of early publicity had indicated that it was to promote John's latest album. Only when I had listened to the album did I understand that *Floating Point* was another Indo-jazz fusion and that John could hardly promote it if there were no Indian musicians in the band. To make matters worse, a week or so before the event, there was news that bass player Hadrien Feraud had broken his finger and had been replaced by Dominique di Piazza.

The London gig was the only British date on an extensive European tour, proof - if proof were needed - of the current state of interest in jazz in the UK. I for one turned up expecting a promotion of the latest album, *Floating Point* (2008) and some tracks from *Industrial Zen* (2006), encouraged by the promotional material handed out on the door and the sale of CDs and DVDs in the foyer. However, that wasn't what we got. Here was the fusion band with Gary Husband on keyboards, Mark Mondesir on drums and Dominique di Piazza, bass. What we got, therefore, was largely a retrospective with numbers from the past including *Little Miss Valley* from the *Free Spirits Tokyo Live* (1994), *Hi-Jacked* from *Qué Allegría* (1992), and the *Unknown Dissident* from *Electric Dreams* (1979).

It seemed as if we were the victims of a much-altered programme so that, with little time for practice, Dominique could play material he already knew. The latter part of the second half was more about an extended drum workout in *Mr D.C.* from *The Heart of Things* (1997) as Mondesir duelled with the slightly over-the-top Husband now playing a second (half-size) drum kit. Nevertheless, despite the absence of Indian musicians who might have been thought necessary for a faithful rendition of the music from *Floating Point*, we did get one of the tracks *Raju* from *Floating Point* and *Señor CS* from *Industrial Zen*. Of course, we got a lot of lightning-fast guitar playing from McLaughlin, spoilt somewhat by a mushy sound quality that could not distinguish the complex playing from these great musicians, except during the slower ballads. John stuck to a single guitar for the whole gig and only about two different sounds.

Gary Husband was clearly a *tour de force*. Born in Yorkshire on 14 June 1960, his mother was a dancer, his father an orchestral musician. He grew up loving all kinds of music from European classical music to big band jazz by Stan Kenton. He began to specialise in piano and drums from an early age, and continues to concentrate on both strands to his career. At 16, he turned professional, taking the drum seat with the Syd Laurence Orchestra. One day, he discovered the music of Billy Cobham, and thence the early records by the first Mahavishnu Orchestra. It was an epiphany, and both Cobham's drums and Hammer's keyboards provided him with large amounts of inspiration.

Moving to London in 1978 he played with all of the top British jazz musicians, including Barbara Thompson's band, Paraphernalia, the Morrisey/Mullen Band, and the Mike Carr Trio. He played piano occasionally for the Ronnie Scott Quintet, Ian Carr's Nucleus and Jeff Clyne's Turning Point. He was also a stalwart member of singer Marion Montgomery's backing group. He released his first (all-synthesizer) album *Diary Of A Plastic Box* (1998) and from 1999 to 2002 he led his own Gary Husband New Trio, with Mick Hutton (bass) and Gene Calderazzo (drums). In the summer of 2003 Gary was awarded a highly coveted place on the Arts Council of England's Contemporary Music Network touring scheme to lead a hand-picked ensemble for a concert tour across the UK in March 2004. This project, entitled *Gary Husband's Force Majeure*, featured Randy Brecker, Matthew Garrison, Jim Beard, Elliot Mason, Jerry Goodman and Arto Tuncboyaciyan. It returned to the UK in March 2005 for a further series of concerts, including a week's residency at Ronnie Scott's Club. Among his several ambitious solo piano recordings is the highly-acclaimed *A Meeting Of Spirits – Interpretations Of The Music of John McLaughlin*. His recent group Gary Husband's Drive released the album *Hotwired* in 2009. [66]

In 2009, John's 4th Dimension tour was celebrated by the release of a DVD recording of the gig in Belgrade on 14 May. It is a professional quality production from Serbian Television and gives an excellent representation of the gig I saw in London. Bass player Dominique di Piazza is a balding forty-something, dressed smartly, as any self-respecting Frenchman should, in black casual sweater and black trousers with sharp creases. His five-string bass is played rather unconventionally without an arched hand, but finger-style with an emphasis on the thumb on which he wears a pick. His abilities are first class, as the music demonstrates. Gary Husband, on the other hand, is untidily dressed in a shapeless, long-sleeve white vest, and shapeless, white linen trousers. His somewhat unkempt hair hangs over his face, but his playing is anything but shapeless. Mark Mondesir is loose and cool, smiling all around in his red vest as he thoroughly enjoys himself and plays extraordinary polyrhythms. John, too, cuts a casual dash in a loose white shirt that hangs outside his dark slacks.

The concert begins with *Señor CS*, played loose and out of tempo over the defined chords at first, as the artist paints a loose outline of his subject. At 2.15 John plays a shout that marks the start of a 4/4 section. Gary solos; Mark looks happy. After Dom plays a lead, John comes in for the final solo section that is long and well developed until 12.00 when he winds it down to close with a flourish at 12.32.

Little Miss Valley first appeared on *Tokyo Live* (1994), the album by John's band, The Free Spirits. It's recognisable here, played in its familiar blues setting over a 16-bar cycle. John goes first with a solo that he develops to a high tension, and when he decides to finish, there is uncertainty in the band about who goes next. Gary's solo is played with an interesting synthesised human voice sound. The rhythmic feel is a blues shuffle, but this changes to a rockier groove later. This is a piece of fun for great players such as these, and it helps get Dominique into shape for the harder stuff to come.

Never one to overindulge in talking to the audience, John says politely how pleased he is to be in Belgrade and introduces his band. Then the band plays *Nostalgia*, a song that has clearly earned its place on the roster by being taken from an elderly collection, *Mahavishnu* (1984). The slow 4/4 tempo of this lovely piece is a welcome invitation to relax, even though John typically resorts to speeds of more than 10 notes per second during his presentation.

The composition *Raju* is one of those recently recorded with his Indian band on *Floating Point*, but with no Indian musicians present, this can only be a westernised version. That matters not. All musicians play solos on this long piece (11.55), and Dom's solo is especially notable as he introduces some clever technical stuff in the form of harmonic, chords and lightning-fast semi-quavers.

The fifth tune is *Sully*, a piece with no provenance, as far as I can discover. Nevertheless, for the older readers amongst us, there are strong echoes of the theme tune from the 1980s American police TV series, *Starsky and Hutch*, itself a tune called *Gotcha*, by Tom Scott (1977). From this era, the tune is inevitably a funk-rock fest with lots of communal freewheeling and solo exhibitionism.

Maharina also appeared on *Floating Point*, but, once again, is very different in the hands of these westernised musicians. Played in 4/4 at a plaintive 60 bpm, this tune is rich with colour and texture, if not singable melody. I feel this is a love song for John's wife, Ina, and she must have been very proud to hear it. Too often John's intense and rapid fireworks can overwhelm us, so it's an even greater joy when we are treated to a glorious celebration of a man's love for a woman.

John introduces *Hi-Jacked* as a feature for Dominique, and its 162 bpm tempo results in a lot of music played at around 11 notes per second by both John and Dominique. As you might expect, this is a high-energy rendition that looks back to the tune's first appearance on *Tokyo Live* (1994) when John's sparring partner was Joey DeFrancesco on Hammond organ.

Track 8 on the DVD is a version of *The Unknown Dissident*, which first appeared on *Electric Dreams* (1992). This is one of John's most soulful compositions, and he hired the great soulful sound of David Sanborn to play on the original. It is tempting to dismiss this as just another straightforward soul-blues, played very slowly in two at 38 bpm, but as you listen more carefully, you hear a count of six beats over those slow two bars. Later you may realise that something is still not right, and careful analysis shows that in each sequence of the main theme, John has introduced two seven-beat bars at bars 5 and 6. In each, there is a downbeat on 1, 3, 5 and 7. It's all clever stuff, but this band play it so fluidly that anyone could be forgiven for not noticing these musical tricks of John's trade.

The DVD ends with an extended medley of two crowd-pleasers: *Five Peace Band* (from *Floating Point*) and *Mother Tongues* (from *The Heart Of Things Live In Paris* (2000)) As with many other live performances, the final piece is usually an opportunity for some high jinks and this is no exception. Played throughout at 160 bpm, they all work to the limit on this one. The later stages are dominated by playing fours in rounds, Mark duelling with Gary who holds his own well on a half-size drum kit with two very battered cymbals. Towards the end of this long (23.24) extravaganza, Dominique finally admits defeat as his lack of experience with the band begins to tell, but this is no problem for by now the music has reached such a fever pitch that anything goes!

As a stand-alone DVD, this release works exceptionally well, and gives an excellent representation of yet another of John's bands at an early stage in its existence. The music draws heavily from John's back catalogue, and there is only occasional use of John's intricate musical constructs. However, we shall see shortly that this band is destined for greater things. The question is, just *how* much better can it get?

Chick Corea and John McLaughlin: *Five Peace Band* - 2009 (*****)

In the autumn of 2008, with the very successful reformed *Return to Forever* tour still ringing in his ears, Chick's next project was similarly imaginative and showed that he had not lost any of his zest for high energy jazz-fusion. He put together a band with John McLaughlin (guitar), Kenny Garrett (saxophone), Christian McBride (bass) and Vinnie Colaiuta (drums). Selections recorded live from the many pieces played during the long tour that followed were compiled for the double CD album *Five Peace Band* (2009), a name conceived by McLaughlin. The cover art is retro - a throwback to the early 1970s psychedelic *Peace and Love* days of Mahavishnu and RTF, but don't think for one moment that the music is.

Three of the numbers are from McLaughlin's recent past: *Raju* is from the magnificent five-star-rated Indo-jazz-fusion album *Floating Point* (2008), whilst *New Blues, Old Bruise* and *Señor CS* are from the very special recording *Industrial Zen* (2006). All three tracks are magnificent here. Being live tracks, they are all sufficiently long to enable development in many imaginative ways that render them different pieces from their previous incarnations. Chick's presence is majestic as he oversees each creative exercise, forsaking his now beloved concert grand piano for the eminently more suitable electronic keyboards of pure jazz-fusion. These days, it's rare to hear Chick play in this style, although with his recent experiences in RTF at his back, he is clearly primed and ready. McLaughlin, of course, has been back to his electric roots for some time and is as fiery as ever, especially on his own numbers. His now preferred Godin guitar/synth is locked into its guitar alias as he leaves the more synthetic sounds to Chick. Thus, there are some excellent hard-rock guitar sounds to enjoy, as well as the slightly more signal-processed tones.

There's a lot of good soloing to get through on this musically rich album so Kenny Garrett's presence feels diluted in places. Nevertheless, his performances in this jazz-fusion context are utterly compelling, his presence is forceful and his imagination boundless. Christian McBride's contributions are equally mind-boggling, if only for the breadth of style, at one point bounding around the ungainly acoustic bass fingerboard like a spring chicken and, at another, playing electric bass as well as anything else so far on record. This must be his finest recording to date and at least 24 hours travelling time away from his (still excellent) acoustic performances for Pat Metheny on the *Day Trip* project.

Anyone who is familiar with Vinnie Colaiuta's playing will expect fireworks, yet for me, his performance is perhaps the most amazing of all. McLaughlin's tendency of late has been to place a strong emphasis on drumming and percussion in his music, perhaps in continued deference to his hero Tony Williams, whose presence was always dominating. For *Industrial Zen* and the 2008 tour, John's latest jazz-fusion band employed both Mark Mondesir and Gary Husband on drum kits, with Husband adding lots of extra percussion (and playing keyboards besides). Similarly, the Indo-fusion band employed for *Floating Point* had both drums and percussion, but drummer Ranjit Barot was a high energy, high presence performer in his own right and, with Anandan Sivamani alongside him, an awesome twosome emerged. Colaiuta, however, constructs a remarkable footprint given that he really does have only two arms and legs. He seems to be playing constantly throughout the album and is almost always doing spectacular things. His drumming is one of the most remarkable performances of any I can think of.

I find each of the McLaughlin tracks to be magnificent and as a trio they are the best of an excellent clutch. *Raju* has been transplanted into a western harmonic layout, with no ill-effects for either version. Indeed, the additional chordal colours from Chick at once emit echoes of his peak with the Elektric Band, and it's then I realise that here he has assembled yet another version of that supergroup. A particularly nice touch is the way Vinnie periodically breaks out into a heavy rock rhythm with the original pulsing 12/8 metre in the background. As one of the shorter tracks at just over 12 minutes, a great deal is fitted into the time-frame and it's a wonderful opener.

A similar deal is on offer for the truly breathtaking *New Blues, Old Bruise*. For this piece, John draws from his Mahavishnu toolbox and uses complex metric and melodic constructions that give the listener the feeling of floating in space-time. In that sense, this piece is truly timeless, and the enigma of the title begins to unravel slightly. It's not just a new blues but one from the next millennium. Chick's sound is right out of his work on the album *Chick Corea Elektric Band* (1986) and once again, the piece is a brilliant fusion of jazz and rock styles. The wonder of the piece is the way the band holds on so well to such complexity. The fourteen minutes of our lives that this music occupies are stupendous. All band members except Christian take a solo, but John and Chick are for once occluded by the two breathtaking performances by Garrett and Colaiuta. Garrett plays a solo of huge proportions in which he takes McLaughlin's multi-coloured strands of harmony and weaves them into a magic carpet of the most intricate melodic patterns. From 3.35 to 7.20 you can listen to saxophone playing of the highest order. At 10.15 it's Colaiuta's turn. For Vinnie to take on a drum solo of such magnitude over this level of complexity whilst continuing to hold on to the timing as his colleagues take him through the written structure is utterly magnificent.

The breathlessness continues on disc 2 for Señor CS, a red-hot track that leaves you exhausted but exhilarated at its twenty-minute end. John starts off with his own kind of jazz cadenza - a solo extemporisation that introduces the melodic theme, but also makes you eager about what is to come, and so it should. First comes an unexpected bass solo, so often left to the end like an afterthought or a courtesy. This one has McBride spewing out notes like streams of molten lava running down the slopes of a volcano. And as he draws to a close, Vinnie is there to provide the clouds of cymbal steam that hiss as the melted rock meets water. Then comes the alto saxophone of the masterful Garrett. This is bright white-hot molten iron compared to McBride's basalt textures and is played with an unusual amount of reverb that creates an aural shimmer. As Garrett's music pours forth with increasing intensity, by 9.15 the notes spew from every tiny orifice of McLaughlin's carefully crafted mould.

For Chick's solo, the rhythm of the piece becomes more mechanistic than spontaneous, the precision of which is enhanced by his crisp, clean electric piano sound. But this is no plodding sequential algorithm. Instead, Chick's brilliant creativity takes John's difficult chord sequence in its stride and sprightly steers its course through the complex form like a nimble mountain goat escaping the lava streams. The music suits Corea perfectly for John's work perfectly matches what Chick might have written. At 12.50 McBride's walking bass leads a brief shift into swing time with some minor complaints from Colaiuta who keeps up an irresistible dynamic pace. Then at 14.07 is the transition into John's solo, for which the pace is at once boosted by another eruption until, by 15.45, the musical edifice set up by the earlier soloists begins to undergo a further meltdown. Even as John brings this inferno under control for the final pass through the theme, the piece now enters a section whereby John, Chick and Kenny take turns in true jazz tradition to cycle through consecutive bars of high octane 12/8, gradually merging into a final burst of tumult and closure at 20.00. Forget Richter, this music is at the extreme of any scale of geological measurement.

Of course, my extravagant praise of the three McLaughlin tracks is the view of a fan of jazz-fusion and it is coloured because, in this case, there are other tracks that do not fall neatly into this sub-genre. It's too easy to view McLaughlin's contributions as more worthy of praise, however, and we should view it as a feature not a fault. Track 2 is *The Disguise*, a new piece by Chick that is calm and reflective yet still bright and full of zest. Garrett's rich flute tones are complimented by the harmony with John's guitar, which has a lot of reverb. The music is very much like pieces from *Inside Out* (1988) or *Beneath the Mask* (1992), although Garrett is a very different player from Eric Marienthal. When he changes to saxophone here, his sound is given some significant effects. This is an excellent straight-ahead jazz organism in the acoustic jazz vein even though it is much infected with fusion genes. It bears few of the hallmarks for which Chick is renowned - Spanish tones and highly convoluted scripting - and is much fresher for it, right through to its lush ending.

Hymn to Andromeda is another title that suggests images of L. Ron Hubbard's galactic fiction. Chick has tried this several times in recent years, notably with the Elektric Band's *To the Stars* (2004). That project was disappointing, but this is a triumph. In the extended introduction Corea indulges in some of his favoured solo piano free improvisations, playing the piano almost as much from the inside as from the outside. To some of us, it seems more like a case of *New Crews, Old News*. However, careful listening uncovers the plot to be much like the one he used on *Inside Out* (1988) where he used carefully designed devices to build a wonderful machine. After the short burst of freedom at the very start, the music develops into a solid melodic form. By 3.15 Chick has joined with Christian and the music is gentle and playful - even blissful; it's meant to be a hymn, after all, but needs to convey that old extra-terrestrial feeling. At 4.50 Christian takes over the lead and Chick moves back as the pair of musicians takes us through the Hymn's second verse. By 7.30, the whole band is at work and the structure is becoming clear: the music is nowhere near as chaotic as it first seems. At 10.05, a moderate swing tempo breaks out and there are loud echoes of *Tales of Daring* from *Inside Out* (1988) which was a hugely innovative suite of carefully orchestrated 'modern' music.

At 12.10 a major new section commences in which Garrett embarks upon one of the stupendous live solos for which he is famous. One of his best-known was for *Human Nature* that he played at the Miles Davis reunion concert at *La Grande Halle de la Villette* in Paris (1991) - fortunately recorded on video. At first, he develops the feel of North Africa, though it could easily be one of the many exotic sets developed for the Star Wars movies. His constructions cycle through periods of increasing and decreasing intensity. Each time, the band tightens the screws to the point where Garrett is screaming to be set free, and each time, as you begin to think he is done, he begins the process again. The first time around, his agonies are played out in distorted altissimo rants. For the second, it's as if he has learnt from the pain of the first and his notes are now full of purity and passion. Garrett's solo is just one of many major features of this album, as it continues to 23.15 - eleven minutes of sheer brilliance.

As you begin to wonder how much longer the piece will continue, it seems that this is no longer a hymn but a saga. The music enters yet another phase as the band breaks into another free-jazz section, as if the spaceship has entered a field of gas and primordial material destined to become a new planet. It is, of course, the indication that the band has returned to the start of the composition for the Hymn's final verse. At 24.40, Andromeda finally comes into view and the 3/4 waltz gentle rocks us from side to side like the solar wind breezing through the asteroid belt. When the piece ends at 27.25, you really feel as if you have been on a journey of discovery.

On the second disc, Corea leads the band through his own arrangement of Jackie McLean's *Dr Jackle*, a standard *up tempo* mainstream piece of blues that is embellished throughout with the dark monstrous tones of an implied Mr Hyde. This develops into a high energy romp that is very satisfying, though not in the same way as McLaughlin's masterpieces, and not for a few moments during this performance do I get the impression that John is less comfortable playing the blues in the way that a mere mortal like me would understand. His solos are really not as satisfying in this very well established harmonic environment as they are when performed with tonal gymnastics in the complex structures of his own making.

Señor CS is surely what Miles Davis would have wished to create when he began his experiments in 1970, and dedicated to his close friend Carlos Santana, this music surely reflects that time. I'm sure he would have been glad to acknowledge the contributions made by his own side-men, inspired over many years by their work alongside him. All this merely highlights the significance of Corea's excellent choice of *In A Silent Way / It's About That Time*, a medley that took both John and Chick back to the days when they first met in the studio in 1969 to record with Miles. Not present then, but one of Miles's most important sidemen was Herbie Hancock, who joins the band on this track - Chick plays electric and Herbie plays acoustic piano. This 21st century version of some of the most significant jazz-fusion music in history is further enhanced by the presence of Garrett who was Miles's preferred saxophonist for the final part of the maestro's career in the late 1980s and the playing of this music by these four men is the source of significant invisible energy to those of us who remember the impact of the originals. There is as much of Miles's aura channelled from this recording as from any other cover of Davis's music and its inclusion for this album is a master-stroke by Corea.

The biggest disappointment is the inclusion of *Someday My Prince Will Come*, played as a Chick/John duet. The piece has been on Chick's list of favourites for years and it might have suited a fourth division bar-band playing sets of old standards for winos, but it's not at all appropriate for a collection of the world's finest musicians. This is a filler track and unsuitable both in its presence on the album and in its position at the end of a stunning collection. I would have so much preferred to hear them spontaneously combust whilst playing Chick's *Got a Match* or kick up dust with John's *For Jaco*. Despite this blemish, the album is more than two and a quarter hours in length, which is excellent value for fans of great jazz, so it can withstand the dismissal of track eight. I therefore urge listeners to ignore it and treat track seven as the end of this fabulous album. There is so much here to astonish and bewilder, especially in these days when all things intellectual are despised. This album is the stuff of genius and there are two men here who indisputably stand out as such, supported by three of the finest musicians on the planet. Despite great successes early in their careers, they didn't get to this point easily or quickly. These five supremely gifted men have devoted their lives to the creation of the finest music; that should be celebrated aloud. I therefore have no hesitation in awarding the album five stars.

John McLaughlin and the 4th Dimension: *To The One* – 2010 (****)

After some years of uncertainty about where his best work was to be done, John decided from 2008 to focus his activities around the new band name – John McLaughlin and the 4th Dimension. Clearly, he had discovered another identity that suited him well, and this band would prove to be especially well founded, even though its members would change. In 2010, John made a new album with a title that continued to demonstrate his love of life and perhaps, a growing awareness of his own mortality, *To The One*. The disc itself even bore a facsimile handwritten dedication – a nice touch, whilst the cover art bore some indications of ambiguity. As John's hands hold the shiny new master disc, it seems he is dedicating it to the reflected partial image of his true love in mortal life. However, the combination of the dedication and the word 'master' doubles as a reference to the 'Immortal One'.

On stage, he looked serenely calm and happy. He had clearly returned to composing at the highest levels of creativity, and to perform his works to appreciative audiences in the company of some of the world's finest musicians. Rather than adopt the elder statesman / wandering troubadour role of *Industrial Zen*, John settled into the traditional small group bandleader style with his new album, a role he had been playing for the past two years on the road. Besides

Gary Husband, who had now become John's closest working partner, John chose Etienne Mbappé (bass) to join the band on a more permanent basis, and his old friend Mark Mondesir (drums).

Etienne (pronounced ATN) Mbappé left his homeland in the Cameroon in 1978 to join his father in Paris. He joined the French National Jazz Band called Orchestre National de Jazz (ONJ) and appeared on the album *African Dream* (1989). Etienne formed a band called Chic Hot and played with the leading French jazz-fusion band Ultramarine, with Nguyen Le (guitar), Mokhtar Samba (drums), Mario Canonge (keyboards), Pierre-Oliver Govin (sax) and Bago (percussion). He appears on their albums *Dé* (1981) and *E Si Mala* (1991). Playing music strongly influenced by Weather Report, and later work by Joe Zawinul, it was natural for Etienne to be attracted to Zawinul's style of world jazz music. He worked with other African musicians such as Salif Keita (appearing on *Amen* (1998)) and Paco Sery, two musicians who were also close to Zawinul. Characterised by his trademark of playing whilst wearing black silk gloves, Etienne found a place in Joe Zawinul's Syndicate from 2000 to 2003 and appeared on *Faces and Places* (2002). His own solo albums were *Misiya* (2004) and *Su La Také* (2008), named after his present Paris-based band with Cate Petit (voice), Clement Janinet (violin), Cedric Baud (guitar) and Nicolas Viccaro (drums). [67]

Mark Mondesir (pronounced Mon-Day-Zee) is a master of his drum kit. Born in Bow, East London, Mark is self-taught: "I say that I'm a graduate of the bedroom school of music!" He learned to play by watching and listening to music on record and TV. [68] Today, he is becoming more involved with passing on his great skills to a younger generation of drummers. Mark is also involved in composing. The great British jazz musician Julian Joseph recently wrote: "Mark Mondesir is undoubtedly one of the finest drummers the UK has ever produced, and has gained the respect and admiration of musicians the world over. A unique talent, he combines technical velocity, complexity and dexterity with an awesome inventiveness and imaginative dynamism, all grounded in an instinctive feel for groove. He has known and worked with Julian for over twenty years, and has made an inspiring and essential contribution to all his projects, bringing a musical integrity and diversity that is, quite simply, humbling. He is comfortable in any genre, from jazz to rock to funk to fusion." [69]

Mark started playing at the age of 12, influenced by people in the fields of rock funk and soul, such as Earth Wind and Fire, Genesis, Wings and David Bowie. "I was playing a lot of groove stuff in my first five years of playing. Then a friend of a friend told me about Jeff Beck and Billy Cobham, describing him as a guy from the States with arms shaped like tree trunks! Way before listening to

Cobham, I was inspired by looking at photos of him and his kit – 3 bass drums, 3 snares, octobans, gong drums, loads of toms, etc… that inspired me and I got into the whole fusion thing at the age of 17 – I started to learn all that before even knowing what rudiments were." [68]

Mark has worked with top jazz artists including Courtney Pine, Julian Joseph, Kevin Eubanks, John Scofield, Jeff Beck, The London Symphony Orchestra, Joe Zawinul, Pee Wee Ellis and many more. He also had a close encounter with a drumming legend. "Tony Williams, who was notoriously hard to impress, was said to have stood behind the stage curtain when Mark was playing at one of the jazz festivals, riveted by Mark's playing. Tony watched the rest of the performance. After this Tony and Mark became friends." [70]

The first track of *To The One* is *Discovery*, a fast (140 beats per minute) composition in standard 4/4 metre with a good, memorable and melodic theme based around sixteen bars. However, nothing is really 'standard' with John and the sixteen beats of bars 13 to 16 are split in such a way (6-6-4?) as to rhythmically disrupt the otherwise mechanical delivery. Two rounds of this theme, separated by an eight bar bridge, set up John and Gary for the usual improvised sections from 0.40 and 2.32 respectively. Gary's solo style is loose, breaking away from the established rhythmic pulse with a floating, airy feel. At 3.40 there is a short argument between drums and guitar/keys in unison. Then at 4.04 Etienne throws his serious weight behind a semiquaver solo that introduces his powerful presence with wonderful clarity. At 5.12 John, accompanied only by drums, performs a cadenza in good classical style before elucidating the theme for the last time. However, there is still more to come as a final argument ensues to see who has last word.

The second track, *Special Beings*, is a delightful contrast to the opener. Set in an unwavering waltz time, this bright, melodic composition is a joy to listen to. Most listeners would be content to know that, but for those with a more analytical interest I must say that the three-beat-to-a-bar metre is played out over a theme consisting of three groups of five bars and five groups of four bars, followed by three groups of five bars. This structure is closely followed throughout the rest of the piece as, from 1.14, Gary takes the lead with another of his delightful, delicate and ethereal creations on electric piano. John returns from 3.09 and the magic continues as we meet the special beings John has in mind.

The Fine Line starts out with a heavy metal guitar sound, but breaks into another memorable melody whilst not diverting from the strong rock vibe. For once, the metre is fixed at 7/4 at a fast pace of 150 bpm. After the heavy metal bass line of four bars in C minor, the main melodic phrase begins at 0.25 and is repeated at

0.47. From 1.02 Gary takes lead on the electric piano, careful to follow the harmonic structure John has laid down. At 2.17 the theme is repeated, cycling in four bars of Cm (2 bars), Abm (1 bar) and Dbm (1 bar). Over this comes a drum extravaganza to 3.20 when the theme is played once before a new section starts at 3.30. A lovely excursion of chords leads into an entirely new JM solo with Etienne's bass defining the harmonic background. This is just another facet of John's brilliant creative imagination that, just when you think the piece has found its destination, he leads you around a corner into new territory. This continues to 5.36 when the metal theme is recycled, with the melody re-run from 5.50. At 6.15 a brief flourish from Gary and John indicates that the end may be approaching, and this is confirmed at 6.32 when John plays another wonderful cadenza with drums until the classic live rock ending brings it all to a close at 7.40.

Lost and Found is a spiritual ballad with John applying his guitar synthesiser to a composition that is in the same mystical vein as he used so wonderfully on *Floating Point*. Mark's steady pulse underpins this loosely formatted composition that seems to be structured around a repeating 8+6+8 pattern, perhaps a 22/8 rhythm. Etienne's crisp, carefully chosen bass notes set the initial harmonic landscape. The piece achieves a wonderful new set of colours as it moves effortlessly into new ground from 1.48, and this gorgeous pastiche is perfectly completed by Gary's acoustic solo from 2.58. As we wander around, lost for words at the spiritual vibe of this great music, an entirely new door opens at 4 minutes and finally shows us what we were looking for...

The energy is back with a vengeance for *Recovery*, another complex composition set loosely in Fm and Abm that only barely describes the rough harmonic terrain of the main theme. The music chugs relentlessly forward in semiquaver rigour, trying at every opportunity to disguise its four beat heritage in a blistering sweep of staccato notes, whether from guitar, keys or bass. At 5.24, listen to the written phrase played by Etienne, then repeated at 5.28 in unison with John, but lengthened. At 5.40 the original phrase occurs again, and is then immediately followed by a different, even longer, version, all played precisely in unison. It is an amazing way to draw the song to an end at 6.18. On a superficial level, the music in this track is exhilarating, bold and busy. On a deeper level it is mesmerising in its intricacy of construction and execution. John is starting to discover a style of composition that is as carefully constructed as any he has used in the past, whilst, to play it, this band is stepping up to a level not achieved since the first Mahavishnu Orchestra. We shall have to wait for the next album for further proof.

The final track on this glorious album is *To The One*, seemingly written in 15/8 for its cycles of (5 groups of 3) beats. The track's title is mirrored by John's synthesiser, which is beautifully smooth as he delivers his sculpted surfaces of sound. The traditional chord sequence of most other compositions in the western idiom is absent here, as John adopts a train of harmonies that steps around in no ordered path. Etienne, defines the way forward with his clear rhythmic marks, as john and then Gary follow his footsteps as if in a musical minefield. But there are no explosions of any kind, just an expression of love and peace that John has been contemplating for so many years.

This is an album of extremely high quality, filled with classic McLaughlin sounds, but boosted by Etienne Mbappé's pulsating bass lines, Gary Husband's strongly creative support and Mark Mondesir's intuitive and complex rhythms. This band is as tight as any musician could wish for, and the interpretations of John's compositions are magnificent. The complexity of the listening experience demands more than just a cursory examination, so it is essential to hear this record more than once. This music may not be easy to sing along to, but it is unquestionably memorable. Furthermore, it has the capacity to penetrate my soul and, once it has migrated to my inner conscience, its musicality and tone invokes a deep-seated satisfaction when I play it. Surely, that is the purpose of music?

John McLaughlin and the 4th Dimension: *Now Hear This* – 2012 (*****)

In the year of his seventieth birthday, John continued the great work started with his new band and released a second album with the title *Now Hear This* (2012), similar to his glorious album *To The One* (2010). It's inevitable that we make a comparison of his age with the quality of the music on offer, and it is a remarkable truth that John McLaughlin, at 70 years of age, is capable of delivering music of the same unique quality that he has done for most of his life. Indeed, some commentators even assessed his music as better than with the Mahavishnu Orchestra – the kind of remark that could easily be accused of being hyperbolic, yet careful analysis shows is perfectly justified. As if to anticipate comment regarding his age, the album cover bears an excellent portrait of John, looking superbly fit and healthy, ready to take on musical challenges at a new creative level.

For his new record, John substituted Mark Mondesir with the brilliant Indian drummer Ranjit Barot, a master of polyrhythmic drumming who had appeared with such distinction on his *Floating Point* (2008) collection. It's tempting to say that the personnel change was another step up in the band's capabilities, though that seems unfair to the wonderfully talented Mondesir.

The title of the opening track is *Trancefusion*, an indicator that all John's early influences are still present for the coming music. And the sounds that instantly emerge are enough to confirm that there is to be no winding down for John's eighth decade on Planet Earth. Whilst the main theme of the music of track 1 is in a regular nine beat pattern, that is child's play compared to the sections that wrap around the memorable spine of the tune.

The opening is led by Ranjit who, with an incomprehensible rhythm, supports John's semiquaver (eighth notes) playing at 9.2 notes per second; that's a basic timing of 552 semiquavers per minute. Trying to divide the first 54 seconds into bars is pointless as John uses the call-and-answer technique to converse with Etienne and Gary. The latter play together in unison with impeccable timing, while John uses sentences that, like any good language, are unequal in length but grammatically correct. At 0.55 the piece settles into its basic 9/4 rhythm, a metre that would be enough to confound many listeners. For me, mathematics is the only true explanation. It takes 3.91 seconds for one bar of 9 crotchets (quarter notes) music containing 36 semiquavers, with a crotchet length of 0.435 sec. The theme length is three repetitions of 15.6 seconds – a twelve-bar model, rather than a sixteen bar model. Over each four-bar segment, the chords cycle through Dm, A7, C7 and A7, chords that have a very Spanish feel. At 1.42 the composition returns to the opening complex modal passage, which is repeated precisely in 54 seconds, although with entirely different sentences. At 2.36, it's back to basics, although, after the first four bars in which we are reminded of the theme, this is Gary's opportunity to improvise while we all whistle the penetrating bass theme. At 3.22, he takes on the unimaginable task of creating through the first scheme until, at precisely 4.16 the main theme returns once more. Some people could say this is the music of robots or computers rather than humans. Well, those who cannot comprehend this most supreme level of skill, let alone play it, *would* say that, wouldn't they? It is the fact that humans can actually create and play this stuff that is truly awesome. Needless to say, the music continues with this pattern; John takes the lead from 5.10, improvising through the opening section before the familiar bass theme is repeated to the end. Sometimes, I'd give anything to see a copy of John's written music!

The next track is *Riff Raff*. On first hearing, this is no more comprehensible than the last. "Here we go again," I hear you say as I tell you that this too has a metronomic structure, with algorithms for its construction that would be more easily formulated by a computer, it seems. For me, it's like unravelling the mysteries of Stonehenge. As I set about the task, I discover to my dismay that it is even *more difficult* to dissect than *Trancefusion*! The simplest explanation I can give is that there is a motif repeated three times at specific placings through the music. It kicks off with what feels like a heavy rock kick-ass four beat, but before the fourth bar is completed, on a *half* beat (i.e. at the 3½ beat of the fourth bar!) the first of the three motifs appears. Each motif therefore lasts for

15½ beats, about 7 seconds in length. Then follows a passage of length 28.5 secs at the same pace, but with (for me, at least) incalculable bar lengths. The structure becomes even more unfathomable when, later in the tune, three of these 28.5 lengths are added to make sections of exactly 1 minute 25.5 seconds through which the musicians flow as easily as water through a straight downpipe. But don't think that smooth timekeeping is matched by smooth playing. At frequent points during his ferocious improvisations, John plays at over 17 notes per second. And as Gary competes on equal terms with John's wizardry, Etienne and Ranjit are totally together in the impossible rhythmic undergrowth. All in all, this seriously jazz-rock piece is a musical maelstrom without recourse to large numbers of decibels. It compares with anything in the Mahavishnu catalogue and is absolutely stunning.

Track 3, *Echoes of Then*, tries a different approach by overlaying familiar rhythms in such a way that we feel at once as if we are listening to this performance from a seat in John's 4th dimension. To try to dissect this multilayered composite of blues-rock-jazz is like unpicking knots of fresh spaghetti: the smooth and slippery strands are tightly intertwined and refuse to comply with the logic of applied hands. So here, again, we have an aptly titled McLaughlin composition that is comfortable listening, as long as you don't try to understand what is going on.

Wonderfall is a beautifully restful piece played in an implied 3/4 rhythm that it is as heavily disguised as a celebrity at a cinema. No-one is prepared to state the pulse explicitly, although it falls to Etienne's bass to return to base more often than the others. Ranjit seems to play in anything but three-quarter time, though he is clearly locked mentally into the pattern, as are they all. John and Gary flit around like butterflies, ignoring everything except the desire to enjoy their brief times in the sunny world offered by this composition.

The respite is brief as, with *Call And Answer*, John returns to his previous formula of fast, foxing flights of notes and complex phrasing. The overlying pulse pumps at 600 notes per minute – ten per second as John's main theme is presented, and this continues through much of the piece. The rhythm is somewhat simpler, in 4/4 mostly, although the main theme is in two pairings with John and Gary shouting the questions and Gary and Etienne providing the answers. Yet again, the sentences are of varying lengths.

Not Here, Not There is a simple construction that looks inside its harmonic structure for colour and meaning. An essential counterweight to energy-laden onslaught of the previous tracks, this is where we draw breath and chill out. No need to worry about timekeeping for this moderate 4/4 number - just a delightful atmosphere of warm melody and sweet sounds. John's slightly edgy guitar voice is balanced by the bright acoustic style of Gary and makes a fine contrast as the pianist traces his path amongst John's innovative chordal threads. As the piece draws to a close, Gary winds us down with delightfully loose noodling that weaves in and out of Ranjit's pulse and leaves me feeling like I've just had a musical massage.

My cry of "More please," seems answered with the early sound of John's weeping instrument on *Guitar Love*. This one is in 4/4 with 12/8 overlaid – complex enough for most people, but nursery stuff for John & Co. The central idea of a composition that describes being at one with his guitar is exciting, and that's pretty much what is on offer as the love affair becomes ever more intense. The erotic dance is interrupted briefly as Gary takes on a solo with his Hammond organ, but the onus is back on John to provide the flowers and chocolates for an ending that climaxes like all good love affairs should. Indeed, the feeling's so good he gets to double-track his playing!

The final track is *Take It Or Leave It*, a composition that at first seems to be written in a funky 4/4 metre underpinned with a slap bass. However, as it stomps its way through a quite short 3 min 46 sec, the steady 160 beats per minute offer a number of ways of interpreting the metre, one of which is to divide it into a six and two fives. To avoid it becoming a musical abacus, I turn my attention to the lead instruments, whereupon it is unclear whether I am listening to John or Gary on synthesizer, but I must suppose this is John in a rather uncharacteristic style, until, with a minute remaining, I hear his usual guitar chops once more, interspersed by Gary's carefully timed chords. This is a straight, road with high cliffs and no end in sight, and I feel lonely and cold as this brilliant album ends.

In summary, *Now Hear This* is as standard an album as John could make: a collection of brilliant numbers with varied design and melodic content such that the album is never dull. The presence of a single band gives coherence and musicality that *Industrial Zen*, for example, with its mix-and-match formula could not match. Yet this is no ordinary record. Indeed, it exhibits extraordinary skill in times when we abhor virtuosity. This semiquaver soup showcases John's style, and he is shadowed by Mbappé, whose piercing bass support is beautifully mixed so that we can always hear his gloved fingers dancing to John's lead. Ranjit Barot brings his great virtuosity and a supernatural understanding of complex rhythm that makes light of John's demanding genius. Gary Husband's playing now puts him in the premier league of modern keyboardists with not so much as cigarette paper between his nimble keys and John's intuitive bursts. Added to that, his capacity for doubling on drums in no way detracts from (or falls short of) the exuberance of Barot. The result is jazz perfection.

Concluding Remarks

It is unfortunate, but there is a single hard statistic that sums up John McLaughlin's career: Eric Clapton 16 – John McLaughlin 0. This is not the result of some casual game of racquet sport, but the number of Grammys won by the two men. I could use it to argue that John McLaughlin holds the record for the greatest disparity between musical prowess and public acknowledgement. It is the result of some forty years of playing guitar under the spotlight of a very large critical audience. The brutal statistic is, of course, not a fair representation of the skills with the guitar or, indeed, of the musical vision of the artist. It could be argued that the two musicians occupy quite different parts of the musical spectrum, but that is an unsound proposition. If anything, McLaughlin's spectrum encompasses Clapton's and he should be advantaged by it. Pat Metheny is eleven years younger than John, yet his haul of Grammys amounts to a massive 18, the biggest by far for a jazz musician. We should now reflect on the reasons for this disgraceful sleight on John McLaughlin, a great musician by any standards.

McLaughlin, in his 70s as I write this, has a career like a compass rose. The east-west paradigm is obvious. The Indian part of his career is remarkable for the degree to which he immersed himself into the music and culture of a distant land. Nevertheless, he loved it deeply and clearly felt very comfortable with the culture. He could play pure Indian music from either north or south India, and he (a Brit!) played as big a role in the fusion of Indian and American music as any other westerner.

In the north, John proved beyond question that he was able to write and perform classical music as well as anyone. His long association – both professional and personal – with Katia Lebèque nurtured a deep-seated love of classical music that he had been given as a child by his mother. His *Concerto for Guitar and Orchestra* and the *Thieves and Poets* suite are substantial pieces that deserve their places in the repertoire of modern European orchestral music. To the south points John's interest in Spanish and Moorish folk music, played with fantastic brio on his clutch of 'guitar super-trio' CDs. So deep was his understanding of the way Flamenco music was constructed and played that it became a fundamental part of his guitar-ethos.

McLaughlin's western pole is, of course, the sharpest. Here he made a mark that is truly indelible in the history of popular music. For a short period, he was a star as bright as any other guitarist, except perhaps for Jimi Hendrix. The power and intensity of the Mahavishnu Orchestra has probably been matched only by Hendrix's 'Experience' or Cream, but the originality and musicianship of the

Mahavishnu Orchestra output is unparalleled. Today (2013), I believe, John is reaching new heights of achievement with his band, as evidenced by his album *Now Hear This* (2012). It is hard to think of any other musician with such a widely disparate polarity of career, and the amount of middle-ground occupied amongst his repertoire of some 50 albums is very small indeed.

It is true to say that John McLaughlin has not been as influential amongst guitar players as he might have been. His fingerwork was simply too fast for most to get near, but McLaughlin's solo style was also too 'off the wall' for many, heavily focussed on fast furious Flamenco flourishes, a single note style that guitarists find difficult to copy. McLaughlin's Flamenco flourishes must have been formed at an early age in his development for it became an intrinsic part of his style and his 'sound'. He developed it by playing alongside Al di Meola and Paco de Lucia, two guitarists who were similarly expert in the art. The kind of guitar playing that builds on American jazz scales harmonies and structures is less obvious in the European McLaughlin's music than it is in the dictionary of Pat Metheny, the pure-bred man from Missouri. Cook describes McLaughlin's style of improvisation as "more akin to running impetuously through a labyrinth of modes, where the object is to build dazzling edifices of many, many notes." [41] Written that way, Cook seems to be unkind, yet his assessment is accurate. McLaughlin saw his style as being like that of Coltrane who, you will recall, is famous for his 'sheets of sound'. What could be more fundamentally based in jazz than that? First impressions are often that this is too large a factor in his playing. However, the more you listen to McLaughlin's CDs, the more facets to his playing begin to surface, such as his deep understanding of harmony, his love of complex chords that make up the vibrant colours in much of his music, and an extraordinary grasp of some of the most complex rhythms ever invented.

There is no doubt that McLaughlin's career suffered, through no fault of his own, from the reaction against musicianship and virtuosity that resulted from the arrival of punk rock in 1978. The two musical qualities most associated with McLaughlin's guitar playing were killed stone dead and John's public profile was wiped out at a stroke as interest in 'clever music' fell victim to the new craze of 'dumbing-down' that has continued to this day. Stump: "Technique was especially damned: it was deemed exclusive and elitist." [71]

Both Cobham and McLaughlin were made into superstars on the basis of their virtuosity; both also fell victim to the dumbing-down in music. Jazz was forced to revert back to its roots and, led by the Wynton Marsalis quartet of 1982, turned the tide away from jazz-fusion, back towards the swing rhythm-based style of classical jazz of the 1960s and the music of the Miles Davis second great quintet. Those who remained behind became tarred with the 'smooth jazz' brush and the focus for the same kind of abuse that jazz-fusion had attracted.

Nicholson describes McLaughlin's style and tone as unique in the field of jazz guitar. His tone was "hard, cutting and metallic", whilst his style was evenly accented with little syncopation or jazz-swing feel. This was a rock-guitar style that no jazzer other than Coryell had used so far. It made him the most influential jazz guitarist since Wes Montgomery. [72]

Cook [41] says that McLaughlin's career suffered by being too diverse. In a commercial sense, that is undeniable, but, like the others, he was forced to change direction when interest in jazz-rock subsided. He could have chosen to continue along the path with an unbroken line of Mahavishnu Orchestra configurations, but he periodically veered off course, first along the path of Indian sensibilities with Shakti and then by taking up the Spanish acoustic guitar in his fiery Flamenco trios, cutting himself off (if need be) from the movers and shakers at Columbia Records. Evidence in this book shows that it is a characteristic of musicians like McLaughlin, who are 'interdisciplinary', that is, they hop and jump about between different genres. John is currently back where he belongs, at the top of the tree of jazz-fusion. The same could be true of the other jazz-fusion musicians. Hancock, Corea, Zawinul and Shorter all experimented across a broad spectrum of styles and, from time to time, got flak from the jazz puritans for doing so. Perhaps McLaughlin has done it more than the rest, but his contributions in the areas where he gained much success are undiminished by those in which he may have been only slightly less successful. When you are so very special at what you do, people find it hard to accept that you might get to a point when you want to do something else. They expect you to go on and on being great. It is, as we have seen in all of these chapters, impossible. That explains why all of these great musicians attract flak at different times.

A highly intelligent European, John lived in America to develop his career, but later chose France for his domicile, a culture he felt more comfortable with. Ignored by the Grammys, John is virtually unknown outside of the world of jazz. Yet, to many of the cognoscenti, he is the world's greatest guitarist. He could have been as rich as any of the rock guitarists – Santana, Clapton, Page - but is not. There were times when his career reached the highest zenith, others when (according to some) he was truly plumbing the depths. He must be given credit for his steadfastness and artistic integrity in the face of much criticism.

At the 1968 Olympic Games in Mexico City, the athlete Bob Beamon leapt a mind-boggling 8.90 metres - over 29ft. The world was stunned for no human had ever come close. In one jump he had conquered both the 28 ft and 29 ft barriers! His world record stood for 23 years, and was named by Sports Illustrated magazine as one of the five greatest sports moments of the 20th century. No-one could have predicted it, and it was all over in the space of ten seconds. Beamon never again jumped over 27 ft, and his career quickly faded to obscurity. But Beamon will never be forgotten and his feat will remain in the history books forever. In music, an assertion is far more difficult to prove. Walter Kolosky named his book *The Mahavishnu Orchestra - The Greatest Band There Ever Was* and, although it can never be proved, anyone who seriously listens to music will find it hard to disagree with his declaration. At once there comes a barrage of doubt. "How can such a thing be true? How can you say that?" That's what I thought when I first picked up his book. However, when you look inside, you survey a collection of startling accolades that attest to the effect the Mahavishnu Orchestra had on people, many of them premier league musicians. I am therefore inclined to agree with Kolosky, with the annotation that today's band comes very close indeed.

The Mahavishnu Orchestra was the first, fully-fledged jazz-rock fusion band. Yes, there had been many experiments in the late 1960s, but most of the attempts were just that. MO was totally focused on fusing all the elements of jazz and rock into a new musical form. McLaughlin admits that it would not have been possible without his experiences with Davis and Williams, but this was the fully formed birth of a new creature with a life of its own, independent from the ridiculous vocals that had been thought of as a necessary part of the formula and bedevilled recordings by Lifetime, Jack Bruce and Dreams, for example. The ridiculous thing is that these bands left vocals behind when they played gigs. MO proved vocals to be irrelevant; the band's music stood on its own instrumental merit and blew people away comprehensively with virtuosity and musicianship that was beyond compare. MO was also the first fusion band to achieve its proper level of commercial success. Lifetime probably had a similar effect on live audiences, but all we are left with are the poor recordings. With MO's wonderful records, no longer were bands confined to invisibility in underground clubs. In this case, you don't have to take the word of a writer that amazing things were going on in clubs - which they were. You can just go out and buy these records and listen to the stunning music for yourself. These CDs are some of the most important you can buy and still some of the most entertaining.

However, there was, I feel, a single and serious mistake made in the naming of the Mahavishnu Orchestra. There are many people, myself included, who, firmly rooted in western culture, simply did not wish to listen to music from the east. No doubt it was a perfectly logical name for John, but in fact the band's name was perfect for driving many people away from its music. As a young 21-year-old in 1971 I had no interest in Indian culture, even though I had followed the Beatles avidly as they too experimented with yogi and sitar. For many years afterwards, as I imbibed the spirits of American jazz, I had no wish to spend my money on tumblers of Indian tonic. I did not hear the music on radio and TV and it simply passed me by as I experimented with the music of Miles, Herbie, Chick, Joe and Wayne (and Stan Getz!) I was, of course, entirely wrong in my judgement, but the MO's marketing – in whatever form – failed to reach me. That prevented me, at least, from becoming an evangelistic young fan. It must have failed to reach many others like me, for I was just a typical young man at the time. With a different name, so many more fans would have been recruited to the Mahavishnu at an early stage. I now regret that omission in my life, but it's never too late.

Today, my admiration for John McLaughlin is immense. I would like to remind you of John McLaughlin's remarkable achievement in stealing so many five-star ratings from my jealous possession. Unlike Bob Beamon, John was not a one-jump wonder, neither did he fade into obscurity. He went on making extraordinary leaps in unexpected directions, making music of the highest quality – not just in jazz. As a publisher of jazz-fusion books for a number of years, my own experience is that John's fanbase is today more extensive than his peers. As one of the world's greatest exponents of guitar playing, he contributed in a variety of other genres. In so doing, just like Herbie Hancock had done, he attracted severe criticism from two quarters. First, there were those with vested commercial interests, who would themselves lose out in some way. Second, were those well-meaning fans that greatly admired his jazz work, but felt he was wasting his talent by not continuing the quest for new frontiers in jazz. Nevertheless, between his periodic sojourns away from the jazz pot-boiler, McLaughlin continued to promote jazz-fusion, arguably better than anyone else, by the many recordings I have described above. Today, in 2013, his work with his band John McLaughlin and the 4th Dimension is solidifying into a new and unparalleled level of excellence in 21st century jazz-fusion. For me, there is no question that Johnny McLaughlin, electric guitarist, is the uncontested Father of Jazz-Fusion. Period!

References

Apart from this, there are three other books about John McLaughlin. The first is by Paul Stump and is entitled *Go Ahead John, The Music of John McLaughlin*, SAF Publishing, 2000. This book is comprehensive and very analytical. It has no index, but does have an excellent discography and, for those interested in the life and work of this master guitarist, it is an essential read, even if the book has attracted some intense adverse criticism.

The second is Walter Kolosky's book about the Mahavishnu Orchestra entitled *Power, Passion and Beauty – The Story of the Legendary Mahavishnu Orchestra*, published by Abstract Logix Books, Cary North Carolina, 2006. This is an excellent source of material about the early period of McLaughlin's career, but does not cover the later part. It is especially good for first-hand quotes from a large number of the people. Written by an enthusiastic fan, it is inevitably biased and rather eccentric in places. Nevertheless, this unique book does convey an excellent sense of the band's impact on the music world, as well as the excitement and novelty of the late 60s and 70s, something that is not acquired simply from listening to recordings. The details of the Mahavishnu albums are comprehensive, but unfortunately this book also has no index which renders it useless as a quick source of reference.

Kolosky has, to some degree, made up for these deficiencies with his 2010 publication *Follow Your Heart John McLaughlin Song By Song A Listeners Guide*, which reviewers have given a long list of glowing references.

Stuart Nicholson's book, *Jazz Rock: A History*, Schirmer Books, New York, 1998, is a standard work on the broader subject, although now out of print. It contains a substantial amount of original material on John McLaughlin's career.

[1] Interview by Paul Gallan, First published in *GRAMBO*, issue 28, July, 1993.
[2] Stump p159
[3] Richard Cook, *Jazz Encyclopedia*, Penguin Books, 2005, p415
[4] Nicholson, p138
[5] Miles Davis with Quincy Troupe, *Miles: The Autobiography*, Picador, 1989, p286
[6] Gene Santoro, sleeve notes for *Apocalypse*, Columbia Legacy CD edition, 1990
[7] John McLaughlin in *John McLaughlin's Jazz Odyssey, Jazz Times*, May 1982, p12; http://www.italway.it/morrone/jml-jazzodyssey.htm
[8] www.45cat.com/record/r5024
[9] John McLaughlin talking to Chuck Berg, *Down Beat,* Vol 45: No 12, 15 June 1978, p15

[10] Kolosky, p15
[11] John McLaughlin talking to Chuck Berg, *Down Beat,* Vol 45: No 12, 15 June 1978, p16
[12] John McLaughlin, Sleeve notes, *Extrapolation*, Polydor, 1969
[13] Ian Carr, *Miles Davis: The Definitive Biography*, Harper Collins, 1999, p244
[14] Niladri Kumar, *Meeting of the Minds - The Making of Floating Point*, DVD, Mediastarz / Abstract Logix 2008
[15] Nicholson, p139
[16] Stump, p46
[17] John McLaughlin talking to Chuck Berg, *Down Beat,* Vol 45: No 12, 15 June 1978, p47
[18] Steven Roby, *Black Gold: The Lost Archives of Jimi Hendrix*, 288 pages, 1 March, 2002, Billboard Books; ISBN: 082307854X
[19] John McLaughlin, Interview for *Guitar Player* magazine, September 1975, http://www.angelfire.com/jazz/jm5/jmjh.html
[20] Kolosky, p1
[21] Kolosky, p52
[22] Kolosky, p58
[23] Kolosky, p60
[24] Kolosky, p63
[25] Kolosky, p89
[26] Kolosky, p68
[27] Kolosky, p100
[28] Mark Gilbert, in Barry Kernfeld (ed), *Blackwell Guide to Recorded Jazz*, Blackwell, Oxford, UK, 2nd edn, 1995, p484
[29] Stephen Davis, *Walk this Way – the Autobiography of Aerosmith*, Avon Books, 1997, 187-8
[30] Kolosky, p102
[31] Kolosky, p100
[32] Bill Bruford
[33] Kolosky, p96
[34] Kolosky, p122
[35] Nicholson, p150
[36] Kolosky, p165
[37] Stump, p66
[38] Stump, p64
[39] Stump, p74
[40] Stump, p75
[41] Richard Cook, *Jazz Encyclopedia*, Penguin Books, 2005, p415
[42] John McLaughlin, Interview for *Guitar Player* magazine, September 1975; http://www.guitarplayer.com/article/john-mclaughlin/Aug-07/31018
[43] [http://www.georgeduke.com/1960s.html

[44] Nicholson p153
[45] Stump, p83
[46] Stump, p89
[47] John Ephland, sleeve notes to *Shakti*, Columbia, 1975
[48] Bill Milkowski, sleeve notes to *Trio of Doom*, Columbia Legacy, 2007; interview #23, abstractlogix.com, 16/4/04
[49] Stump, p107
[50] Stump, p104
[51] Stump, p123
[52] Stump, p125
[53] Stump, p129
[54] Stump, p128
[55] Stump, p128
[56] Nicholson, p154
[57] Stump p130
[58] John McLaughlin: sleeve notes to *The Mediterranean Concerto for Guitar and Orchestra*, CBS, 1990
[59] Stump, p142
[60] John McLaughlin, sleeve notes to *Time Remembered*, Verve, 1993.
[61] Wikipedia biography; http://www.wikipedia.com
[62] Stump, p147-8
[63] Stump, p154
[64] John McLaughlin, sleeve notes to *The Believer*, Verve, 2000
[65] John McLaughlin, sleeve notes to *Thieves and Poets, Verve*, 2003
[66] www.garyhusband.com
[67] www.etiennembappe.com
[68] www.miledolbear.com
[69] www.julianjoseph.com
[70] www.drummerworld.com
[71] Stump, p158ff
[72] Nicholson, p146

Discography

John McLaughlin
***** 1969 Extrapolation
CD Polydor 841598-2, UIN/UPC: 042284159821
Length: (40.37)
Musicians: John McLaughlin (guitar), John Surman (saxophone), Tony Oxley (drums), Brian Odges (bass)
Tracks: 1 Extrapolation (2.57), 2 It's Funny (4.25), 3 Arjen's Bag (4.25), 4 Pete the Poet (5.00), 5 This is For Us To Share (3.30), 6 Spectrum (2.45), 7 Binky's Beam (7.05), 8 Really to Know (4.25), 9 Two for Two (3.35), 10 Peace Piece (1.50)
Recorded: 18 January, 1969
Notes: The album was recorded at Advision Studios in London and released on Marmalade Records. All subsequent releases were on the Polydor label. It was not released in the USA until 1972, after the success of the Mahavishnu Orchestra.

The Tony Williams Lifetime
* 1969 Emergency
CD Verve 314 539 117 2 UIN/UPC: 731453911727
Length: (70.35)
Musicians: Tony Williams (drums), John McLaughlin (guitar), Larry Young aka Khalid Rasin (organ)
Tracks: 1 Emergency (9.35), 2 Beyond Games (8.17), 3 Where (12.10), 4 Vashkar (4.59), 5 Via The Spectrum Road (7.49), 6 Spectrum (8.50), 7 Sangria For Three (13.07), 8 Something Special (5.37)
Recorded: 26-28 May 1969

The Tony Williams Lifetime
* 1970 Turn It Over
CD Verve 314 539 118-2 UIN/UPC: 731453911826
Length: (38.35)
Musicians: Tony Williams (drums), John McLaughlin (guitar), Larry Young aka Khalid Rasin (organ), Jack Bruce (bass)
Tracks: 1 To Whom It May Concern - Them (4.20), 2 To Whom It May Concern - Us (2.55), 3 This Night, This Song (3.44), 4 Big Nick (2.43), 5 Right On (1.49), 6 Once I Loved (5.08), 7 Vuelta Abajo (4.57), 8 A Famous Blues (4.10), 9 Allah Be Praised (4.36), 10 One World (3.45)
Recorded: 1970
Notes: Jack Bruce plays on 10, which was not included on the original album.

John McLaughlin
* 1970 Marbles
CD Brook BROOK 1040, UIN/UPC: 883717700506
Length: (35.30)
Musicians: John McLaughlin (guitar), Buddy Miles (drums) Billy Rich (bass), Larry Young aka Khalid Rasin (organ)
Tracks: 1 Marbles (4.13), 2 Devotion (11.22), 3 Don't Let The Dragon Eat You Mother (5.14), 4 Purpose of When (4.42), 5 Dragon Song (4.12), 6 Siren (5.44)
Recorded: Feb 1970
Notes: Originally issued as the album Devotion (1970).

John McLaughlin
* 1970 Devotion
CD CHARLY SNAP 232 CD, UIN/UPC: 803415123223
Length: (35.17)
Musicians: John McLaughlin (guitar), Larry Young aka Khalid Rasin (organ), Buddy Miles (drums), Billy Rich (bass)
Tracks: 1 Devotion (4.11), 2 Dragon Song (5.37), 3 Marbles (5.13), 4 Siren (4.42), 5 Don't Let the Dragon Eat Your Mother (4.12), 6 Purpose of When (11.22)
Recorded: Feb 1970
Notes: Originally published on the Douglas label. Re-released on the Brook label as Marbles (2006).

John McLaughlin, John Surman, Karl Berger, Stu Martin, Dave Holland
** 1971 Where Fortune Smiles
CD Dawn Records ARC 7129, UIN/UPC: n/a
Length: (35.17)
Musicians: John McLaughlin (guitar), John Surman (saxophone), Dave Holland (bass), Stu Martin (drums), Karl Berger (vibraphone)
Tracks: 1 Glancing Backwards (For Junior) (8.54), 2 Earth Bound Hearts (4.15), 3 Where Fortune Smiles (4.01), 4 New Place, Old Place (10.24), 5 Hope (7.19)
Recorded: May, 1970

John McLaughlin
** 1971 My Goal's Beyond
CD Douglas AD-03, UIN/UPC: 3660341122297
Length: (41.41)
Musicians: John McLaughlin (guitar), Dave Liebman (saxophone), Jerry Goodman (violin), Charlie Haden (bass), Eve McLaughlin (tamboura), Billy Cobham (drums), Airto Moreira (percussion), Badal Roy (percussion)
Tracks: 1 Peace One (7.15), 2 Peace Two (12.18), 3 Goodbye Pork Pie Hat (3.15), 4 Something Spiritual (3.35), 5 Hearts and Flowers (2.05), 6 Phillip Lane

(3.35), 7 Waltz for Bill Evans (2.00), 8 Follow Your Heart (3.17), 9 Song for My Mother (3.30), 10 Blue in Green (2.37)
Recorded: Mar, 1971

Mahavishnu Orchestra
***** 1971 The Inner Mounting Flame
CD Columbia Legacy CK 65523, UIN/UPC: 5099706552321
Length: (46.31)
Musicians: John McLaughlin (guitar), Rick Laird (bass), Jan Hammer (keyboard), Jerry Goodman (violin), Billy Cobham (drums)
Tracks: 1 Meeting of the Spirits (6.52), 2 Dawn (5.10), 3 Noonward Race (6.28), 4 A Lotus on Irish Streams (5.39), 5 Vital Transformation (6.16), 6 The Dance of Maya (7.17), 7 You Know, You Know (5.07), 8 Awakening (3.32)
Recorded: 21 July 1971

John McLaughlin and Carlos Santana
** 1973 Love Devotion Surrender
CD Columbia 468871-2, UIN/UPC: 9399746887121
Length: (38.52)
Musicians: John McLaughlin (guitar), Carlos Santana (guitar), Larry Young aka Khalid Rasin (organ), Doug Rauch (bass), Don Alias (percussion), Jan Hammer (keyboard), Billy Cobham (drums), Michael Shrieve (drums), James (Mingo) Lewis (percussion), Armando Peraza (percussion)
Tracks: 1 A Love Supreme (7.46), 2 Naima (3.12), 3 The Life Divine (9.22), 4 Let Us Go Into the House of the Lord (15.43), 5 Meditation (2.38)
Recorded: October 1972, March 1973

Mahavishnu Orchestra
***** 1973 Birds of Fire
CD Columbia Legacy CK 66081, UIN/UPC: 5099706608127
Length: (40.24)
Musicians: John McLaughlin (guitar), Rick Laird (bass), Jan Hammer (keyboard), Jerry Goodman (violin), Billy Cobham (drums)
Tracks: 1 Birds of Fire (5.43), 2 Miles Beyond (4.40), 3 Celestial Terrestrial Commuters (2.55), 4 Sapphire Bullets of Pure Love (0.21), 5 Thousand Island Park (3.20), 6 Hope (1.55), 7 One Word (9.55), 8 Sanctuary (5.02), 9 Open Country Joy (3.53), 10 Resolution (2.09)
Recorded: August, 1972

Mahavishnu Orchestra
**** 1999 The Lost Trident Sessions
CD Columbia Legacy CK 65959, UIN/UPC: 5099706595922
Length: (39.44)

Musicians: John McLaughlin (guitar), Rick Laird (bass), Jan Hammer (keyboard), Jerry Goodman (violin), Billy Cobham (drums)
Tracks: 1 Dream (11.06), 2 Trilogy: The Sunlit Path, La Mere de la Mer, Tomorrow's Story Not the Same (9.30), 5 Sister Andrea (6.43), 6 I Wonder (3.07), 7 Steppings Tones (3.09), 8 John's Song (5.53)
Recorded: June 1973

Mahavishnu Orchestra
***** 1973 Between Nothingness and Eternity
CD Columbia 32766, UIN/UPC: 07464327662
Length: (42.24)
Musicians: John McLaughlin (guitar), Rick Laird (bass), Jan Hammer (keyboard), Jerry Goodman (violin), Billy Cobham (drums)
Tracks: 1 Trilogy Medley, The Sunlit Path, La Mere de la Mer, Tomorrow's Story Not the Same (12.16), 2 Sister Andrea (8.44), 3 Dream (21.24)
Recorded: August, 1973

Mahavishnu Orchestra
*** 1974 Apocalypse
CD Columbia Legacy CK 46111, UIN/UPC: 07464461112
Length: (52.11)
Musicians: John McLaughlin (guitar), Jean-Luc Ponty (violin), Gayle Moran (voice), Ralph Armstrong (bass), Marsha Westbrook (viola), Carol Shive (violin), Phillip Hirsch (cello), Narada Michael Walden (drums), Michael Tilson Thomas (conductor), London Symphony Orchestra (orchestra)
Tracks: 1 Power of Love (4.13), 2 Vision is a Naked Sword (14.18), 3 Smile of the Beyond (8.00), 4 Wings of Karma (6.06), 5 Hymn to Him (19.19)
Recorded: March, 1974

Mahavishnu Orchestra
*** 1975 Visions of the Emerald Beyond
CD Columbia Legacy COL 467904-2, UIN/UPC: 5099746790424
Length: (40.23)
Musicians: John McLaughlin (guitar), Jean-Luc Ponty (violin), Narada Michael Walden (drums), Gayle Moran (voice), Ralph Armstrong (bass), Stephen Kindler (violin), Carol Shive (violin), Phillip Hirsch (cello), Bob Knapp (trumpet), Russel Tubbs (saxophone)
Tracks: 1 Eternity's Breath I (3.10), 2 Eternity's Breath II (4.48), 3 Lila's Dance (5.34), 4 Can't Stand Your Funk (2.09), 5 Pastoral (3.41), 6 Faith (2.00), 7 Cosmic Strut (3.28), 8 If I Could See (1.18), 9 Be Happy (3.31), 10 Earth Ship (3.42), 11 Pegasus (1.48), 12 Opus 1 (0.15), 13 On the Way Home to Earth (4.34)
Recorded: 4-14 December, 1974

Shakti
** 1975 Shakti with John McLaughlin
CD Columbia COL 467905-2, UIN/UPC: 5099746790523
Length: (52.05)
Musicians: John McLaughlin (guitar), L. Shankar (violin), R V Raghavan (mridangam), T H (Vikku) Vinayakaram (ghatam), Zakir Hussain (tabla)
Tracks: 1 Joy (18.15), 2 Lotus Feet (4.46), 3 What Need Have I For This (29.04)
Recorded: 5 July, 1975

Mahavishnu Orchestra
** 1976 Inner Worlds
CD Columbia Legacy 476905-2, UIN/UPC: 5099747690525
Length: (44.06)
Musicians: John McLaughlin (guitar), Ralph Armstrong (bass), Narada Michael Walden (drums), Stu Goldberg (keyboard)
Tracks: 1 All in the Family (6.01), 2 Miles Out (6.44), 3 In My Life (3.22), 4 Gita (4.28), 5 Morning Calls (1.23), 6 The Way of the Pilgrim (5.15), 7 River of my Heart (3.41), 8 Planetary Citizen (2.14), 9 Lotus Feet (4.24), 10 Inner Worlds Pt 1 and 2 (6.33)
Recorded: 1976

Shakti
*** 1976 A Handful of Beauty
CD Columbia COL 494448-2, UIN/UPC: 5099749444829
Length: (47.55)
Musicians: John McLaughlin (guitar), L. Shankar (violin), T H (Vikku) Vinayakaram (ghatam), Zakir Hussain (tabla)
Tracks: 1 La Danse du Bonheur (4.50), 2 Lady L (7.28), 3 India (12.38), 4 Kriti (3.00), 5 Isis (15.13), 6 Two Sisters (4.43)
Recorded: August, 1976

Shakti
**** 1977 Natural Elements
CD Columbia 489773-2, UIN/UPC: 5099748977328
Length: (39.30)
Musicians: John McLaughlin (guitar), L. Shankar (violin), T H (Vikku) Vinayakaram (ghatam), Zakir Hussain (tabla)
Tracks: 1 Mind Ecology (5.47), 2 Face to Face (5.57), 3 Come on Baby Dance With Me (1.56), 4 The Daffodil and the Eagle (7.00), 5 Happiness is Being Together (4.27), 6 Bridge of Sighs (3.52), 7 Get Down and Sruti (7.00), 8 Peace of Mind (3.22)

John McLaughlin
*** 1978 Johnny McLaughlin - Electric Guitarist
CD Columbia CK 46110, UIN/UPC: 07464461102
Length: (38.53)
Musicians: John McLaughlin (guitar), Stanley Clarke (bass), Chick Corea (keyboard), Jack DeJohnette (drums), Jack Bruce (bass), Tony Williams (drums), Billy Cobham (drums), Stu Goldberg (keyboard), Fernando Saunders (bass), Jerry Goodman (violin), Tom Coster (organ), Carlos Santana (guitar), Neil Jason (bass), Narada Michael Walden (drums), Alyrio Lima (percussion), Armando Peraza (percussion), David Sanborn (saxophone), Alphonso Johnson (bass), Tony Smith (drums), Patrice Rushen (keyboard)
Tracks: 1 New York on my Mind (5.45), 2 Friendship (7.00), 3 Every Tear from Every Eye (6.50), 4 Do You Hear the Voices You Left Behind? (7.39), 5 Are You the One? Are You the One? (4.41), 6 Phenomenon: Compulsion (3.21), 7 My Foolish Heart (3.22)
Recorded: January, February, 1978

John McLaughlin, Jaco Pastorius, Tony Williams
*** 2007 Trio of Doom
CD Columbia Legacy 82796964502, UIN/UPC: 827969645024
Length: (39.39)
Musicians: John McLaughlin (guitar), Jaco Pastorius (bass), Tony Williams (drums)
Tracks: 1 Drum Improvisation (Live) (2.46), 2 Dark Prince (Live) (6.36), 3 Continuum (Live) (5.11), 4 Para Oriente (Live) (5.42), 5 Are You the One, Are You The One? (Live) (4.51), 6 Dark Prince (Studio) (4.11), 7 Continuum (Studio) (3.49), 8 Para Oriente Alt Take 1 (Studio) (1.05), 9 Para Oriente Alt Take 2 (Studio) (0.20), 10 Para Oriente (Studio) (5.28)
Recorded: 3 and 8 March, 1978

John McLaughlin with the One Truth Band
*** 1979 Electric Dreams
CD Columbia Legacy 472210-2, UIN/UPC: 5099747221026
Length: (39.03)
Musicians: John McLaughlin (guitar), Stu Goldberg (keyboard), L. Shankar (violin), Fernando Sanders (bass), Tony Smith (drums), Alyrio Lima (percussion), David Sanborn (saxophone)
Tracks: 1 Guardian Angels (0.52), 2 Miles Davis (4.54), 3 Electric Dreams, Electric Sighs (6.27), 4 Desire and the Comforter (7.35), 5 Love and Understanding (6.39), 6 Singing Earth (0.38), 7 The Dark Prince (5.17), 8 The Unknown Dissident (6.18)
Recorded: November, December, 1978
Notes: David Sanborn plays on 8.

Al DiMeola, John McLaughlin, Paco De Lucia
*** 1981 Friday Night in San Francisco
CD Columbia Legacy COL 489007-2, UIN/UPC: 5099748900722
Length: (41.10)
Musicians: John McLaughlin (guitar), Paco de Lucia (guitar), Al di Meola (guitar)
Tracks: 1 Mediterranean Sundance / Rio Ancho (11.31), 2 Short Tales of the Black Forest (8.43), 3 Frevo Rasgado (7.55), 4 Fantasia Suite (8.50), 5 Guardian Angel (4.01)
Recorded: 5 December, 1980

John McLaughlin
*** 1981 Belo Horizonte
CD Warner Bros Jazz Masters 8122-73755-2, UIN/UPC: 081227375522
Length: (37.27)
Musicians: John McLaughlin (guitar), Katia Labeque (keyboard), Francois Couturier (keyboard), Francois Jeaneau (saxophone), John Paul Celea (bass), Paco de Lucia (guitar), Tommy Campbell (drums), Jean Pierre Drouet (percussion), Steve Sheman (percussion), Augustin Dumay (violin)
Tracks: 1 Belo Horizonte (4.28), 2 La Baleine (5.57), 3 VeryEarly (Homage to Bill Evans) (1.12), 4 One Melody (6.27), 5 Stardust on your Sleeve (6.01), 6 Waltz for Katia (3.25), 7 Zamfir (5.46), 8 Manitas d'Oro (For Paco de Lucia) (4.11)
Recorded: June, July, 1981

John McLaughlin
*** 1982 Music Spoken Here
CD Warner Bros WEA 0630-17157-2, UIN/UPC: 706301715727
Length: (38.31)
Musicians: John McLaughlin (guitar), Katia Labeque (keyboard), Francois Couturier (keyboard), John Paul Celea (bass), Tommy Campbell (drums)
Tracks: 1 Aspan (5.39), 2 Blues for L. W. (6.20), 3 The Translators (2.37), 4 Honky-Tonk Haven (4.07), 5 Viene Clareando (0.28), 6 David (7.44), 7 Negative Ions (3.51), 8 Brise de Coeur (5.19), 9 Loro (2.08)
Recorded: June, July, 1982

John McLaughlin, Al di Meola, Paco de Lucia
** 1983 Passion Grace and Fire
CD Phillips 811 334-2, UIN/UPC: 042281133428
Length: (31.49)
Musicians: John McLaughlin (guitar), Al di Meola (guitar), Paco de Lucia (guitar)

Tracks: 1 Aspan (4.08), 2 Orient Blue (7.05), 3 Chiquito (4.42), 4 Sichia (3.48), 5 David (6.29), 6 Passion, Grace and Fire (5.26)

Mahavishnu Orchestra
**** 1984 Mahavishnu
CD Wounded Bird WOU 5190, UIN/UPC: 664140519022
Length: (42.01)
Musicians: John McLaughlin (guitar), Billy Cobham (drums), Jonas Hellborg (bass), Bill Evans (sax) (saxophone), Mitch Forman (keyboard), Danny Gottlieb (drums), Katia Labeque (keyboard), H P Chaurasia (bansuri), Zakir Hussain (tabla)
Tracks: 1 Radio-Activity (6.54), 2 Nostalgia (5.58), 3 Nightriders (3.50), 4 East Side, West Side (4.49), 5 Clarendon Hills (6.00), 6 Jazz (1.45), 7 The Unbeliever (2.50), 8 Pacific Express (6.32), 9 When Blue Turns to Gold (3.23)
Recorded: April, May, 1984

John McLaughlin and Mahavishnu
**** 1986 Adventures in Radioland
CD Verve 519 397-2, UIN/UPC: 731451939723
Length: (41.28)
Musicians: John McLaughlin (guitar), Bill Evans (saxophone), Mitch Forman (keyboard), Jonas Hellborg (bass), Danny Gottlieb (drums), Abraham Wechter (guitar)
Tracks: 1 The Wait (5.35), 2 Just Ideas (2.00), 3 Jozy (5.25), 4 Half Man - Half Cookie (2.56), 5 Florianapolis (5.21), 6 Gotta Dance (4.18), 7 The Wall Will Fall (6.00), 8 Reincarnation (2.57), 9 Mitch Match (3.54), 10 20th Century Ltd (2.31)
Recorded: January, February, 1986

John McLaughlin
**** 1990 The Mediterranean Concerto for Guitar and Orchestra
CD CBS MK 45578, UIN/UPC: 07464455782
Length: (61.09)
Musicians: John McLaughlin (guitar), Katia Labeque (keyboard), Michael Tilson Thomas (conductor), London Symphony Orchestra (orchestra), Michael Gibbs (orchestrator)
Tracks: 1 Concerto for Guitar and Orchestra - The Mediterranean - I Rhythmic (11.58), 2 II - Slow and Sad (15.34), 3 III - Animato (8.36), 4 Brise de Coeur (7.45), 5 Montana (4.28), 6 Two Sisters (3.53), 7 Until Such Time (4.29), 8 Zakir (4.13)
Recorded: July 1988

John McLaughlin Trio
**** 1990 Live at the Royal Festival Hall
CD Winter & Winter JMT 919 035-2, UIN/UPC: 025091903528
Length: (64.15)
Musicians: John McLaughlin (guitar), Kai Eckhardt (bass), Trilok Gurtu (percussion)
Tracks: 1 Blue in Green (5.28), 2 Just Ideas (1.40), 3 Jozy (3.28), 4 Florianapolis (14.35), 5 Pasha's Love (7.16), 6 Mother Tongues (18.37), 7 Blues for L.W. (8.25)
Recorded: 27 November, 1989

John McLaughlin Trio
*** 1992 Que Allegria
CD Verve 837 280-2, UIN/UPC: 042283728028
Length: (64.43)
Musicians: John McLaughlin (guitar), Trilok Gurtu (percussion), Dominique di Piazza (bass), Kai Eckhardt (bass)
Tracks: 1 Belo Horizonte (6.34), 2 Baba (for Ramana Maharshi) (6.50), 3 Reincarnation (11.52), 4 1 Nite Stand (5.26), 5 Marie (1.58), 6 Hijacked (8.34), 7 Mila Repa (7.31), 8 Que Alegria (10.31), 9 3 Willows (5.14)
Recorded: 29 November 1991 to 12 March, 1992

John McLaughlin
** 1993 Time Remembered - John McLaughlin Plays Bill Evans
CD Verve 519 861-2, UIN/UPC: 731451986123
Length: (40.06)
Musicians: John McLaughlin (guitar), Yan Maresz (guitar), Francois Szony (guitar), Pascal Rabatti (guitar), Alexandre Del Fa (guitar), Philippe Loli (guitar)
Tracks: 1 Prologue (2.14), 2 Very Early (4.20), 3 Only Child (5.06), 4 Waltz for Debby (4.55), 5 Homage (2.16), 6 My Bells (3.22), 7 Time Remembered (3.59), 8 Song for Helen (1.54), 9 Turn Out the Stars (6.26), 10 We Will Meet Again (4.20), 11 Epilogue (1.14)
Recorded: 25-30 March 1993

The Free Spirits featuring John McLaughlin
*** 1994 Tokyo Live
CD Verve 521 870-2, UIN/UPC: 731452187024
Length: (74.51)
Musicians: John McLaughlin (guitar), Dennis Chambers (drums), Joey DeFrancesco (keyboard)
Tracks: 1 1 Nite Stand (7.05), 2 Hijacked (10.25), 3 When Love is Far Away (4.56), 4 Little Miss Valley (10.56), 5 Juju at the Crossroads (5.15), 6 Vuhovar (12.11), 7 No Blues (4.27), 8 Mattinale (19.42)

Recorded: 16, 18 December, 1993

John McLaughlin
** 1995 Molom - A Legend of Mongolia
CD Verve 529 034-2, UIN/UPC: 731452903426
Length: (58.23)
Musicians: John McLaughlin (guitar), Trilok Gurtu (percussion)
Tracks: 1 Um Mani Padme Hum (1.19), 2 Molom Theme Song 1 (3.19), 3 The Boy's Theme 1 (2.19), 4 Breakfast - The Cave (5.48), 5 The Four Seasons (0.33), 6 Horses (4.22), 7 Boudamchou (2.07), 8 Little Girl's Theme 1 (2.56), 9 Cows in the Water (1.09), 10 The Man Hunts (1.43), 11 The Camel Walk (1.02), 12 Hunting - the Witch (4.41), 13 The Boy Walks (1.02), 14 Melody (4.02), 15 The Dream of the Boy (1.56), 16 The Boy Cries (1.26), 17 Traditional Song (2.59), 18 Introduction of the Boy to the Monk (3.42), 19 The Little Girl Says Goodbye to the Boy (1.10), 20 The Boy Leaves (5.02), 21 National Song (1.36), 22 Molom Theme Song end (4.17)
Recorded: February, 1994

John McLaughlin
*** 1995 After the Rain
CD Universal 80100660, UIN/UPC: 5050801006607
Length: (57.14)
Musicians: John McLaughlin (guitar), Joey DeFrancesco (keyboard), Elvin Jones (drums)
Tracks: 1 Take the Coltrane (6.01), 2 My Favourite Things (6.16), 3 Sing Me Softly of the Blues (6.31),   4 Encuentros (7.32), 5 Naima (4.43), 6 Tones for Elvin Jones (6.34), 7 Crescent (7.41), 8 Afro Blue (6.54), 9 After the Rain (4.54)
Recorded: 4, 5 October, 1994

John McLaughlin
**** 1996 The Promise
CD Verve 529 828-2, UIN/UPC: 731452982827
Length: (73.35)
Musicians: John McLaughlin (guitar), Jeff Beck (guitar), Tony Hymas (keyboard), Pino Palladino (bass), Mark Mondesir (drums), Joey DeFrancesco (keyboard), Dennis Chambers (drums), Yan Maresz (guitar), Paco de Lucia (guitar), Al di Meola (guitar), Michael Brecker (saxophone), Jim Beard (keyboard), James Genus (bass), Don Alias (percussion), Zakir Hussain (tabla), Trilok Gurtu (percussion), Nishat Khan (sitar), Sting (bass), Vinnie Colaiuta (drums), David Sanborn (saxophone), Philippe Loli (guitar)
Tracks: 1 Django (7.24), 2 Thelonius Melodius (5.22), 3 Amy and Joseph (2.28), 4 No Return (7.20), 5 El Ciego (9.10), 6 Jazz Jungle (14.45), 7 The Wish (8.39), 8 English Jam (1.12), 9 Tokyo Decadence (0.39), 10 Shin Jin Rui (10.47), 11

The Peacocks (5.53)
Recorded: 1995

Paco De Lucia, Al Di Meola, John McLaughlin
** 1996 The Guitar Trio
CD Verve 533 215-2, UIN/UPC: 731453321526
Length: (53.02)
Musicians: John McLaughlin (guitar), Paco de Lucia (guitar), Al di Meola (guitar)
Tracks: 1 La Estiba (5.51), 2 Beyond the Mirage (6.10), 3 Midsummer Night (4.36), 4 Manha de Carnaval (6.11), 5 Letter from India (3.54), 6 Espiritu (5.30), 7 Le Monastère dans les Montagnes (6.15), 8 Azzura (7.58), 9 Cardeosa (6.36)
Recorded: June, July, 1996

John McLaughlin
**** 1997 The Heart of Things
CD Verve 539 153-2, UIN/UPC: 731453915329
Length: (47.16)
Musicians: John McLaughlin (guitar), Gary Thomas (saxophone), Matthew Garrison (bass), Jim Beard (keyboard), Dennis Chambers (drums)
Tracks: 1 Acid Jazz (8.19), 2 Seven Sisters (10.17), 3 Mr D. C. (7.07), 4 Fallen Angels (9.29), 5 Healing Hands (7.36), 6 When Love is Far Away (4.34)
Recorded: 1997

Remember Shakti
*** 1999 Remember Shakti
2 CD Verve 559 945-2, UIN/UPC: 731455994520
Length: (132.22)
Musicians: John McLaughlin (guitar), Zakir Hussain (tabla), H P Chaurasia (bansuri), T H (Vikku) Vinayakaram (ghatam), Uma Metha (tanpura)
Tracks: 1 Chandrakauns (33.36), 2 The Wish (18.48), 3 Lotus Feet (7.21), 4 Mukti (63.31), 5 Zakir (9.06)
Recorded: 24-27 September 1997

John McLaughlin
***** 1998 The Heart of Things Live in Paris
CD Verve 543 536-2, UIN/UPC: 731454353625
Length: (77.37)
Musicians: John McLaughlin (guitar), Dennis Chambers (drums), Gary Thomas (saxophone), Matthew Garrison (bass), Otmaro Ruiz (keyboard), Victor Williams (percussion)
Tracks: 1 Seven Sisters (8.30), 2 Mother Tongues (12.57), 3 Fallen Angels (10.33), 4 The Divide (16.41), 5 Tony (13.56), 6 Acid Jazz (14.53)

Recorded:4, 5 November, 1998

Remember Shakti
** 2000 The Believer
CD Verve 549 044-2, UIN/UPC: 731454904421
Length: (77.11)
Musicians: John McLaughlin (guitar), Zakir Hussain (tabla)
U Shrinivas (guitar), V Selvaganesh (kanjira)
Tracks: 1 5 in the Morning, 6 in the Afternoon (18.13), 2 Ma No Pa (14.56), 3 Lotus Feet (7.07), 4 Maya (13.40), 5 Anna (10.35), 6 Finding the Way (12.40)
Recorded: 1999

Remember Shakti
** 2001 Saturday Night in Bombay
CD Universal Music S.A. France 014 164-2, UIN/UPC: 044001416422
Length: (61.58)
Musicians: John McLaughlin (guitar), Zakir Hussain (tabla)
U Shrinivas (guitar), V Selvaganesh (kanjira), Shankar Mahadevan (voice), Sivamani (percussion), Debashish Bhattacharya (slide guitar), Bhavani Shankar (dholak), Roshan Ali (dholak), Aziz (dholak), Taufiq Qureshi (percussion), A K Pallanivel (tavil)
Tracks: 1 Luki (5.39), 2 Shringar (26.38), 3 Giriraj Sudha (10.45), 4 Bell'Alla (18.48)
Recorded: 8, 9 December, 2000

John McLaughlin
** 2003 Thieves and Poets
CD Universal Music France 0602498010754, UIN/UPC: 602498010754
Length: (44.20)
Musicians: John McLaughlin (guitar), I Pommeriggi Musicali di Milano (orchestra), Renato Rivolta (conductor), Viktoria Mullova (violin), Philippe Loli (guitar), Matt Haimovitz (cello), Paul Meyer (clarinet), Bruno Frumento (percussion), Yan Maresz (guitar), Marcus Wippersberg (programming), Olivier Fautrat (guitar), Francois Szony (guitar), Alexandre Del Fa (guitar), Helmut Schartlmueller (guitar)
Tracks: 1 Thieves and Poets Pt 1 (12.36), 2 Thieves and Poets Pt 2 (8.18), 3 Thieves and Poets Pt 3 (5.38), 4 My Foolish Heart (5.03), 5 The Dolphin (4.16), 6 Stella By Starlight (4.26), 7 My Romance (4.09)
Recorded: June, 2002

John McLaughlin
**** 2006 Industrial Zen
CD Verve 9839328, UIN/UPC: 602498393284

Length: (61.26)
Musicians: John McLaughlin (guitar), Bill Evans (sax) (saxophone), Gary Husband (keyboard), Hadrian Feraud (bass), Mark Mondesir (drums), Eric Johnson (guitar), Vinnie Colaiuta (drums), Ada Rovatti (saxophone), Dennis Chambers (drums), Zakir Hussain (tabla), Tony Grey (bass), Matthew Garrison (bass), Marcus Wippersberg (programming), Otmaro Ruiz (keyboard), Shankar Mahedevan (voice)
Tracks: 1 For Jaco (5.15), 2 New Blues Old Bruise (7.14), 3 Wayne's Way (7.06), 4 Just So Only More So (9.56), 5 To Bop or Not To Be (6.41), 6 Dear Dalai Lama (12.28), 7 Señor CS (7.38), 8 Mother Nature (5.08)
Recorded: 2005

John McLaughlin
***** 2008 Floating Point
CD Mediastarz/Abstract Logix ABLX 011, UIN/UPC: 827912075106
Length: (62.28)
Musicians: John McLaughlin (guitar), Louiz Banks (keyboard), Ranjit Barot (drums), Sivamani (percussion), Hadrian Feraud (bass), George Brooks (saxophone), Debashish Bhattacharya (slide guitar), Shashank (flute), Shankar Mahedevan (voice), U Rajesh (mandolin), Naveen Kumar (flute), Niladri Kumar (electric sitar)
Tracks: 1 Aggaji (for Alla Rakha) (9.01), 2 Raju (8.21), 3 Maharina (6.09), 4 Off the One (6.55), 5 The Voice (9.19), 6 Inside Out (8.30), 7 1 4 U (7.07), 8 Five Peace Band (7.06)
Recorded: April, 2007
Notes: George Brooks plays on 1; Debashish Bhattacharya plays on 2; Shashank plays on 4; Shankar Mahedevan sings on 5; U Rajesh plays on 6; Naveen Kumar plays on 7; Niladri Kumar plays on 8.

John McLaughlin
**** 2008 Meeting of the Minds - The Making of Floating Point [DVD]
DVD Mediastarz/Abstract Logix 827912075090, UIN/UPC: 827912075090
Length: (90.00)
Musicians: John McLaughlin (guitar), Louiz Banks (keyboard), Ranjit Barot (drums), Debashish Bhattacharya (slide guitar), Naveen Kumar (flute), Niladri Kumar (electric sitar), U Rajesh (mandolin), Shankar Mahedevan (voice), Shashank (flute), Sivamani (percussion)
Tracks: 1 Inside Out (15.00), 2 Raju (15.00), 3 The Voice (15.00), 4 Five Peace Band (15.00), 5 Off the One (15.00), 6 1 4 U (15.00)
Recorded: April, 2007

John McLaughlin and the 4th Dimension
**** 2009 Live @ Belgrade [DVD]

DVD Mediastarz/Abstract Logix ABLX016, UIN/UPC: 82791208737
Length: (104.00)
Musicians: Eve McLaughlin (tamboura), Gary Husband (keyboard), Mark Mondesir (drums), Dominique di Piazza (bass)
Tracks: 1 Señor CS (12.32), 2 Little Miss Valley (10.55), 3 Nostalgia (7.03), 4 Raju (11.55), 6 Maharina (6.59), 7 Hi-Jacked (10.13), 8 The Unknown Dissident (9.22), 9 5 Peace Band / Mother Tongues (23.34), 5 Sully (7.54)
Recorded: 16 May, 2008
Notes: Recorded at Dvoranan Dom Sindikata, Belgrade by Radio Television of Serbia.

Chick Corea and John McLaughlin
***** 2009 Five Peace Band
CD Concord Records 0888072313972, UIN/UPC: 888072313972
Length: (139.00)
Musicians: Chick Corea (keyboard), John McLaughlin (guitar), Kenny Garrett (saxophone), Christian McBride (bass), Vinnie Colaiuta (drums)
Tracks: 1 Raju (12.29), 2 The Disguise (13.32), 3 New Blues, Old Bruise (14.06), 4 Hymn to Andromeda (27.45), 5 Dr Jackle (22.53), 6 Senor CS (20.15), 7 In a Silent Way / It's About That Time (20.06), 8 Someday My Prince Will Come (7.42)
Recorded: September, October 2008

John McLaughlin and the 4th Dimension
**** 2010 To The One
CD Mediastarz/Abstract Logix ABLX 027, UIN/UPC: 700261290829
Length: (40.04)
Musicians: John McLaughlin (guitar), Gary Husband (keyboard), Etienne Mbappé (bass), Mark Mondesir (drums)
Tracks: 1 Discovery (6.16), 2 Special Beings (8.38), 3 The Fine Line (7.43), 4 Lost and Found (4.26), 5 Recovery (6.21), 6 To The One (6.34)
Recorded: 2009

John McLaughlin and the 4th Dimension
***** 2012 Now Hear This
CD Mediastarz/Abstract Logix ABLX 037, UIN/UPC: 7002613595570
Length: (49.59)
Musicians: John McLaughlin (guitar), Ranjit Barot (drums), Gary Husband (keyboard), Etienne Mbappe (bass)
Tracks: 1 Trancefusion (7.16), 2 Riff Raff (7.02), 3 Echoes From Then (6.07), 4 Wonderfall (6.27), 5 Call And Answer (5.53), 6 Not Here Not There (6.17), 7 Guitar Love (7.08), 8 Take It Or Leave It (3.46)
Recorded: 2012

BOX SETS

John McLaughlin
**** 2007 Original Album Classics (5 CD Box Set)
5 CD Columbia 886971454529, UIN/UPC: 886971454529
Length: (217.26)
Musicians: John McLaughlin (guitar)
Tracks: 1 Album: Shakti (52.05), 2 Album: A Handful of Beauty (47.55), 3 Album: Natural Elements (39.30), 4 Album: Electric Guitarist (39.03), 5 Album: Electric Dreams (38.53)
Recorded: July, 1975 to December, 1978

Recording Career of John McLaughlin

John plays on some or all tracks of the following albums. Years quoted are those in which the albums were first released.

1969 *Extrapolation* by John McLaughlin: Polydor (841598-2)
1969 *Super Nova* by Wayne Shorter: Blue Note (CDP 7 84332-2)
1969 *Emergency!* by The Tony Williams Lifetime: Verve (314 539 117 2)
1969 *In A Silent Way* by Miles Davis: Columbia (CBS-450982-2)
1969 *Infinite Search* by Misoslav Vitous: Atlantic ATS ST 05520 (Italy)/Embryo SD 524 (USA). Re-released on LP in 1972 by Atlantic (SD 1622) as *Mountain In The Clouds*.
1970 *Marbles* by John McLaughlin: Brook (BROOK 1040)
1970 *Things We Like* by Jack Bruce: Polydor (0656042)
1970 *Moto Grosso Feio* by Wayne Shorter: Blue Note / One Way Records (BN-LA 014-G / S21 17373)
1970 *Turn It Over* by The Tony Williams Lifetime: Verve (314 539 118-2)
1970 *Devotion* by John McLaughlin: CHARLY (SNAP 232 CD)
1970 *Solid Bond* by Graham Bond Organisation: Rhino / Warner (8122799065)
1970 *Spaces* by Larry Coryell: Vanguard (VMD 79345)
1970 *Bitches Brew* by Miles Davis: Columbia (G2K 40577)
1970 *Purple* by Miroslav Vitous: Sony (J) (SOPC 57101-J)
1971 *The Inner Mounting Flame* by Mahavishnu Orchestra: Columbia Legacy (CK-65523)
1971 *Live-Evil* by Miles Davis: Columbia (C2K-65135)
1971 *My Goal's Beyond* by John McLaughlin: Douglas (AD-03)
1971 *A Tribute To Jack Johnson* by Miles Davis: Columbia (CK-519264)
1971 *Innovations* by Duffy Power: Transatlantic Records (TRA 229)
1971 *Where Fortune Smiles* by John McLaughlin, John Surman, Karl Berger: Dawn Records (ARC 7129)
1971 *Escalator Over The Hill* by Carla Bley and Paul Haines: ECM / Watt (1802)
1972 *On The Corner* by Miles Davis: Columbia (CK-63980)
1973 *Love Devotion Surrender* by John McLaughlin and Carlos Santana: Columbia (468871-2)
1973 *Welcome* by Santana: Columbia Legacy (511130-2)
1973 *Between Nothingness and Eternity* by Mahavishnu Orchestra: Columbia (32766)
1973 *Birds of Fire* by Mahavishnu Orchestra: Columbia Legacy (CK 66081)
1974 *Apocalypse* by Mahavishnu Orchestra: Columbia Legacy (CK 46111)
1974 *Big Fun* by Miles Davis: Columbia (C2K-63973)
1974 *Get Up With It* by Miles Davis: Columbia (C2K-63970)
1975 *Metamorphosis* by the Rolling Stones: ABKCO

1975 *Shakti* with John McLaughlin by Shakti: Columbia (COL 467905-2)
1975 *Journey To Love* by Stanley Clarke: Epic (EPC 468221 2)
1975 *Visions of the Emerald Beyond* by Mahavishnu Orchestra: Columbia Legacy (COL 467904-2)
1976 *Inner Worlds* by Mahavishnu Orchestra: Columbia Legacy (476905-2)
1976 *A Handful of Beauty* by Shakti: Columbia (COL 494448-2)
1976 *School Days* by Stanley Clarke: Epic (EPC 468219 2)
1977 *Natural Elements* by Shakti: Columbia (489773-2)
1978 *Johnny McLaughlin - Electric Guitarist* by John McLaughlin: Columbia (CK 46110)
1979 *Electric Dreams* by John McLaughlin with the One Truth Band: Columbia Legacy (472210-2)
1979 *Circle in the Round* by Miles Davis: Columbia (COL 467898 2)
1981 *Belo Horizonte* by John McLaughlin: Warner Bros Jazz Masters (8122-73755-2)
1981 *Friday Night in San Francisco* by Al DiMeola, John McLaughlin, Paco De Lucia: Columbia Legacy (COL 489007-2)
1982 *Music Spoken Here* by John McLaughlin: Warner Bros WEA (0630-17157-2)
1983 *Passion Grace and Fire* by John McLaughlin, Al di Meola, Paco de Lucia: Phillips (811 334-2)
1984 *Mahavishnu* by Mahavishnu Orchestra: Wounded Bird (WOU 5190)
1985 *The Alternative Man* by Bill Evans: Blue Note (CDP 7 46336-2)
1985 *You're Under Arrest* by Miles Davis: Columbia (468703-2)
1986 *Adventures in Radioland* by John McLaughlin and Mahavishnu: Verve (519 397-2)
1986 *Round Midnight* by Dexter Gordon / Herbie Hancock: Columbia Legacy (507924-2)
1986 *The Other Side of Round Midnight* by Dexter Gordon: Blue Note (CDP 7 46397 2)
1987 *Making Music* by Zakir Hussain: ECM (1349)
1989 *Aura* by Miles Davis: Columbia (463351-2)
1990 *Live at the Royal Festival Hall* by John McLaughlin Trio: Winter&Winter JMT (919 035-2)
1990 *The Mediterranean Concerto for Guitar and Orchestra* by John McLaughlin: CBS (MK 45578)
1992 *Black Devil* by Miles Davis: Beech Marten (BM 053/2)
1992 *Que Allegria* by John McLaughlin Trio: Verve (837 280-2)
1993 *Time Remembered* - John McLaughlin Plays by John McLaughlin: Verve (519 861-2)
1994 *Tokyo Live* by The Free Spirits featuring John McLaughlin: Verve (521 870-2)
1995 *Molom - A Legend of Mongolia* by John McLaughlin: Verve (529 034-2)

1995 *After the Rain* by John McLaughlin: Universal (80100660)
1996 *The Promise* by John McLaughlin: Verve (529 828-2)
1996 *The Guitar Trio* by Paco De Lucia, Al Di Meola, John McLaughlin: Verve (533 215-2)
1997 *The Heart of Things* by John McLaughlin: Verve (539 153-2)
1998 *The Complete Bitches Brew Sessions* by Miles Davis: Columbia (COL 516251-2)
1998 *The Heart of Things Live in Paris* by John McLaughlin: Verve (543 536-2)
1999 *The Lost Trident Sessions* by Mahavishnu Orchestra: Columbia Legacy (CK-65959)
1999 *Remember Shakti* by Remember Shakti: Verve (559 945-2)
2000 *The Believer* by Remember Shakti: Verve (549 044-2)
2001 *The Complete In A Silent Way Sessions* by Miles Davis: Columbia (C3K-65362)
2001 *At La Villette* by Miles Davis: JVC (JVC 493) [DVD]
2001 *Saturday Night in Bombay* by Remember Shakti: Universal Music S.A. France (014 164-2)
2003 *The Complete Jack Johnson Sessions* by Miles Davis: CBS (C5K86359)
2003 *Thieves and Poets* by John McLaughlin: Universal Music France (0602498010754)
2005 *The Cellar Door Sessions* 1970 by Miles Davis: Columbia (C6K 93614)
2006 *Industrial Zen* by John McLaughlin: Verve (9839328)
2007 *Trio of Doom* by John McLaughlin, Jaco Pastorius, Tony: Columbia Legacy (82796964502)
2007 *Original Album Classics* (5 CD Box Set) by John McLaughlin: Columbia (886971454529)
2008 *Floating Point* by John McLaughlin: Mediastarz/Abstract Logix (ABLX 011)
2008 *Meeting of the Minds - The Making of Floating Point* by John McLaughlin: Mediastarz/Abstract Logix (827912075090) [DVD]
2008 *The Complete On The Corner Sessions* by Miles Davis: Sony / BMG (88697062392)
2009 *Five Peace Band* by Chick Corea and John McLaughlin: Concord Records (0888072313972)
2009 *Live @ Belgrade* by John McLaughlin and the 4th Dimension: Mediastarz/Abstract Logix (ABLX 016) [DVD]
2010 *To The One* by John McLaughlin and the 4th Dimension: Mediastarz/Abstract Logix (ABLX 027)
2012 *Now Hear This* by John McLaughlin and the 4th Dimension: Mediastarz/Abstract Logix (ABLX 037

John McLaughlin's Recordings with Miles Davis

February 18, 1969
Personnel: Miles Davis, Wayne Shorter, Joe Zawinul, Chick Corea, Herbie Hancock, John McLaughlin, Dave Holland, Tony Williams,
Location: Columbia Studio B, NYC
Tracks: Shhh / Peaceful; In a Silent Way (rehearsal); In a Silent Way; It's About That Time; Shhh / Peaceful (LP version); In a Silent Way / It's About That Time (LP version)
On albums: The Complete in a Silent Way Sessions; In a Silent Way

February 20, 1969
Personnel: Miles Davis, Wayne Shorter, Joe Zawinul, Chick Corea, Herbie Hancock, John McLaughlin, Dave Holland, Joe Chambers,
Location: Columbia Studio B, NYC
Tracks: The Ghetto Walk; Early Minor
On albums: The Complete in a Silent Way Sessions

August 19, 1969
Personnel: Miles Davis, Bennie Maupin, Wayne Shorter, Chick Corea, Joe Zawinul, John McLaughlin, Dave Holland, Harvey Brooks, Jack DeJohnette, Lenny White, Don Alias, Jim Riley,
Location: Columbia Studio B, NYC
Tracks: John McLaughlin, Bitches Brew, Sanctuary, Pharaoh's Dance (rehearsal), Orange Lady (rehearsal)
On albums: Bitches Brew, The Complete Bitches Brew Sessions

August 20, 1969
Personnel: Miles Davis, Bennie Maupin, Wayne Shorter, Chick Corea, Joe Zawinul, John McLaughlin, Dave Holland, Harvey Brooks, Jack DeJohnette, Don Alias, Jim Riley,
Location: Columbia Studio B, NYC
Tracks: Miles Runs the Voodoo Down
On albums: Bitches Brew, The Complete Bitches Brew Sessions

August 21, 1969
Personnel: Miles Davis, Bennie Maupin, Wayne Shorter, Chick Corea, Joe Zawinul, Larry Young, John McLaughlin, Dave Holland, Harvey Brooks, Jack DeJohnette, Lenny White, Don Alias, Jim Riley,
Location: Columbia Studio B, NYC
Tracks: Pharaoh's Dance; Spanish Key
On albums: Bitches Brew, The Complete Bitches Brew Sessions

November 19, 1969
Personnel: Miles Davis, Bennie Maupin, Steve Grossman, Chick Corea, Herbie Hancock, Khalil Balakrishna, John McLaughlin, Ron Carter, Harvey Brooks, Billy Cobham, Bihari Sharma, Airto Moreira
Location: Columbia Studio E, NYC
Tracks: Great Expectations, Orange Lady, Yaphet, Corrado
On albums: Big Fun; The Complete Bitches Brew Sessions

November 28, 1969
Personnel: Miles Davis, Bennie Maupin, Steve Grossman, Larry Young, Chick Corea, Herbie Hancock, Khalil Balakrishna, John McLaughlin, Dave Holland, Harvey Brooks, Jack DeJohnette, Billy Cobham, Bihari Sharma, Airto Moreira
Location: Columbia Studio E, NYC
Tracks: Trevere, The Big Green Serpent, The Little Blue Frog (alternate take), The Little Blue Frog (master take) (edited)
On albums: The Complete Bitches Brew Sessions

January 27, 1970
Personnel: Miles Davis, Bennie Maupin, Wayne Shorter, Chick Corea, Joe Zawinul, Khalil Balakrishna, John McLaughlin, Dave Holland, Billy Cobham, Jack DeJohnette, Airto Morcira
Location: Columbia Studio B, NYC
Tracks: Lonely Fire, Guinnevere, His Last Journey (rehearsal)
On albums: Big Fun; Circle in the Round, The Complete Bitches Brew Sessions

January 28, 1970
Personnel: Miles Davis, Bennie Maupin, Wayne Shorter, Chick Corea, Joe Zawinul, John McLaughlin, Dave Holland, Billy Cobham, Jack DeJohnette, Airto Moreira
Location: Columbia Studio B, NYC
Tracks: Feio, Double Image
On albums: The Complete Bitches Brew Sessions

February 6, 1970
Personnel: Miles Davis, Wayne Shorter, Chick Corea, Joe Zawinul, John McLaughlin, Dave Holland, Jack DeJohnette, Billy Cobham, Airto Moreira
Location: Columbia Studio B, NYC
Tracks: Recollections, Take It or Leave It, Gemini / Double Image
On albums: The Complete Bitches Brew Sessions; Live/Evil

February 18, 1970
Personnel: Miles Davis, Bennie Maupin, Chick Corea, John McLaughlin, Sonny Sharrock, Dave Holland, Jack DeJohnette,
Location: Columbia Studio B, NYC
Tracks: Willie Nelson
On albums: A Tribute to Jack Johnson, The Complete Jack Johnson Sessions

February 27, 1970
Personnel: Miles Davis, Steve Grossman, John McLaughlin, Dave Holland, Jack DeJohnette,
Location: Columbia Studio B, NYC
Tracks: Willie Nelson, Johnny Bratton
On albums: Directions, The Complete Jack Johnson Sessions

March 3, 1970
Personnel: Miles Davis, Steve Grossman, John McLaughlin, Dave Holland, Jack DeJohnette,
Location: Columbia Studio B, NYC
Tracks: Archie Moore, Go Ahead John
On albums: Big Fun, The Complete Jack Johnson Sessions

March 17, 1970
Personnel: Miles Davis, Wayne Shorter, Benny Maupin, John McLaughlin, Dave Holland, Billy Cobham,
Location: Columbia Studio C, NYC
Tracks: Duran
On albums: The Complete Jack Johnson Sessions

March 20, 1970
Personnel: Miles Davis, Steve Grossman, John McLaughlin, Dave Holland, Lenny White,
Location: Columbia Studio B, NYC
Tracks: Sugar Ray
On albums: The Complete Jack Johnson Sessions

April 7, 1970
Personnel: Miles Davis, Steve Grossman, Herbie Hancock, John McLaughlin, Michael Henderson, Billy Cobham,
Location: Columbia Studio B, NYC
Tracks: Right Off, Yesternow
On albums: A Tribute to Jack Johnson, The Complete Jack Johnson Sessions

May 19, 1970
Personnel: Miles Davis, Steve Grossman, Keith Jarrett, Herbie Hancock, John McLaughlin, Michael Henderson, Gene Perla, Billy Cobham, Airto Moreira,
Location: Columbia Studio C, NYC
Tracks: Honky Tonk, Ali
On albums: Get Up With It, The Complete Jack Johnson Sessions

May 21, 1970
Personnel: Miles Davis, Keith Jarrett, John McLaughlin, Jack DeJohnette, Airto Moreira,
Location: Columbia Studio C, NYC
Tracks: Konda
On albums: Directions, The Complete Jack Johnson Sessions

May 27, 1970
Personnel: Miles Davis, Keith Jarrett, Herbie Hancock, John McLaughlin, Michael Henderson, Airto Moreira, Hermeto Pascoal
Location: Columbia Studio C, NYC
Tracks: Nem Um Talvez
On albums: The Complete Jack Johnson Sessions

June 4, 1970
Personnel: Miles Davis, Steve Grossman, Chick Corea, Keith Jarrett, Herbie Hancock, John McLaughlin, Dave Holland, Jack DeJohnette, Airto Moreira
Location: Columbia Studio C, NYC
Tracks: The Mask, Pt. 1, The Mask, Pt. 2, The Mask
On albums: Live/Evil, The Complete Jack Johnson Sessions

December 19, 1970
Personnel: Miles Davis, Gary Bartz, Keith Jarrett, John McLaughlin, Michael Henderson, Jack DeJohnette, Airto Moreira,
Location: Cellar Door, Washington, DC
Tracks: Directions, Honky Tonk, What I Say, Directions, Improvisation 4, Inamorata, Sanctuary, It's About That Time
On albums: Live Evil, The Cellar Door Sessions

June 1, 1972
Personnel: Miles Davis, Dave Liebman, Harold Williams, Chick Corea, Herbie Hancock, Collin Walcott, John McLaughlin, Michael Henderson, Jack DeJohnette, Al Foster, Billy Hart, Badal Roy
Location: Columbia Studios, NYC
Tracks: On the Corner, New York Girl, Thinkin' One Thing and Doin' Another, Vote for Miles, Black Satin

On albums: On the Corner, The Complete On The Corner Sessions

January 10-14, 1985
Personnel: Miles Davis, Robert Irving, John McLaughlin, Darryl Jones, Vincent Wilburn, Steve Thornton,
Location: Record Plant Studios, NYC
Tracks: Ms. Morrisine, Katia Prelude, Katia
On albums: You're Under Arrest

January 31- February 4, 1985
Personnel: Miles Davis, Palle Bolvig, Perry Knuden, Benny Rosenfeld, Idrees Sulieman, Jens Winther, Jens Engel, Ture Larsen, Vincent Nilsson, Ole Kurt Jensen, Axel Windfeld, Niels Eje,, Per Carsten, Bent Jaedig, Uffe Karskov, Flemming Madsen, Jesper Thilo, Lillian Thornquist, Thomas Clausen, Kenneth Knudsen, Ole Koch-Hansen, John McLaughlin, Bjarne Roupe, Niels-Henning Orsted Pedersen, Bo Stief, Lennart Gruvstedt, Vincent Wilburn, Marilyn Mazur, Ethan Weisgaard, Eva Hess Thaysen, Palle Mikkelborg
Location: Easy Sound Studios, Copenhagen, Denmark
Tracks: White, Orange, Violet
On albums: Aura

July 10, 1991
Personnel: Miles Davis, Wayne Shorter, Bill Evans, Kenny Garrett, Jackie McLean, Steve Grossman, Chick Corea, Herbie Hancock, Deron Johnson, Joe Zawinul, John McLaughlin, John Scofield, Joe "Foley" McCreary, Dave Holland, Richard Patterson, Darryl Jones, Ricky Wellman, Al Foster
Location: La Grande Halle de la Villette, Paris, France
Tracks: Katia, Jean Pierre
On albums: Black Devil

Index

1 4 U, 125, 163
1 Nite Stand, 102, 104, 159
3 Willows, 103, 159
4th Dimension (band), 8, 12, 126, 128, 135, 139, 147, 163, 164, 168
5 Peace Band / Mother Tongues, 164
A Famous Blues, 28, 151
A Handful of Beauty, 7, 69, 98, 155, 167
A Lotus on Irish Streams, 40, 153
A Love Supreme, 14, 54, 153
A Remark You Made, 115
A Tribute To Jack Johnson, 166
Abercrombie, John, 37
Acid Jazz, 111, 117, 161
Adventures in Radioland, 8, 87, 93, 96, 99, 102, 158, 167
Afro Blue, 106, 160
After the Rain, 8, 106, 160, 168
Aggaji (for Alla Rakha), 124, 163
Aighetta guitar quartet, 103
Al Jarreau, 56
Ali, Roshan, 162
Alias, Don, 34, 108, 109, 153, 160, 169
All in the Family, 64, 155
Allah Be Praised, 28, 151
Amandla, 104
Amy and Joseph, 107, 160
And the Wind Cries Mary, 45
Apocalypse, 7, 55, 59, 60, 97, 148, 154, 166
Apostolic Studios NYC, 31
Archie Moore, 171
Are You the One? Are You the One?, 74, 78
Arista Records, 65
Armstrong, Ralphe, 154, 155
As We Speak, 77
Aspan, 84, 86, 157, 158
Auger, Brian, 13, 37
Aura, 167, 173
Awakening, 41, 153
Aziz, 162
Azzura, 110, 161
Baba (for Ramana Maharshi), 159
Bacharach, Burt, 97
Bailey, Derek, 32
Baker, Peter (Ginger), 13, 14, 21
Balakrishna, Khalil, 170

Banks, Louiz, 123, 125, 163
Barot, Ranjit, 123, 131, 139, 140, 141, 142, 163, 164
Bartz, Gary, 172
Basie, William Allen, 9, 35
Be Happy, 61, 154
Beamon, Bob, 145, 147
Beard, James Arthur, 93, 108, 109, 111, 112, 114, 127, 160, 161
Beatles (band), 13, 23, 32, 38, 56, 146
Beck, Gordon, 15
Beck, Jeff, 21, 63, 107, 136, 137, 160
Beck, Joe, 23
Belgrade, 8, 126, 128, 163, 164, 168
Bell, Jean, 63
Belo Horizonte, 7, 81, 82, 84, 86, 101, 157, 159, 167
Beneath the Mask, 133
Benson, George, 23, 35
Berger, Karl, 7, 31, 152, 166
Berklee Music College, 20, 36, 37, 81, 98
Berlin, Jeff, 98, 101
Berry, Chuck, 41, 80, 102
Between Nothingness and Eternity, 7, 45, 48, 154, 166
Beyond Games, 25, 151
Beyond the Mirage, 109, 161
Bhattacharya, Debashish, 119, 124, 162, 163
Big Fun, 31, 166, 170, 171
Big Nick, 28, 151
Bill Evans, 20, 34, 36, 37, 82, 83, 87, 90, 92, 94, 103, 104, 121, 122, 158, 163, 167, 173
Birdfingers, 52
Birds of Fire, 7, 45, 59, 153, 166
Bitches Brew, 23, 24, 64, 76, 166, 168, 169, 170
Black Devil, 167, 173
Black Satin, 172
Bley, Carla, 26, 166
Bley, Paul, 37
Blue in Green, 34, 99, 100, 153, 159
Blues, 28, 70, 84, 100, 103, 104, 106, 157, 159
Blues for L. W., 103, 157
Blues for L.W., 70, 84, 100, 103, 159
Blues for Pablo, 84

Bollywood, 122
Bolvig, Palle, 173
Bond, Graham, 13, 14, 166
Bossa Nova, 28
Boudamchou, 160
Bowie, David, 15, 136
Braxton, Anthony, 78
Breakfast - The Cave, 160
Brecker, Michael, 88, 121, 160
Brecker, Randy, 35, 52, 127
Bridge of Sighs, 72, 155
Brise de Coeur, 85, 98, 157, 158
Broadbent, Alan, 37
Brooks, George, 163
Brooks, Harvey, 169, 170
Broonzy, Big Bill, 12, 17
Brown, Pete, 17
Brubeck, Dave, 35
Bruce, Jack, 13, 17, 21, 27, 28, 29, 74, 146, 151, 156, 166
Bruford, Bill, 44, 149
Burton, Gary, 21
Butler, Frank, 20
Byrd, Charles L., 82
California, 66
Call And Answer, 141, 164
Campbell, Tommy, 81, 82, 157
Cardeosa, 110, 161
Carey, Mariah, 56
Carnaval, 109
Carr, Ian, 15, 127, 149
Carsten, Per, 173
Carter, Ron, 15, 20, 170
Celea, Jean Paul, 81, 157
Celestial Terrestrial Commuters, 46, 153
Central Park, 48
Chambers, Dennis, 104, 107, 108, 111, 113, 117, 159, 160, 161, 163
Chambers, Joe, 22, 169
Chandrakauns, 118, 161
Chaurasia, Hari Prasad, 158, 161
Chennai, 123, 124
Chick Corea Elektric Band, 87, 111, 131, 133
Chinmoy, Sri, 33, 34, 56, 59, 62, 67, 73
Chiquito, 86, 158
Circle in the Round, 31, 167, 170
Clapton, Eric Patrick, 21, 143
Clarendon Hills, 90, 158
Clark, Petula, 14

Clarke, Stanley, 74, 156, 167
Clausen, Thomas, 173
Clyne, Jeffrey, 127
Cobham, Billy, 11, 31, 34, 35, 52, 56, 60, 74, 87, 92, 111, 121, 127, 136, 152, 153, 154, 156, 158, 170, 171, 172
Colaiuta, Vincent, 108, 130, 131, 160, 163, 164
Cole, Nat King, 35
Coleman, Ornette, 68
Coltrane, John, 33, 53, 54, 55, 68, 106
Columbia Records, 22, 35, 38, 48, 53, 54, 67, 73, 78, 79, 145, 148, 150, 153, 154, 155, 156, 157, 165, 166, 167, 168, 169, 170, 171, 172
Come on Baby Dance With Me, 155
Compulsion, 74
Concerto, 97, 98, 143, 150, 158
Concerto for Guitar and Orchestra - The Mediterranean, 97, 98, 143, 150
Concierto de Aranjuez, 97
Continuum, 78, 121, 156
Corea, Chick, 8, 11, 28, 34, 40, 56, 63, 64, 74, 78, 80, 87, 97, 106, 112, 123, 130, 131, 156, 164, 168, 169, 170, 171, 172, 173
Corrado, 170
Coryell, Larry, 21, 33, 52, 79, 166
Cosey, Peter, 31
Cosmic Strut, 61, 62, 154
Coster, Tom, 74, 156
Couturier, Francois, 157
Cows in the Water, 160
Cream (band), 21, 27, 28, 29, 78, 143
D.C., 113, 127
Dankworth, John, 15
Dark Prince, 77, 78, 156
Davis, Clive, 38, 65
Davis, Miles, 8, 9, 11, 12, 13, 15, 18, 19, 20, 21, 22, 23, 24, 25, 28, 30, 31, 34, 36, 37, 38, 44, 45, 53, 55, 64, 67, 68, 76, 77, 83, 84, 87, 91, 92, 94, 97, 99, 103, 104, 107, 124, 133, 134, 144, 147, 148, 149, 156, 166, 167, 168, 169, 170, 171, 172, 173
Davis, Richard, 21
Dawson, Alan, 20
Day Trip, 131
de Lucia, Paco, 7, 8, 79, 83, 86, 107, 109, 144, 157, 160, 161, 167

Dear Dalai Lama, 121, 163
Decoy, 91
DeFrancesco, Joey, 104, 106, 129, 159, 160
deJohnette, Jack, 20, 21, 22, 74, 156, 169, 170, 171, 172
Del Fa, Alexandre, 159, 162
deLucia, Paco, 79, 83, 86, 107, 109, 144
Dennert, Michael, 36
dePlata, Manitas, 83
Desire and the Comforter, 76, 156
Deuchar, BigPete, 13
Deutsche Kammerphilharmonie, 120
Devotion, 7, 29, 30, 33, 34, 40, 53, 152, 166
di Meola, Al, 144, 157, 160, 161, 167
di Piazza, Dominique, 126, 127, 128, 159, 164
Directions, 31, 171, 172
Django, 12, 107, 160
Dolphy, Eric Allan, 20
Donkey, 88, 91, 92
Double Image, 170
Douglas, Alan, 30, 34
Down, 15, 70, 72, 148, 149, 169
Downbeat (magazine), 19, 69, 101, 104
Doxy, 13
Dr Jackle, 134, 164
Dragon Song, 152
Dream, 49, 51, 136, 154
Dreams, 75, 76, 127, 146
Driscoll, Julie, 13
Drouet, Jean Pierre, 82, 157
Drum Improvisation (Live), 156
drum machines, 96
Duke, George, 55, 62
Dumay, Augustin, 83, 157
Duran, 171
Duster, 21
Dylan, Bob, 33
Early Minor, 169
Earth Bound Hearts, 32, 152
Earth Ship, 61, 154
Echoes, 141, 164
Echoes From Then, 164
Eckhardt, Kai, 85, 98, 101, 102, 159
Ego, 28
Eje, Niels, 173
El Ciego, 107, 160
Electric Dreams, 7, 75, 76, 127, 129, 156, 167
Elegant Gypsy, 79
Elements, 70, 71, 83
Ellington, Ray, 14
Emergency!, 7, 24, 25, 27, 151, 166
Emmerson Lake and Palmer ELP (band), 43, 44
Encuentros, 106, 160
Engel, Jens, 173
Eric, 20, 21, 133, 143, 163
Escalator Over The Hill, 166
Espiritu, 110, 161
Eubanks, Kevin, 137
Eubanks, Robin, 81
Evans, Bill, 158, 163
Evans, Gil, 12, 84
Every Tear from Every Eye, 74, 156
Extrapolation, 7, 15, 16, 26, 27, 34, 42, 46, 149, 151, 166
Face to Face, 71, 155
Fallen Angels, 113, 115, 161
Fame, Georgie, 13, 29
Fantasia Suite, 80, 157
Far Away, 105, 114
Farlow, Tal, 12
Farmer, Arthur, 37
Fautrat, Olivier, 162
Fender Rhodes (keyboard), 41, 42, 74
Feraud, Hadrian, 121, 163
Filles de Kilimanjaro, 15, 45
Finding the Way, 162
Fishman, Larry, 99
Fitzgerald, Ella, 35
Five Peace Band, 8, 124, 129, 130, 163, 164, 168
Flamenco, 12, 18, 80, 83, 105, 143, 144, 145
Flamingo (club), 13
Fleischmann, Ernest, 97
Floating Point, 8, 122, 123, 126, 127, 129, 130, 131, 138, 139, 149, 163, 168
Florianapolis, 94, 99, 158, 159
Follow Your Heart, 34, 148, 153
For Jaco, 121, 135, 163
Forman, Mitchel, 93, 99, 158
Foster, Al, 172, 173
Franklin, Aretha, 56
Freeway of Love, 56
Frevo Rasgado, 80, 157
Friday Night in San Francisco, 7, 79, 119,

157, 167
Frumento, Bruno, 120, 162
Funk, 60, 154
Gambale, Frank, 54
Garrett, Kenny, 130, 131, 164, 173
Garrison, Matthew, 111, 127, 161, 163
Gemini / Double Image, 170
Geneva Switzerland, 71
Genus, James, 108, 160
Get Down and Sruti, 70, 72, 155
Get Up With It, 31, 166, 172
Getz, Stan, 37, 78, 82, 147
Giant Steps, 74
Gibbs, Michael, 15, 56, 98, 158
Gibson (guitar), 30, 65, 67, 93, 94, 119
Gibson Les Paul (guitar), 65, 93
Gillespie, John Birks 'Dizzy', 39, 81
Giriraj Sudha, 119, 162
Gita, 64, 155
Give Peace a Chance, 33
Glancing Backwards (For Junior), 152
Go Ahead John, 148, 171
Godin (guitar), 125, 130
Goldberg, Stu, 63, 73, 75, 155, 156
Goodbye Pork Pie Hat, 34, 152
Goodman, Jerry, 34, 36, 38, 52, 56, 59, 62, 83, 127, 152, 153, 154, 156
Goodrick, Mick, 37
Gordon, Dexter, 167
Gorelick, Kenneth, 130, 131, 164, 173
Gotcha, 129
Gotta Dance, 94, 158
Gottlieb, Danny, 92, 158
Grande Halle de la Villette (concert hall), 133, 173
Grapelli, Stephane, 12
Great Expectations, 170
Greatest Hits, 107, 109
Grey, Tony, 163
Grossman, Steve, 37, 170, 171, 172, 173
Grusin, David, 82
Gruvstedt, Lennart, 173
Guardian Angel, 75, 80, 156, 157
Guardian Angels, 75, 156
Guinnevere, 170
Guitar Love, 142, 164
Gurtu, Trilok, 85, 98, 101, 102, 108, 110, 159, 160
Haden, Charlie, 34, 152
Haimovitz, Matt, 120, 162

Haines, Paul, 166
Half Man - Half Cookie, 158
Hall, Jim, 18
Hammer, Jan, 36, 42, 49, 91, 121, 153, 154
Hancock, Herbie, 11, 20, 21, 61, 64, 65, 91, 96, 123, 134, 147, 167, 169, 170, 171, 172, 173
Happiness is Being Together, 72, 155
Harriott, Joe, 66
Harrison, George, 32, 75
Hart, William, 172
Havana Cuba, 78
Havana Jam, 78
Healing Hands, 113, 161
Hearts and Flowers, 34, 152
Heckstall-Smith, Richard Malden, 9, 14
Hellborg, Jonas, 88, 158
Henderson, Michael, 171, 172
Hendrix, Jimi, 21, 30, 45, 78, 143, 149
Hi-Jacked, 127, 129, 164
Hijacked, 102, 103, 159
Hills, 90
Hirsch, Phillip, 57, 60, 154
His Last Journey, 170
Holdsworth, Allan, 54
Holland, Dave, 7, 15, 19, 20, 22, 30, 31, 64, 152, 169, 170, 171, 172, 173
Holliday, Billie, 35
Hollywood Bowl, 97
Honky Tonk, 85, 172
Honky-Tonk Haven, 157
Hot Rats, 55
Houston, Whitney, 56, 65
Hubbard, Frederick Dewayne, 21, 37
Human Nature, 133
Husband, Gary, 121, 127, 128, 131, 136, 139, 142, 163, 164
Hussain, Zakir, 66, 69, 70, 91, 108, 118, 119, 155, 158, 160, 161, 162, 163, 167
Hutcherson, Bobby, 21
Hymas, Tony, 107, 160
Hymn to Andromeda, 133, 164
Hymn to Him, 58, 154
I Saw Her Standing There, 13
I Wonder, 52, 154
If I Could See, 61, 154
In A Silent Way, 134, 166
In A Silent Way / It's About That Time, 134
Inamorata, 172

177

India, 14, 66, 70, 91, 109, 118, 119, 122, 143, 155
Indo-Jazz Fusions, 66, 68
Indo-Jazz Suite, 66
Industrial Zen, 8, 16, 120, 122, 123, 127, 130, 131, 135, 142, 162, 168
Infinite Search, 24, 166
Inner Worlds, 7, 62, 63, 65, 69, 155, 167
Innovations, 13, 166
Inside Out, 125, 133, 163
Isis, 70, 155
Jaco Pastorius, 7, 37, 78, 101, 121, 156, 168
Jaedig, Bent, 173
Jagger, Mick, 14
Jamaica, 72
James, Robert McElhiney, 82
Jarreau, Al, 56
Jarrett, Keith, 37, 172
Jason, Neil, 74, 156
Jazz Jungle, 108, 112, 113, 160
Jean Pierre, 82, 157, 173
Jeaneau, Francois, 157
Jensen, Ole Kurt, 173
Joel, Billy, 78
John Scofield, 104, 137, 173
Johnny Bratton, 171
Johnny McLaughlin - Electric Guitarist, 156, 167
Johnson, Alphonso, 156
Johnson, Deron, 173
Johnson, Eric, 163
Jones, Darryl, 173
Jones, Elvin, 69, 106, 160
Jones, Tom, 14
Jordan, Clifford, 81
Joseph, Julian, 136, 137
Journey To Love, 167
Jozy, 93, 99, 158, 159
Juju at the Crossroads, 105, 159
Just Ideas, 93, 99, 158, 159
Just So Only More So, 163
Kammerphilharmonie, Deutsche, 120
Karnatic music, 70
Karskov, Uffe, 173
Katia, 70, 81, 82, 83, 84, 85, 86, 91, 98, 143, 157, 158, 173
Keita, Salif, 136
Kenton, Stan, 127
Kermode, Mark, 105

Khan, Nishat, 108, 160
Khayal (Indian), 103
Kilimanjaro, 15, 45
Kind of Blue, 19, 99
Kindler, Stephen, 154
King Crimson (Band), 43, 44
Knapp, Bob, 60, 61, 154
Knudsen, Kenneth, 173
Koch-Hansen, Ole, 173
Konda, 172
Kooper, Al, 24
Kramer, Joey, 43
Kriti, 70, 155
Kumar, Naveen, 125, 163
Kumar, Niladri, 124, 149, 163
La Baleine, 81, 82, 84, 157
La Cigale Paris, 114
La Danse du Bonheur, 69, 155
La Estiba, 109, 161
La Mere de la Mer, 154
La Villette, 168
Labeque, Katia, 157, 158
Lady L, 70, 155
Laird, Rick, 37, 41, 42, 52, 56, 66, 153, 154
Larsen, Ture, 173
Le Faro, Scott, 37
Le, Nguyen, 136
Leadbelly,, 12
LeFaro, Scott, 37
Lennon, John, 33
Let Us Go Into the House of the Lord, 54, 153
Letter from India, 109, 161
Levin, Tony, 37
Lewis, James, 153
Lewis, John, 107
Liebman, Dave, 34, 152, 172
Lifetime, 7, 21, 24, 25, 27, 29, 38, 43, 44, 74, 78, 146, 151, 166
Lima, Alyrio, 74, 75, 156
Little Girl's Theme 1, 160
Little Miss Valley, 105, 127, 128, 159, 164
Little Theatre (club), 31
Live at the Royal Festival Hall, 8, 70, 98, 115, 159, 167
Live-Evil, 166
Loli, Philippe, 109, 120, 159, 160, 162
London Symphony Orchestra, 56, 137, 154, 158

Lonely Fire, 170
Loro, 157
Los Angeles Philharmonic Orchestra, 97
Lost and Found, 138, 164
Lotus Feet, 65, 69, 110, 118, 155, 161, 162
Love and Understanding, 77, 156
Love Devotion Surrender, 153, 166
Low-Lee-Tah, 52
Lowther, Henry, 15
Lucas, Reggie, 31
Luki, 119, 162
Ma No Pa, 162
Macero, Teo, 23
Mademoiselle Mabry, 45
Madsen, Flemming, 173
Mahadevan, Shankar, 119, 124, 162, 163
Maharina, 124, 129, 163, 164
Mahavishnu, 7, 8, 9, 12, 27, 29, 30, 33, 34, 35, 36, 38, 43, 44, 45, 46, 48, 51, 52, 53, 55, 56, 57, 59, 60, 61, 62, 63, 66, 67, 69, 73, 74, 87, 88, 91, 92, 93, 96, 118, 121, 127, 128, 130, 131, 138, 139, 141, 143, 145, 146, 148, 151, 153, 154, 155, 158, 166, 167, 168
Mahavishnu Orchestra (band), 7, 8, 9, 12, 27, 29, 30, 35, 36, 38, 43, 44, 45, 46, 48, 51, 52, 53, 55, 57, 59, 60, 62, 63, 66, 67, 69, 73, 74, 87, 91, 92, 121, 127, 138, 139, 143, 145, 146, 148, 151, 153, 154, 155, 158, 166, 167, 168
Making Music, 119, 167
Mancini, Henry, 80
Mandel, Mike, 52
Manha de Carnaval, 109, 161
Manhattan Transfer (band), 81
Manitas d'Oro (For Paco de Lucia), 157
Marbles, 30, 152, 166
Maresz, Yan, 103, 107, 109, 120, 159, 160, 162
Marienthal, Eric, 133
Marquee (club), 13
Marsalis, Wynton, 144
Martin, George, 23, 56
Martin, Stuart, 7, 31, 152
Mattinale, 105, 159
Maupin, Bennie, 35, 169, 170, 171
Maya, 41, 60, 162
Mayer, John, 66
Mazur, Marilyn, 173
Mbappe, Etienne, 136, 137, 138, 139, 140, 141, 164
M-Base Collective (band), 111
McBride, Christian, 130, 131, 164
McLaughlin, Eve aka Mahalakshmi, 152, 164
McLean, Jackie, 20, 134, 173
Mediterranean Sundance, 80
Mediterranean Sundance / Rio Ancho, 157
Meeting of the Minds, 8, 122, 123, 149, 163, 168
Meeting of the Minds - The Making of Floating Point, 122, 123, 149
Meeting of the Spirits, 38, 153
Melody, 82, 83, 160
Metamorphosis, 14, 166
Metha, Uma, 118, 161
Metheny, Pat, 37, 45, 46, 91, 92, 131, 143, 144
Mexico City, 145
Meyer, Paul, 120, 162
Miami Vice (TV Series), 91
Michael Brecker, 88, 121, 160
Midsummer Night, 109, 161
Mikkelborg, Palle, 173
Mila Repa, 102, 159
Milano, 120
Miles Davis, 7, 8, 9, 11, 12, 13, 15, 18, 19, 20, 21, 22, 23, 24, 25, 27, 28, 30, 31, 34, 36, 37, 38, 44, 45, 53, 55, 64, 67, 68, 76, 77, 83, 84, 87, 91, 92, 94, 97, 99, 103, 104, 107, 124, 133, 134, 144, 147, 148, 149, 153, 155, 156, 166, 167, 168, 169, 170, 171, 172, 173
Miles Ahead, 84
Miles and Coltrane, 15, 124
Miles Beyond, 45, 153
Miles Out, 64, 155
Miles, Buddy, 30, 152
Milestones, 19
Mind Ecology, 71, 155
Mirage, 109
Mitch Match, 95, 158
Mitchell, Mitch, 29
Modern Jazz Quartet, 107
Molom - A Legend of Mongolia, 160, 167
Mondesir, Mark, 107, 121, 127, 128, 131, 136, 139, 160, 163, 164
Monk, Thelonius, 107
Montgomery, John Leslie (Wes), 15, 18, 37, 145

Montreux Jazz Festival, 88
Moran, Gayle, 56, 58, 63, 154
Moreira, Airto, 34, 152, 170, 172
Morning Calls, 64, 155
Mother Nature, 122, 163
Mother Tongues, 100, 115, 129, 159, 161
Moto Grosso Feio, 24, 166
Mountain In The Clouds, 166
Mr D. C., 161
Mraz, George, 36
Mukti, 118, 161
Mullova, Viktoria, 120, 162
Music Spoken Here, 7, 84, 86, 98, 157, 167
Musicali di Milano, I Pommeriggi, 162
My Bells, 104, 159
My Favourite Things, 106, 160
My Foolish Heart, 75, 120, 156, 162
My Goal's Beyond, 152
My Romance, 120, 162
Naima, 54, 106, 153, 160
National Song, 110, 160
Natural Elements, 7, 70, 71, 155, 167
Negative Ions, 85, 157
Nelson Rangell, 125
Nelson, Willie, 171
Nem Um Talvez, 172
New Blues, 121, 130, 131, 163, 164
New Blues Old Bruise, 163
New York, 9, 15, 20, 21, 31, 35, 37, 38, 48, 67, 69, 73, 78, 97, 148, 156, 172
New York Girl, 172
New York on my Mind, 156
Nightriders, 89, 91, 158
Nilsson, Vincent, 173
Nimbler, Jürgen, 120
No Blues, 104, 159
No Return, 107, 160
Noonward Race, 40, 42, 153
North Africa, 133
North Carolina, 148
Nostalgia, 88, 89, 128, 158, 164
Not Here Not There, 164
Now Hear This, 8, 139, 142, 144, 164, 168
Odges, Brian, 15, 17, 19, 151
Off the One, 124, 163
On the Corner, 31, 166, 168, 172, 173
On the Way Home to Earth, 61, 154
Once I Loved, 28, 151
One Melody, 82, 83, 157

One Word, 46, 153
One World, 151
Only Child, 159
Ono, Yoko, 33
Open Country Joy, 47, 153
Opus 1, 61, 154
Orange Lady, 169, 170
Orchestra, London Symphony, 56, 137, 154, 158
Orient Blue, 86, 158
Oriente, 78
Original Album Classics (5 CD Box Set), 165, 168
Out to Lunch, 20
Ovation guitar, 110
Oxley, Tony, 15, 17, 151
Pacific Express, 90, 158
Palladino, Pino, 107, 160
Pallanival, A K, 162
Panama, 35
Para Oriente, 78, 156
Paraphernalia, 127
Parliament/Funkadelic (band), 104
Pascoal, Hermeto, 172
Passion Grace and Fire, 7, 85, 86, 109, 157, 167
Pastorius, Jaco, 7, 37, 78, 101, 121, 156, 168
Patterson, Richard, 173
Payne, Sonny, 35
Peace of Mind, 72, 155
Peace One, 34, 152
Peace Piece, 18, 151
Peace Two, 34, 152
Peacock, Gary, 21
Peacocks, 109
Pearly Gates, 54, 120
Pee Wee, 137
Pegasus, 61, 62, 93, 154
Peraza, Armando, 74, 153, 156
Perhaps, 12, 13, 25, 28, 56, 61, 72, 81, 82, 86, 87, 98, 101, 111, 112, 114, 145
Perry, Joe, 43
Pete the Poet, 17, 151
Peterson, Oscar, 123
Phenomenon, Compulsion, 74, 156
Phi Tech, 99
Phillip Lane, 34, 152
Photon MIDI interface, 99
Planetary Citizen, 65, 155

Polydor Records, 24, 149, 151, 166
Pommeriggi Musicali di Milano, 120
Ponty, Jean-Luc, 55, 62, 93, 154
Power of Love, 57, 154
Power, Duffy, 13, 166
Prince of Darkness, 77
Pukwana, Dudu, 15
Purpose of When, 152
Que Allegria, 81, 159, 167
Qureshi, Taufiq, 162
Rabatti, Pascal, 159
Radio-Activity, 89, 158
Raghavan, Ramnad V, 155
Rajesh, U, 163
Raju, 124, 127, 129, 130, 131, 163, 164
Rangell, Nelson, 125
Rauch, Doug, 153
Really to Know, 18, 151
Record Plant (studio), 30, 173
Reincarnation, 95, 102, 158, 159
Remember Shakti, 8, 98, 118, 119, 161, 162, 168
Rendell, Don, 15
Return to Forever (band), 87, 130
Rheinhardt, Django, 107
Rich, Billy, 30, 152
Rich, Buddy, 37
Riff Raff, 140, 164
Right Off, 18, 30, 171
Right On, 28, 151
Riley, Jim, 169
Rio Ancho, 80
Ritenour, Lee, 82
River of my Heart, 155
Rivers, Sam, 20, 21
Rivolta, Renato, 120, 162
Road to St Ives, 31
Roberts, Tony, 15
Rodrigo, 97
Rolling Stones, 14, 166
Rollins, Sonny, 14, 37, 81
Ronnie Scott's (club), 37
Rosenfeld, Benny, 173
Round Midnight, 97, 167
Round Midnight (movie), 97, 167
Roupe, Bjarne, 173
Rovatti, Ada, 121, 122, 163
Roy, Badal, 34, 152, 172
Royal Festival Hall London, 70, 85, 98, 99, 115

Rubber Soul, 33
Ruiz, Otmaro, 114, 161, 163
Rushen, Patrice, 74, 156
San Francisco, 37, 76, 79, 119
Sanborn, David William, 74, 75, 77, 108, 129, 156, 160
Sanctuary, 47, 153, 169, 172
Sanders, Fernando, 75, 77, 156
Sangria For Three, 151
Santana, Carlos, 7, 53, 74, 104, 134, 153, 156, 166
Santisi, Ray, 36
Sapphire Bullets of Pure Love, 46, 153
Saturday Night in Bombay, 8, 119, 124, 162, 168
Saunders, Fernando, 77, 156
Schartlmueller, Helmut, 162
Schneider, Richard, 83
School Days, 167
Scissor Sisters (band), 61
Scofield, John, 104, 137, 173
Scott, Shirley, 35
Scott, Tom, 129
Sees, Cees, 36
Selvaganesh, V, 162
Sembello, Michael, 77
Senor CS, 16, 122, 127, 164
Sery, Paco, 136
Seven Sisters, 112, 114, 117, 161
Seven Steps to Heaven, 20
Shakti (band), 7, 12, 63, 65, 66, 67, 69, 71, 73, 79, 98, 118, 119, 145, 150, 155, 167, 168
Shakti with John McLaughlin, 7, 66, 155, 167
Shankar, Bhavani, 162
Shankar, Lakshminarayana, 75, 118, 155, 156
Shankar, Ravi, 33
Sharma, Bihari, 170
Sharma, ShivKumar, 119
Sharrock, Sonny, 21, 171
Shashank, 124, 163
Shearing, George, 35
Sheman, Steve, 157
Shhh / Peaceful, 169
Shin Jin Rui, 108, 160
Shive, Carol, 57, 60, 154
Short Tales of the Black Forest, 157
Shorter, Wayne, 11, 20, 24, 53, 77, 93,

166, 169, 170, 171, 173
Shrieve, Michael, 153
Shringar, 119, 162
Shrinivas, U, 162
Sichia, 86, 158
Silver, Horace, 35
Simmons (drums), 93, 96
Simon, Carly, 38
Sinatra, Frank, 35
Sing Me Softly of the Blues, 106, 160
Singing Earth, 77, 156
Sister Andrea, 49, 52, 154
Sivamani, Anandan, 123, 124, 131, 162, 163
Skidmore, Alan, 15
Smile of the Beyond, 58, 154
Smith, Anthony Allen, 74, 75, 156
Smith, Tony, 74, 75
Solid Bond, 13, 166
Someday My Prince Will Come, 135, 164
Something Special, 26, 151
Something Spiritual, 34, 152
Song for Helen, 159
Song for My Mother, 153
Sony Legacy, 78
South Africa, 15
South Hampton College NY, 67
Spaces, 52, 166
Spain, 79, 84, 85
Spanish Key, 169
Special Beings, 137, 164
Spectrum, 17, 26, 151
Spiritual, 34
Spontaneous Music Ensemble (band), 31
Spyrogyra (band), 94
Stanley Clarke, 74, 156, 167
Star People, 91
Stardust, 83, 157
Stardust on your Sleeve, 157
Starsky and Hutch (TV series), 65, 129
Steely Dan (band), 104
Steif, Bo, 173
Stella By Starlight, 162
Steppings Tones, 52, 154
Stern, Mike, 104
Sting, 108, 160
Stuff, 55
Sugar Ray, 171
Sulieman, Idrees, 173
Sullivan, Big Jim, 14

Sully, 129, 164
Sundance, 80
Super Nova, 166
Surman, John, 7, 15, 31, 151, 152, 166
Sydney, 37
Synclavier guitar synthesiser, 88, 91, 93, 94
synthesisers, 81
Szony, Francois, 159, 162
Take It Or Leave It, 142, 164
Take the Coltrane, 106, 160
Taylor, James, 38
The Alternative Man, 94, 167
The Believer, 8, 119, 150, 162, 168
The Big Green Serpent, 170
The Blue Note Tokyo Jazz Club, 104
The Bodyguard, 56
The Boy Cries, 160
The Boy Leaves, 160
The Boy Walks, 160
The Boy's Theme 1, 160
The Camel Walk, 160
The Cellar Door Sessions 1970, 168
The Complete In A Silent Way Sessions, 168
The Complete Jack Johnson Sessions, 168, 171, 172
The Daffodil and the Eagle, 72, 155
The Dance of Maya, 153
The Dark Prince, 77, 156
The Disguise, 133, 164
The Divide, 115, 117, 161
The Dolphin, 120, 162
The Dragon, 152
The Dream, 160
The Dream of the Boy, 160
The Fine Line, 137, 164
The Four Seasons, 160
The Ghetto Walk, 169
The Goon Show, 14
The Grass Is Greener, 13
The Guitar Trio, 8, 109, 161, 168
The Heart of Things, 8, 111, 114, 127, 161, 168
The Heart of Things Live in Paris, 161, 168
The Inner Mounting Flame, 7, 38, 42, 153, 166
The Jean-Luc Ponty Experience with the George Duke Trio, 55

The Life Divine, 54, 153
The Little Blue Frog, 170
The Little Girl Says Goodbye to the Boy, 160
The Lost Trident Sessions, 7, 51, 153, 168
The Man Hunts, 160
The Mask, 172
The Mediterranean Concerto for Guitar and Orchestra, 8, 97, 150, 158, 167
The Other Side of Round Midnight, 167
The Peacocks, 109, 161
The Promise, 8, 106, 107, 111, 118, 160, 168
The Sunlit Path, 49, 154
The Translators, 85, 157
The Unbeliever, 90, 158
The Unknown Dissident, 77, 129, 156, 164
The Voice, 124, 163
The Wait, 93, 158
The Wall Will Fall, 95, 158
The Way of the Pilgrim, 65, 155
The Who (band), 29
The Wish, 108, 118, 160, 161
The World of David Bowie, 15
Thelonius Melodius, 107, 160
Thieves and Poets, 8, 84, 93, 120, 143, 150, 162, 168
Thilo, Jesper, 173
Things We Like, 166
This is For Us To Share, 151
Thomas, Gary, 111, 112, 113, 114, 161
Thomas, Michael Tilson, 56, 98, 154, 158
Thompson, Danny, 13
Thornton, Steve, 173
Thousand Island Park, 46, 153
Time Remembered, 8, 82, 103, 109, 120, 150, 159, 167
To Bop or Not To Be, 163
To The One, 8, 135, 137, 138, 139, 164, 168
To the Stars, 133
To Whom It May Concern - Them, 151
To Whom It May Concern - Us, 151
Together, 15, 55, 72
Tokyo Decadence, 108, 160
Tokyo Live, 8, 104, 127, 128, 129, 159, 167
Tones for Elvin Jones, 106, 160
Tony Williams, 7, 11, 19, 20, 21, 24, 27, 30, 43, 44, 74, 78, 117, 124, 131, 137, 151, 156, 166, 169
Tony Williams Lifetime (band), 7, 21, 24, 25, 27, 29, 38, 43, 44, 74, 78, 146, 151, 166
Traditional Song, 160
Trancefusion, 140, 164
Trevere, 170
Trilogy Medley, 154
Trinity (band), 13, 37
Trio of Doom, 7, 78, 150, 156, 168
Truth in Shredding, 54
Tubbs, Russel, 60, 154
Tuncboyaciyan, Arto, 128
Turn It Over, 7, 27, 151, 166
Turn Out the Stars, 159
Turrentine, Stanley, 35
Two for Two, 18, 151
Two Sisters, 70, 98, 155, 158
Um Mani Padme Hum, 160
Until Such Time, 158
vanGelder, Rudy, 36
Vasconcelos, Nana, 101
Vashkar, 26, 151
Vaughan, Sarah, 37
Verve Records, 24, 101, 106, 150, 151, 158, 159, 160, 161, 162, 166, 167, 168
Very Early, 82, 159
VeryEarly (Homage to Bill Evans), 157
Via The Spectrum Road, 151
Viene Clareando, 85, 157
Vinayakaram, T H, 155, 161
Vinnie Colaiuta, 108, 130, 131, 160, 163, 164
Vision is a Naked Sword, 57, 154
Visions of the Emerald Beyond, 7, 60, 93, 154, 167
Vital Transformation, 40, 153
Vitous, Miroslav, 24, 36, 166
Vuelta Abajo, 151
Vuhovar, 105, 159
Walden, Narada Michael, 63, 74, 154, 155, 156
Walesa, Lech, 84, 100
Waltz for Bill Evans, 34, 153
Waltz for Debby, 159
Waltz for Katia, 83, 157
Warfield Theatre, 79
Warners Records, 84, 87
Warwick, Dionne, 14
Washington, Dinah, 35

Waters, Muddy, 12
We Will Meet Again, 159
Weather Report (band), 11, 17, 39, 52, 64, 76, 90, 115, 136
Webster, Ben, 37
Wechter, Abraham, 67, 83, 99, 158
Weckl, Dave, 111
Weisgaard, Ethan, 173
Weiss, Nat, 38
Wellman, Ricky, 173
Westbrook, Marsha, 57, 154
Westbrook, Michael, 15
What I Say, 172
What Need Have I For This, 69, 155
When Blue Turns to Gold, 91, 118, 158
When Love is Far Away, 105, 114, 159, 161
Where Fortune Smiles, 7, 31, 152, 166
White, Lenny, 169, 171
Wilburn, Vincent, 173
Williams, Anthony, 7, 11, 19, 20, 21, 24, 27, 30, 43, 44, 74, 78, 117, 124, 131, 137, 151, 156, 166, 169
Williams, Victor, 111, 113, 161
Willie Nelson, 171
Windfeld, Axel, 173
Wings of Karma, 58, 154
Winther, Jens, 173
Wippersberg, Marcus, 79, 162, 163
Wonderfall, 141, 164
Woodstock, 33
Yaphet, 170
Yes (band), 25, 43, 44, 112, 146
Yesternow, 171
You Gotta Take a Little Love, 36
Young, Larry aka Khalid Rasin, 22, 30, 151, 152, 153
Zakir, 66, 69, 70, 91, 98, 108, 118, 119, 155, 158, 160, 161, 162, 163, 167
Zamfir, 83, 157
Zamfir, Gheorghe, 83
Zappa, Frank, 43, 54, 55
Zawinul, Josef, 11, 68, 73, 92, 93, 96, 97, 136, 137, 145, 169, 170, 173